3 9153 00942353 6

DISCARD

Socialism Since Marx

Marx

A CENTURY OF THE EUROPEAN LEFT

Socialism Since Marx

A CENTURY OF THE EUROPEAN LEFT

Leslie Derfler

St. Martin's Press   New York

Library of Congress Catalog Card Number: 72–95838
Copyright © 1973 by St. Martin's Press, Inc.
All Rights Reserved.
Manufactured in the United States of America.
For information write: St. Martin's Press, Inc., 175 Fifth Avenue,
New York, N.Y. 10010

Affiliated Publishers: Macmillan Limited, London
—also at Bombay, Calcutta, Madras, and Melbourne.

Preface

This book is less concerned with socialist thought than with socialist movements. The two, of course, cannot be separated, but a great deal has already been said about the former (George Lichtheim's description of the relationship between Marxism and Marxist parties has rightly been called a model of intellectual history). I have tried here to report on what socialists did, in the conviction that what they did was at least as important as what they said. In so doing, I have kept an eye on socialism's clientele and chief body of support, the "laboring classes." The discussion that has emerged may be both broad and short enough for use as an introduction by students having even a limited knowledge of modern European history. The account is not intended and cannot serve as a substitute for those of G. D. H. Cole, Carl Landauer, Jacques Droz, or George Lichtheim. The extent of my reliance on these and other writers will be apparent to anyone familiar with them. Whatever originality my contribution to socialist history has may be found not in the information provided but in its focus and organization.

A major difficulty arose from the need to identify movements (which, in an admittedly arbitrary way, I have equated with viable political parties) as in fact socialist. I have resorted to the expedient of taking literally a party's own designation and accepting as sufficient the reasons it has offered for such self-identification usually, its refusal to treat labor as merely another commodity and its holding as objectives the accomplishment of basic changes in the status of the economically underprivileged and the establishment of public direction over productive property.

I have attempted to identify experiences common to the major socialist movements: specifically, their early willingness to work within democratic forms, their partial return to revolutionary tactics, their growing commitment before World War I to measures of national preservation, and their more or less similar responses to the rival mass movements of communism and fascism. I have also examined some experiences that were distinctive: the activities of socialists in tsarist Russia, for example, in contrast with those of their counterparts in Western Europe. In accounting for such differences, we may see to what extent socialism was given tactical and even theoretical expression by the particular milieu in which it developed. The relationships set forth are tentative, and I trust that this book will be regarded as an essay in working-class politics and comparative history, not as an attempt to formulate laws. No doubt some of my generalizations will require further validation; I hope the examples I have chosen to support them are representative.

I have confined my account to European parties for a number of reasons, not the least of which is the consideration given to space. It is of course true that developments in the United States, like the New Deal, and in Australia and New Zealand, like industrial conciliation systems, have affected the history of socialism. However, socialism remained an essentially European affair until after World War II. The First Workingmen's International involved mainly England and France. The Second, while boasting of Latin American and Japanese representation, was resticted to European parties. The socialism practiced at the time was found inadequate by economically underdeveloped lands unaccustomed to parliamentary institutions. Nor was it found attractive by workers in the United States, where it was declining even before 1914. Moreover, Europe constituted an area in which societal forms and labor markets were reasonably similar. Movements in Britain, France, Germany, and Russsia serve in this book to illustrate the major themes. Other movements, like Austro-Marxism before and after World War I and Scandinavian socialism during the depression of the 1930s, are brought into the account when they play a role or constitute a variation on a theme.

The major omission is that of Soviet communism. Or more precisely, it is not so much omitted as limited to one party in a description of socialist-communist relations. I would rather not enter the debate over whether democratic socialism as preferred by parties in the West or communism is the heir to the socialist tradition, though it will be apparent that I think the best case can be made for the former. I consider the domestic activities of the CPSU as belonging essentially to Soviet rather than socialist history.

Carl Landauer has again revealed his readiness to assist less adept scholars by consenting to read the manuscript. Those recommendations I was wise enough to follow have strengthened it greatly, as have the suggestions offered by several colleagues. One final acknowledgment must be made: to my students, who, having been exposed to the subject in various class and seminar rooms, have often responded with insight and perception. They have contributed importantly to the writing of this book.

L. D.

Contents

ONE

The

Preconditions

Well before the
turn of the cen-
tury, Marxism
represented the most dynamic and
complete articulation of socialist
thinking. The origins of modern
socialism, however, are diverse. The French Revolution at the end of
the eighteenth century may be considered the chief source, while the
uprisings of 1830 and 1848 (and the writings of the arch-conspirator
of the July Monarchy and Second Empire, Auguste Blanqui) added
impetus to the revolutionary tradition. Stress laid on community organization and factory legislation by Robert Owen, as well as Pierre-Joseph
Proudhon's *mutualism,* contributed to fashioning more gradualist
alternatives. *Chartism* imbued socialism with an awareness of the need
to win political rights. Louis Blanc's demands for national workshops
pointed to the need for state help, a theme further elaborated by
Ferdinand Lassalle. In urging that labor be the agent of its own
emancipation and that society be transformed "from below," Blanc
separated himself from his more utopian predecessors. Marx, however,
synthesized the influences of the French and Industrial revolutions and
the ideas of early socialists. The adoption by socialists of the principles
and practices he set forth directly influenced socialism's greatest expansion between 1870 and 1914.

THE MARXIST LEGACY

What strikes one most about the legacy to socialism left by Karl Marx is
its ambiguity. Both his writings and politics (and those of Friedrich Engels) have been used by peaceful as well as by the more revolutionary
socialists. The latter were originally called *orthodox* and later *Bolsheviks;*
the former were called *revisionists* or *reformists* and represented socialist development in Western Europe.

1

ANTECEDENTS OF MARXISM

The politics first practiced by Marx conformed to the orthodox model of socialism. His part in the secret Communist League in the late 1840s and early 1850s was as conspiratorial as it was utopian, and his writings of the period, in apparent contrast to the earlier humanistic *Economic and Philosophical Manuscripts of 1844,* in large part reflected his emerging radical orientation. They also reflected, particularly the *Manifesto* of 1848, the ideas in French and German radical intellectual circles formulated during the two previous decades. Writers had observed the dichotomy between the optimistic Hegelian historical perspective of progress and growing human mastery of the universe, contrasting the widening poverty that followed industrialization and urban expansion. An "emotional and intellectual rebellion" turned on the old order and presented sketchy utopian alternatives that were vaguely socialistic in nature. Two undefined phrases became catchwords for the reformers: "organization of labor," or the planned use of human and material resources, and "association," or the cooperative control of the means of production.[1]

Communism in the mid-1840s thus represented a vision of a perfect society for intellectuals, artists, and writers, although its real power was exaggerated by friend and foe alike. The point is that these people now denounced the bourgeoisie as the real oppressors of the masses, and, with the possible exception of England, held that class in general contempt. Hence the idea of reform through class conflict came to replace benevolent methods favored by early "utopian" reformers. This hardened line had its counterpart in a growing concern with political power. Democracy was the order claimed by all radical factions. They consequently made attempts to join forces with liberals, although most liberals like Alphonse Lamartine, Giuseppi Mazzini, and Camillo Cavour rejected cooperation with socialists.

Such events as a revolt in 1844 of Silesian weavers, the Peterloo Massacre, and Chartist riots served to highlight the existence of well-rooted class antagonisms. Engels predicted revolution in England and France for the same year. French and German authorities showed concern over the threat of communist attacks. Although the specter of communism appeared real enough in the "hungry forties," the threat proved to be much overrated.

THE COMMUNIST MANIFESTO

Marx drew the various strands of radical thought into a coherent whole. The 1848 Manifesto identified labor as the only revolutionary class of the time and described the stages of development in its struggle against the bourgeoisie in terms of an organized and concerted effort. Reinforced by those fallen from the ranks of the ruling classes, and internationalized in opposition to capitalism's ever-wider concentration to maximize profits, workers were assured of ultimate victory. Marx repeatedly identified communist or socialist interests with those of the proletariat. (From a doctrinal point of view, he saw socialism as a transition period; communism was never described in detail, but the name was used by the organization—the Communist League—with which he was then affiliated.) The communists, then, were not a party or a sect, but the self-conscious vanguard of the proletariat itself. Unlike other groups claiming working-class support, they were to identify with the common interests of the proletariat in its entirety, regardless of nationality, and to place particular issues in the context of the larger and enduring conflict with capitalism.

In view of the state's inability to change itself into a democratic instrument (and Marx never admitted that it could reflect other than bourgeois interests while under bourgeois control), communists felt they would ultimately achieve their goal "only by a forcible overthrow of all existing social conditions." The tactics specifically called for in the Manifesto, however, were considerably more moderate. First steps aimed at winning the "battle of democracy" and stressed the need for cooperation with democratic forces. When and how to cooperate would depend on place and time. For example, alliance with the middle classes would be possible in Germany if the German bourgeoisie opposed feudalism and monarchy The workers would achieve and then use their political supremacy to wrest by degrees all capital from the bourgeoisie in order to centralize instruments of production in the hands of the state—that is, the proletariat organized as the ruling class.

THE REVOLUTIONS OF 1848

This outburst of revolution—or more precisely, its outcome— reinforced Marx's awareness of the advantages of bourgeois democracy for the proletariat. The democratic and liberal state offered workers a legal basis for economic association as well as the opportunity for representation in a political party. Trade unions and parties would defend and further working-class interests. Their very existence would provide countless occasions to develop class consciousness. Marx could detect few signs of large-scale revolt in Germany and was hostile to the proposed *German Legion* that his fellow exiles in Paris were then outfitting. In Cologne, where he went to join and write for the Democratic party (it was not socialist, but contained a socialist wing led by Ferdinand Lassalle), Marx soon estimated that the period of active revolution was over and rejected efforts to continue insurrection by conspiratorial means. (Together with Engels, Marx did visit the scene of the

Baden and Palatinate insurrections, however, and received a mandate to represent the German revolutionary party in Paris.) From these decisions, from the inaugural speech given 13 years later to the Council of the (First) International, and from his last reflections of the Paris Commune, social democrats sketched a picture of peaceful change sought through legal procedures from Marx.

In the interim Marx pursued the study of economics. He also produced his histories of the revolution in France and subsequent accession of Napoleon III. In terms of the legacy for political action, these analyses pointed to the class nature of the June Days—a struggle into which the unprepared workers were forced. They demonstrated as well the counterrevolutionary tendencies of the peasants. Marx implied (and Engels was to make explicit in his 1895 introduction to the *Class Struggles in France*) that general elections, once "a means of deception," had turned into "an instrument of emancipation." His newspaper articles written during these years pointed out the difficulties in staging successful coups (a tactic advocated during Marx's earlier and more radical *Blanquist* period) where, as in Germany, decentralization was paramount and labor was insufficiently concentrated.[2]

THE FIRST INTERNATIONAL

Like Eduard Bernstein after him, Marx's years in London reinforced his conviction that universal socialist strategies were useless. What might be appropriate on the continent could be absurd in England. His Inaugural Address to the newly founded International (composed largely of British and French workers) revealed a concern with the aims of organized labor, an interest influenced by his own personal poverty and by recognition that more would be achieved by working with legislatures still under bourgeois control. The address was later referred to as *Charter* for social democracy. The utopianism of the forties had given way to the realism of the sixties, and this attitude, although temporarily abandoned at the outset of the Paris Commune (the radical uprising of the city in 1871), stamped the mature Marx.[3]

Marx's position as a theorist of the labor movement and his desire to influence British trade unionists helped to fashion a commitment to democratic socialism. His address depicted the misery of the workers and measured the gulf between them and the upper classes. It also hailed the *10-Hour-Day Law* for the immediate benefits it brought and because it was a victory of principle won by the exertion of working-class pressure. Elsewhere in his speech Marx rejected the cooperative movement. He suspected it would never reach national dimensions, and he continued to lay stress on political rather than economic action. The conquest of political power became "the great duty of the working classes." This was reaffirmed in the first volume of *Capital,* which appeared three years later. Marx here called for the "removal of all legally removable hindrances to the free development of the working class imposed by its rulers." This explains the book's emphasis on English factory legislation; its usefulness may have been oversimplified, but it was intended to serve as a model:

One nation can and should learn from others. And when a society has got upon the right track for the discovery of the natural laws of its movement . . . it can neither clear by bold leaps, nor remove by legal enactments the obstacles offered by the successive phases of its development. But it can shorten and lessen the birth pangs.[4]

In the Inaugural Address, he offered tactics dictated by circumstances. To appease English trade unionists Marx acknowledged the importance of the immediate objectives of labor. To placate French socialists, who preferred mutualist (independent associations of producers) to collectivist (state ownership of production) solutions, he stated a willingness to develop cooperatives to nationwide proportions and avoided any calls for nationalization. However, the overriding importance of the First International rests on the fact that for the first time the need to win political power was clearly stated and made the focal point of working-class activity. The International was to concern itself with the development of an organization required to win power—the modern socialist political party—and not the sporadic, secret, and usually isolated activity previously undertaken.[5]

The antecedents of the International were varied, ranging from Tom Paine and the Corresponding Societies to the Holy Alliance and Chartism. It was created not by Marx but by the two most advanced working classes in Britain and France. Composed largely of skilled workers, enjoying competent leadership, and becoming nationally organized, British unions were far from ideologically oriented. They rejected the idea of the class struggle and were willing to rely on existing parties, particularly the Liberal party, for desired legislation. Their internationalism originated in the understandable effort to prevent the importation by industrialists of cheap continental labor. The London Trades Council invited European workers to join forces and exert collective pressure on their governments against the use of foreign strikebreakers. This led to the meeting in Saint Martin's Hall on September 28, 1864 and the rise of the International.

French workers were mostly Proudhonists favoring mutual credit and economic rather than political action. Some favored the more direct confrontations urged by Blanquists. The delegation of workers sent by Napoleon III to the Universal Exposition of 1862 in London had contained few republicans. Impressed by the efficiency of the trade unions, the delegation called on French labor to redouble its efforts to win the right to combine. These French Proudhonists, British trade unionists, and various political exiles in London, including Polish and German emigrés (Marx himself) and followers of Louis Kossuth, Mazzini, and Lassalle, founded the International and accounted for the variations in its makeup. It was initially a hesitant and prudent Marx who agreed to help draft rules and write the inaugural address, working to balance the more conservative English and radical continental groups. He sought to impose no doctrine. He refrained from attacking Proudhon and insisted only on the need for workers to emancipate themselves and not deprecate the advantages found in winning political power through political organization. The International's structure became a model for that of the national parties. Sovereignty rested in a congress, composed of delegates of the diverse branches, meeting annually and electing an executive council responsible to it. Component workers' organizations were considered subdivisions of the International, yet there was little contact among the various movements in separate countries.

The size of the International should not be exaggerated. In June, 1870, a *procureur général* claimed a total membership of over 800,000 and almost 450,000 for the French section. He failed to distinguish between individual members (perhaps 2,000 in France, fewer than 300 in England) and trade unions and parties that joined collectively. Still, there were more than 30,000 in England, representing primarily collective membership (out of over 800,000 union members) and somewhat less than that in France.[6] The type of membership varied according to country. In England, Belgium, and France, workers' associations proved the chief support. In Germany it came from a political party, composed largely of dissident Lassalleans who had organized one in 1868-1869. The impact of the International was felt less in England, where it exerted only limited influence on the trade unions, but on the continent there were several successful interventions in strikes like that of the Paris metals workers in 1867. The Second Empire prosecuted the French section, but its leaders were not arrested or forced into exile until the time of the Commune.

Marx placed high hopes in the International. "And in the next revolution," he wrote to Engels in 1867, "*We* (i.e., you and I) will have this powerful *engine in our hands*" (*sic*).[7] However, the well-documented struggle within and for control of the International dissipated its strength and in large part accounted for its collapse. Conflicting groups included the followers of Proudhon in the mid-sixties, Marxists in the late sixties, and anarchists loyal to Michael Bakunin in the early seventies. Only Marxists demanded political action. Others favored various federative economic forms. Clashes between anarchists, on the one hand, and Marx and British unionists, on the other, did not break out until the late sixties, thanks in large measure to Marx's willingness to compromise. Consequently, the International offered no political resolutions (like calling for the reestablishment of an independent Poland) or antimutualist ones (like calling for the general strike). By the time of the Brussels Congress of 1868, however, a majority had been formed able to ask for the collectivization of land, mines, and railroads.

ANARCHISM

At the following year's Basle Congress, Bakunin made his appearance and won his first major success. The great Russian revolutionary and anarchist had been in Italy since 1864, trying unsuccessfully to persuade Mazzinians of the usefulness of his secret organization. He was now able to have the International adopt a resolution advocating in principle the complete abolition of the right of inheritance. Bakunin favored communal autonomy and was a Germanophobe. Still, the differences between him and Marx were as much over method as doctrine. He repudiated political action, social reforms, and the framework of the state in which they were to take place, preferring to rely on peasants rather than workers.

Bakunin saw in Marxist ideas the seeds of a new middle class, one composed of bureaucratic salaried employees. To the degree to which his fears that the "radical intellectual" would replace the bourgeoisie with the bureaucrat as the new exploiter of the worker were valid, the struggle between the two men is still being fought. It may well be that the difference between them was mainly one of objectives, with Marx riding the crest of scientific socialism in his fight against capitalism. In championing wage earners and peasants, Bakunin was opposed even to those forms of exploitation anticipated after a proletarian victory. The conflict between them was basic, Bakunin seeking the destruction of the state versus the more Jacobin Marx looking toward its capture.[8]

Marx saw in Bakunin, particularly in the latter's *International Brotherhood,* a revival of the old methods of political conspiracy and secret organization, the reverse of the approach adopted by the First International.[9] The teachings of both men influenced subsequent socialist movements. Elements of Marxism appeared in revolutionary syndicalism and in bolshevism but were oriented particularly to democratic socialism; Bakuninist ideas were revealed primarily in anarchism, revolutionary syndicalism, and bolshevism.

These internal divisions remained secondary until 1870. After that their embodiment in national contexts proved ruinous to the International. National parties, especially those in the Latin countries of Europe, resented the authority and authoritarianism of the general council. Marx in 1871 abandoned his earlier flexibility and pragmatism. Because of the experience of the Commune, he had a private council convened in London to equate working-class action with the establishment of a political party of its own. The 23 delegates who attended also adopted restrictive and centralizing resolutions. Bakuninist reaction split the International, his proponents among the Italian, Spanish, Belgian, French, and Swiss sections breaking with the parent organization. At the Hague in 1872 Marx succeeded in having Bakunin expelled.

Marx then decided to move the International's council to New York City. Evidently he expected it to find renewed vigor in the United States. In any event, he was convinced it was too divided in Europe. The basis for his support was diminishing, and he preferred that it not fall into the hands of his adversaries. Most southern states were Bakuninist; French emigrés in London were chiefly Blanquists; the English were trade-union oriented; and only some German Social Democrats, too heavily involved in German national problems to provide much help, remained loyal. The political situation after 1870, moreover, had changed. The creation of a unified Italy and Germany, and the beginning of extensive domestic and foreign tranquility were not conducive to international socialist organization. Marx's council and hence the International were dissolved in 1876 in Philadelphia.

As with its successor, the different outlooks of its national sections overrode international claims on working-class solidarity. Nor did the First International ever reach the new industrial workers it was supposed to serve.   Still, in its short life it established the principle of working-class unity and made possible the development of all-inclusive socialist parties on the national level. Briefly, it bequeathed a legacy of political action.   In England it had aided in the campaign for initiating electoral reform.   It had also attracted worldwide publicity to trade union struggles, slowed the recruitment of continental labor, and helped the Newcastle engineers win the 9-hour day in 1871. The First International was more important for what it anticipated than for what it accomplished.   It was also considerably more than a myth.

THE PARIS COMMUNE

Was it the experience of the Commune that accounted for Marx's shift from a pragmatic to a more doctrinaire position? His gyrations here were remarkable.   It would appear that he first urged French workers to abandon revolution.   In his *Second Address to the General Council,* delivered after the French defeat at Sedan on September 3, 1870, Marx called on workers to support the provisional government and to reject the revolution intended to create a working-class commune as "a hopeless piece of folly."

The French workers must do their duty as citizens. . . . Let them quietly and with determination make the most of the republican freedom granted to them in order to carry out thoroughly the organization of their own class. This will give them new strength for the rebirth of France and for our common task—the emancipation of the proletariat.

The words were ignored. Marx and Engels ultimately defended the Communards and derived lessons from their experience.

From a doctrinal point of view the Commune cast some doubt on the need to retain the old form of the state as the basis of society after the victorious revolution. The direct democracy of the Commune impressed him, and he saw local councils responsible to the voters, rather than to national parliaments, as "the political form under which to work out the economic emancipation of labor." Until the disappearance of all classes the state was to remain a class organization but would now represent the interests of the proletariat. However, unlike the bourgeois state, it would consciously "prepare the way for its own extinction." Marx developed this position in his *Critique of the German Social Democratic Party's Gotha Program* in 1875. He was concerned primarily with repudiating the Lassallean insistence on the importance of cooperatives. However, he maintained in a classic phrase that the revolutionary transformation of a capitalist into a communist society corresponded to a political transformation "in which the state can be nothing but the revolutionary dictatorship of the proletariat." Dictatorship here was largely equated with popular rule. This remark was seized upon by Lenin and the Bolsheviks to justify the insurrection and used to maintain powerful party control after its completion.

The Civil War in France enabled both social democrats and communists to claim that they were following in Marx's footsteps. He demonstrated the inability of the working class to "simply lay hold of ready-made State machinery . . . and wield it for its own purposes." Consequently, he could allow reformists to argue that for all practical purposes he was seeking time precisely for the development of those abilities by winning the "battle of democracy" and by raising the proletariat to the position of the ruling class. In defending the Commune as a working-class uprising and assigning it a key place in socialist history, he permitted revolutionaries to point to the legitimacy of insurrection.

Marx described the Commune as "the most glorious deed of our party since the June insurrection." Previously he had disavowed Blanquist notions of conspiracy and had deemphasized Jacobin dictatorship. His treatment of the Commune revived both traditions. George Lichtheim has written that by "abandoning his realistic outlook of 1864 and reverting to the utopianism of the Communist Manifesto," Marx discouraged British trade unions from remaining associated with the International, widened the split between anarchism and socialism, and so contributed to its destruction. Bourgeois repression of Communards would doubtless have required socialists to identify with the Commune. By making it part of socialist legend, he imposed on social democracy a "political myth" opposed to its daily practice. He thus endowed it with a "split personality," which after 1871 plagued all socialist parties.[10]

Ten years later, however, and historically this must be regarded as Marx's final verdict, he described the Paris Commune as "merely the rising of a city under exceptional conditions; the majority of the Commune was in no way socialist nor could it be." In the same letter he said that "a socialist movement does not come into power . . . unless conditions are so developed that it can immediately take the necessary measures . . . for permanent action."[11] In 1880, when he drafted a program for the socialist organization founded by the Frenchman Jules Guesde, Marx hailed the new party with all its reformist demands as the "first real labor movement in France." The Commune, he persisted, had revealed France's backwardness and had shown how repeated proletarian rebellions were signs of "political immaturity."[12]

In retrospect, then, Marx's revolutionary periods seem short-lived. Even in 1872, after ousting Bakuninists from the International, he had pointed to the possibility of a peaceful transition to socialism if societal institutions were sufficiently democratic. Immediately following the Hague Congress of that year he argued that different lands required different methods of revolution. In Britain, America, and possibly Holland, revolution—here equated with the establishment of socialism and hence an end rather than a means—might be won by successfully accumulating sufficient political power. Such opportunities did not exist in Germany and several other countries, and, for the most part, force was recognized as the "lever of revolution." Engels' 1891 *Critique* of the German socialist party's Erfurt Program provided further support for those convinced of Marx's belief that revolution, at least in some countries, might not be necessary. Engels' introduction to the 1895 edition of Marx's *Class Struggles in France* played down insurrection and dwelt on the advantages of universal suffrage and parliamentary machinery. These texts, as well as the Marxist condemnation of anarchists for holding as their objective the destruction rather than the control of the state, would all be brought into play by participants in the revisionist-revolutionary controversy at the turn of the century.

CONCLUSION

The Marxist legacy, then, is a mixed one. It provided rationales for both the revolutionary and the peaceful transitions to socialism. This was more true of his writings than for his personal involvement (as a member of the International's executive), although it is difficult to separate the two since Marx invariably wrote with an audience in mind. He thus set the stage for the "dilemma" of modern socialism: to attain a socialist society by a parliamentary and piecemeal path, or to follow a revolutionary one. Concern with reform, however, was forced upon even those who stressed the revolutionary aspects of the legacy. Marx had postulated the winning of a politically democratic and economically liberal revolution by the bourgeoisie against anticapitalist forces as necessary to create the conditions for proletarian development and ultimate social revolution. In view of their progressive democratic norms and advanced capitalist holdings, England and later Germany were regarded as ripe for proletarian uprising. For precisely the opposite reasons a notoriously unprepared Russia might first have to undergo a successful bourgeois revolution. No Marxist saw socialism as possible in preindustrial or economically underdeveloped areas. But between the two revolutions, both to satisfy legitimate working-class demands and to instill greater class consciousness within workers, minimum reforms could be sought within the framework of the existent bourgeois state. The *Communist Manifesto* had itself provided a model for subsequent socialist party programs by providing both maximum and minimum programs. The former took the form of an orthodox analysis demonstrating the need for and inevitability of revolution. The latter listed immediate reforms and offered advice on how to cooperate with the middle classes in order to obtain them. Despite these references to parties, there is still no evidence that Marx was concerned with the distinction between parties and classes. He regarded the former as groups of like-minded men. Lenin was the first major figure among Marxists to provide socialist theory on the role and nature of political parties.

These issues are important because after 1870 socialism became a political force and was no longer an intellectual struggle for theoretical bases. They were to be universally fought out at the turn of the century and again after World War I. Until then, the forces making for the democratization of socialism largely commanded the arena. The Jacobin model of the revolutionary vanguard was reserved for those occasions requiring rhetoric. The political game was played to the utmost —where, to be sure, playing fields were available. Electoral campaigns, increasingly attractive programs, and electoral and parliamentary alliances with nonsocialist groups became the order of the day. Earlier warnings of opportunist pitfalls and accompanying admonitions to regard parliamentary activities as only one of several available tactics would appear wholly justified in the opinion of those who had delivered them. Still, insistence on political action probably constitutes the chief legacy left to socialism by Marx. Insofar as he had the proletariat ac-

cept the leadership of a political party, he transformed the character of
the movement from a conspiracy to a more viable organization.

LABOR AND SOCIALISM

Mass parties require mass constituencies, and socialists understandably anticipated receiving support from those on whose behalf the new parties
were to act. As the history of the Left over the last century reveals, however, the cooperation of labor (acting as potential party members or even
as voters) could not be taken for granted. Accordingly, it may also be
useful to establish the preconditions, insofar as they can be determined,
of socialism's political growth and in so doing examine the relationship
between the socialist and labor movements. Because socialism became
an important political force in the last third of the nineteenth century,
a survey of the economic conditions then prevailing seems an appropriate
point of departure.

CONCENTRATION AND DEPRESSION

In spite of a "great depression" during the 1870s and 1880s, the last
few decades of the century was a period of immense industrialization and
urbanization for Europe and most of North America. The pattern
varied in Europe according to location, a development already visible by
the end of the eighteenth century. Like the revival of commerce before
it, industrialization came earlier in the West, and the capitalist, like the
merchant who preceded him, gained control of power. In central and
eastern Europe the nobility remained politically as well as socially supreme; it had merely sanctioned commercial activity and similarly ac-
commodated industry.[13] Because capitalism carried the seeds of liberal
institutions, the political development of labor was to be affected accordingly.

Innovations in technology, particularly in metallurgy and electricity,
affected industry in such a way as to bear out Marx's prediction of increasing concentration of ownership. Production became centered in
the factory (although factories in countries like France remained small),
and the modern corporation, with limited liability and later with separation of ownership and management, became the agent of industrial development. Vastly expanded output and the rise of large-scale credit
institutions permitted concentration in the form of pools, cartels, and
combines, driving out smaller, less successful firms. Concentration also
took place in the holding of private wealth. In Great Britain, fewer
than 5 percent of those over the age of 25 possessed 60 percent of the
nation's wealth in 1911. Even in France, which prided itself on the
widespread ownership of land, fewer than 2 percent of those who paid

an inheritance tax owned 34 percent of the wealth bequeathed as late as 1933. Rapid industrial growth meant a rise in real wages. But the worker's share of the national income decreased; his labor was intensified and his living conditions remained harsh. The inquiry made by Charles Booth in 1887 revealed that over a third of the inhabitants of London lived in below-poverty status.[14]

Did the great depression in the quarter century from 1873 to 1896 adversely affect economic development? Some commentators have doubted it. Not all the indices of a depressed economy were present. In large part the decline was relative and not absolute; that is, some sectors showed an actual fall but many showed a fall only in their rate of growth. Critics nevertheless acknowledged a drop in such indices as prices, industrial and agricultural production, trade, and—relevant for our purposes—employment. Not as severe as the economic crisis of the 1930s, the depression nonetheless cut sharply into production figures and shook business confidence. In the decade and a half before 1873 the annual rate of British industrial growth (excluding the cotton and building industries) averaged almost 3 percent. During the decade and a half after, it averaged little more than half that figure.[15]

There is no single explanation for the depression, and its causes varied from country to country. Those offered for the decline of prices in England include insufficient monetary supplies, reduced and unproductive investments, technological developments making cost reductions possible, a lessening in the growth of world trade, and inadequate responses on the part of businessmen. Reasons for the aggravation of the depression also varied according to location. One common factor was increased competition in one form or another from outside of Europe, although in Germany the trade boom of the early seventies appears to have contributed most, and the metals industries continued to grow. In England, export markets shrank as overseas lands industrialized. Improvements in transportation opened great virgin farmlands in America, Australia, and Russia, bringing cheaper grain, meat, and wool to Europe. Lowered costs of labor (as in Russia) or greater use of farm machinery (as in America) allowed imports to swamp European growers. The agricultural crisis affected the entire European economy because the reduced purchasing power of the farming population shrank the domestic market for manufactured goods.

The crisis was also intensified by an unparalleled series of misfortunes: excessive rain, cold, and drought; and animal and plant disease. In France, the home market was further limited by a longstanding tendency toward depopulation and by a reliance on the production of luxury goods that inevitably fare poorly in times of depression. What, then, was the social impact? Did the depression help to arouse or spur the growth of mass social movements?

LABOR AND THE ECONOMY

The relationship between the great movements identified with late nineteenth-century Western history and the depression has yet to be worked out.[16] The general return to protectionism and surge of interest in pooling arrangements seems a clear enough result; the growth of national sentiment, militarism, imperialism, and socialism less so. All these trends shared a tendency to withdraw from an earlier, optimistic world of laissez-faire. Each nationality, each class was urged to close ranks and show concern for its own interests. Within the nation each group fought for a greater share of return. It was precisely during the period of the depression that socialism became a mass movement with well-organized and highly developed national parties. Of the 37 European socialist parties affiliated with the Labor and Socialist International in 1931, all but 6 were founded in the period 1873–1892; and of the rest, four were established between 1898 and 1902.[17]

It must be said at once that no adequate explanation exists for sudden advances in social movements affecting labor. They appear related in some way to cyclical fluctuations, but there is no truly discernible relationship. Each advance in trade union growth and action, for example, must be analyzed individually in order to determine the "specific combination of tensions responsible." The fact remains that every significant jump (1871–1873, 1889–1891, and 1911–1913) in England about doubled the strength of the trade union movement.[18]

Perhaps the most relevant indicator—as well as cause—of working-class discontent was the extent of unemployment and the level of real wages (what wages will buy, as contrasted to monetary wages). Was there more unemployment after 1873 than before, and before 1896 than after? If not, there could hardly have been much of a depression. One of the difficulties in arriving at an answer, in this as in other indices, is the lack of statistical evidence available. No government figures on unemployment were compiled, there being no national insurance scheme then in existence. What figures there are come from trade union sources, and because trade unions were most numerous and best organized in England, it is that country's labor history that has been most thoroughly documented and described. Unemployment during the period 1874–1895 (the depression) was about 2 percent greater than during 1851–1873 and 1896–1914, averaging 7.2 percent.[19] Significantly, unemployment was very low between 1870 and 1873, following a great export spurt, and remained low for another 5 years after that. Put another way, during the 3 or 4 years before the date usually assigned as marking the outset of the depression, employment figures were exceptionally high and few could anticipate that they would not continue to remain so.

A no-less-important indicator of depressed labor conditions was the level of real wages. Apparently they did not decline during the depression. Monetary wages remained stable (workers tended to resist wage cuts thus creating an initial lag), but the reasons for their prolonged stability were not clear. Consequently, in a period of falling prices, real wages had necessarily to inch forward. Professor Henry Pelling has concluded that because real wages not only did not fall but continued to advance, and because periods of high unemployment were short-lived and present only in heavy industry, workers in England were not particularly hurt by the "great depression."[20]

Examination of wage levels raises some questions. Real wages (disregarding unemployment) may be assigned an arbitrary value of 100 for the period 1850–1860. They reached 117 for 1865–1869, and then surged to 133 by 1874, the fastest known increase before World War I.[21] During the next dozen years and for the reasons offered above, real wages eased ahead. Both direction and speed of change were significant. In the quarter century 1850–1874 real wages increased by a total amount of 33 percent. In only the 5 years between 1869 and 1874 they shot forward by 16 percent, a rate nearly two and a half times greater than that for the longer period. But in the dozen years between 1876 and 1888 they advanced from about 137 to 148, an increase of only 8 percent. Although our information is sketchy (how much more so for the continent than for England!), it is reasonable to estimate that the rate of growth in real wages during the depression was considerably smaller than before it began. If we recall that at the same time there was a steady, if small, increase in unemployment, the economic crisis could very well have generated widespread working-class discontent.

Manifest economic trends were only part of the problem. As important must have been the psychological responses to changes, real or anticipated, in wealth or power. Marx himself argued that dissatisfaction is measured not by absolute realities but by relative expectations. "Our desires and pleasures," he said, "spring from society. We measure them, therefore, by society and not by the objects which serve for their satisfaction. Because they are of a general nature, they are of a relative nature." De Tocqueville held a similar view.[22] Frustration is generated when a rise and then a lapse in real income occurs, or when a rise in the economic position in society of one's relevant group is followed by an increase in real income slower than of other groups. Both circumstances may produce a decline in status. Modern reference-group theory relates satisfaction not to existing conditions but to the conditions of the social group against which one measures his situation.

THE ECONOMY AND SOCIALISM

The distinction between political and economic action must clearly be drawn. Depressions do not always or even necessarily favor trade union growth. The mass unemployment generated by severe ones can cause workers to lose the gains previously won. The loss of union membership that follows weakens or destroys organizational strength and in so doing may be a factor in turning workers to socialism.[23] In an expansionist phase, with its greater profits, the problem is seen as lying with their distribution but within existing political and social frameworks. During the periods of high unemployment and general business contraction, labor may feel cut off from economic opportunity and conscious of suffering from inadequacies in social justice. Trade union struggles for improved conditions, then, seem less than vital and the union itself less than indispensable. Permanent improvements appear impossible without basic transformations in society, and these transformations are best attained by recourse to political activity, either by means of the ballot box to give labor a greater or controlling voice in government or by extralegal methods.

Radicalism in working-class politics was also related to the process and state of industrialization, a phenomenon first noted by Engels.[24] Labor moved to the left when industrialization was undergoing rapid growth and when many workers were dislocated. (Although this contention does not fit German industrial development in the period 1890–1914, particularly in power and chemicals when labor became more reformist.) Conversely, when the industrialization process was mature or grew very gradually (as was the case in Denmark), only a small percentage of the labor force, often recent arrivals, was discontented. Working-class politics then tended to be conservative. On the other hand, labor could become more radical when the state of industrialization did not allow for a reduction in the gulf separating the very rich from the very poor.

The economic history of nineteenth-century England offered some illustration of these themes. The crisis of 1846, brought about by the collapse of credit and bad harvests, together with the February Revolution in Paris two years later, evoked recirculation of the People's Charter and the demand of the Workingmen's Association for annual elections based on universal suffrage. Feargus O'Connor went so far as to proclaim the need for an armed uprising. Chartism had turned to political demands during the previous decade of depression, between 1837 and 1847. Shortly after mid-century, however, good harvests throughout the world ensured continued and large-scale supplies of food imports. Consequently, the British export trade almost tripled in the period 1850–1875, with accompanying increases in profits and, to a lesser extent, wages. The action undertaken by labor again became economic in nature, seeking specific improvements in working conditions and placing emphasis on mutual assistance. This *new model* unionism looked to practical-minded leaders who had risen through the ranks. Its ideology, if the term is at all appropriate, was middle-class laissez-faire, which attributed difficulties experienced by workers not to wicked employers but to the inexorable demands of the marketplace.

Strikes and other aggressive tactics were still carried out. It was argued, however, that they could not upset the law of supply and demand. The objective was seen as one of making supply and demand work for labor through more stringent apprenticeship rules, enlargement of union treasuries, and development of adequate benefit programs. The Amalgamated Society of Engineers formulated the *new model* in 1850–1851, and other trade unions adopted it. Mechanics and other skilled workers instituted businesslike approaches and paid their officials well. Organized in administratively autonomous units, they ignored politics. Nor did they formulate any plans to combat depression in the late 1870s. Critics like Tom Mann and John Burns unsuccessfully sought a more decisive policy, one that called for more than the continuance of the the status quo and adequate insurance for union members. The unwillingness of the Trades Union Congress to defeat (although narrowly) a resolution calling for universal suffrage revealed the extent of labor's commitment to economic—or, it may be argued, in this context, conservative—action.

This pattern was roughly similar to that followed in the United States. During the first three-quarters of the nineteenth century labor might be described as relatively prone to militant procedures. However, with industrial expansion and capitalist growth beginning in the decades following the Civil War, the American Federation of Labor (AFL) accepted the "pure and simple" trade unionism urged by Samuel Gompers. This set the tone for American labor at least for the half-century that followed. Still, in the depression of the 1870s, the Knights of Labor supported various local labor parties. Similarly, during the peak of industrial development in tsarist Russia, a segment of labor disavowed the political solutions favored by the intelligentsia, and in its *economism,* turned to more traditional trade union procedures.

We may pursue our British example a step further. The great depression set in after the mid-seventies. With its resources eaten away and its faith shaken, but with its ranks swelled by unskilled workers, British labor turned to a *new unionism*. It drew inspiration from socialism. Trade unions were to work for a new social order based upon the welfare of the working class in its entirety. Socialists like Mann, Burns, and the Scots miners' official, Keir Hardie, held key posts. Great strikes, like those of the gas workers and the dockers were staged successfully. In the period 1882–1892, the number of trade union workers in England doubled from 750,000 to one and a half million.[25]

New unionism accepted as necessary the political changes asked by socialism. The contours it assumed were shaped by English tradition, but the old ideal of individual self-help, which had marked labor at mid-century, was clearly found wanting. Parliament's disastrous Taff-Vale Decision holding trade unions responsible for damages caused during strikes and the apparent uselessness of relying for improvements on the Liberal party completed the transformation at the turn of the century. Large segments of French labor revealed a willingness to resort to political, if not necessarily parliamentary, solutions in the late eighties, by their support of General Boulanger.[26] In the United States, the more politically oriented Congress of Industrial Organizations (CIO) grew up in the depressed 1930s.

Again, we must distinguish between economic and political action, because it was the latter that made socialism a mass movement. Professor Selig Perlman has argued that trade unions are inherently pragmatic, continually seeking to preserve and add to the benefits already acquired, and very much aware of the risks involved in hasty political involvement.[27] In a well-functioning economy, the union's role, insofar as it accepts the system in which the wealth was produced, is that of fighting for the worker's rightful share. Given the opportunity to act freely in defense of its interests, the means envisioned are largely economic. But with a real or anticipated reduction of wages and status, or when deprived of their full freedom of action by unfriendly governments, societal changes are explored and political solutions considered.

Socialist ideas were not new, but it is characteristic for dissatisfied elements during times of crisis to implement theories already devised rather than cast about for new ones. Rousseau's writings did not cause the Revolution in France. However, French revolutionaries after its outbreak were willing to turn to them. Likewise, socialism seemed more relevant in the late 1870s and early 1880s, particularly the ideas of Marx. In a climate of chronic unemployment, socialism could more easily accommodate itself to practical working-class demands for improvements. Marxism represented the one variety of social theory based on the dynamic role to be played by labor. Part of the Marxist legacy concerned the realization of immediate reforms and the consequent use of existing state machinery to obtain them, leading the entire socialist movement in a reformist direction and defeating the revolutionary, as well as the anarchist and mutualist, competition. The issue fought out by organized socialism in the decades before World War I, as well as the areas in which it triumphed, depended on the strength of existing liberal and democratic traditions and practices. Thus it was most successful in Western Europe and progressively less so as we move to the East.[28]

SOCIALISM AND THE SOCIAL CONTEXT

Dissimilar social structures and traditions made for diverse socialist responses. The presence in Germany, for example, of a rigid class structure and military tradition and in Britain of a relatively enlightened nobility, liberal tradition in politics, and basically empirical approach to political and social questions might alone suggest a pragmatism and flexibility in the one movement and a more doctrinaire and abstract orientation in the other. There was as clear a distinction between the development of the British and German movements as there was between British and German workers. Intellectuals everywhere, because they were needed as editors, attorneys, and parliamentarians, held a disproportion ately higher share of leading positions. Even so, the experiences and outlook of German labor, as contrasted to British, may have accounted for its greater reliance on them. They provided not only the theory for, but the leadership of, the party. The more these distinctions and settings are appreciated, the more one is led to consider that what requires explanation are the similarities and not the differences in the paths taken by the different socialist movements.

Less obvious in explaining these differences is the interplay of social forces acting as determinants of labor protest. The organizational development of British and German coal miners, for example, illuminated the respective socialist movements each came to support.[20] German miners before 1850 worked either directly for the state (as in the Saar Basin), or for an employer holding a state concession and thereby subject to its regulations. British mines, however, were individually owned and operated, and when the state intervened, it did so largely to safeguard employer interests. British miners protected themselves only by recourse to well-established traditions of mutual aid and to their "riotous disposition."

They lacked the ability to organize successfully, however, and had to await the coming of two historical phenomena: the rise of middleclass political reform and the growth of Methodism. In managing to oppose aristocratic pretensions, liberals both set an example and provided an ideological basis for the self-reliance already implanted. The miners were now convinced that trade union growth took place when market conditions permitted it. Methodism generated greater self-respect and developed techniques of organization, with worker-preachers becoming organizers and leaders. The point is that British miners initially relied for reforms on their own abilities and on the dictates of the marketplace, as well as on social legislation. This endured until the great depression rendered their situation as unskilled workers more precarious. Then newer and more radical protests were made. Welfare legislation was more arduously sought and emphasis placed on collective and social rather than on civil rights. The socialist groupings then emerging encouraged the growth of militancy, while the miners' history and tradition of protest helped to account for their repudiation of the early Marxist organizations and ultimate receptivity to the reforms promised by a labor not a socialist party.

Unlike that of their British counterparts, the protest movements of

German miners in the Ruhr and Saar regions were not divorced from ideology, at least not until the twentieth century. State intervention meant guildlike regulations affecting everything from dress to deportment. It also brought such privileges as exemption from certain taxes, in some cases from military service, as well as positive assistance in the event of accident, sickness, or death. In this way the legacy of dependence on a paternalistic state was fashioned. When the state began to abandon its supervision of mining shortly after mid-century (except for the Saar), workers continued to expect protection. They could not easily shift loyalty to their fellows, a shift required in the larger effort to shape techniques of self-defense. Their protest movement came to depend instead on those with higher social status, in this case groups with ideological underpinnings. German miners were thus led to movements organized along political and ideological lines and not to those concerned with directly relevant bread-and-butter issues. In the degree to which this analysis is valid, we understand more easily the appearance of parties like the socialist and Catholic (the latter with Christian socialist overtones) before that of well-established trade unions.

Miners tended to support those who thought in terms of changing society rather than of seeking improvements in working conditions. In Britain, socialists found union members suspicious of political solutions. In Germany, the growth of unions was furthered by existing political parties, which saw in them sources of recruitment. There was to be a conflict, and ultimately a compromise, between party and trade unions when the latter felt sufficiently strong to assert themselves and the primacy of economic interests in the first decade of the twentieth century. It was then that the relationships between party and unions in Germany and Britain converged, with workers in both countries reaffirming the desirability of economic roles. There would be other consequences as well, but enough has been said to indicate the importance of the part played here by tradition. Germans substituted dependence on party for dependence on the state. (Subsequent German governments would seek to prevent that dependence on party precisely by reestablishing dependence on the state. The "social" legislation of both Bismarck and Hitler illustrated this.)

That British workers came to support a labor and not a socialist party was consistent with the precedent of trade union (or economic), and not political, organization. For the Labour party was largely the creation of workers determined to defend professional and not political interests. In fact, they turned to a party only when they saw the two could not be separated. The chief political organization in Britain representing working-class interests was to adopt no ideological basis until after World War I.

Still, in one major respect both British and German labor had more in common with each other than with their counterpart in France, and French labor may be said to have conformed to yet a third pattern. Both the British and German labor movements for different reasons and in different ways were either integrated into their respective nations or preferred to work within national political frameworks. In Britain, the transition to modern industrial society was carried out by relatively peaceful compromise. Older landed elements may or may not have relinquished their power, but they did blend into the new society. In Germany, on the other hand, what remained of the feudal nobility entered into an alliance with heavy industry. Thanks to the former's prestige and large role in administration and in the military, it was able to retain control over the middle classes. The consequence of this control meant retarded democratic forms and unresponsive representative institutions. An unaccomplished liberalism, in turn, helped to account for the exclusion of workers from society and prompted them to establish their own institutions, from political parties to social clubs. They did this so effectively, however, that their growing strength constituted a unifying feature and made them a force to be reckoned with.[30]

French labor remained both outside of established society and incapable of extensive organization. The twofold economy consisted of a large peasant class alongside a modern, but still decentralized and diminutive industrial sector. French capitalism, in large part family-owned, small in size, and unencumbered by the demands of labor, was among the most oppressive in Western Europe, and the French state one of the most backward in social legislation. The structure of French capitalism best explains the persistent reliance on economic action by French labor. *Syndicalism,* the ideology that was to embrace and legitimize economic action, was more the product of the workshop than the factory. However, other and more historical reasons explain the continued popularity of professional, as contrasted to political, solutions on the part of French workers. The antiparliamentarianism taught by Proudhon was strengthened by the political "betrayals" of 1848 and 1871 and reinforced by the most dynamic element within French socialism. The simplistic Marxism of Jules Guesde persuaded his Workers party to place all emphasis on politics and reject economic alternatives. The Guesdist-controlled grouping of unions established in 1886, the National Federation of Trade Unions, was viewed as a source of recruitment for the party and as a receptacle for its propaganda. Thus it was that hostility between trade unions, many of whose members regarded job grievances as more relevant than prescriptions for future society, and socialists early emerged as a major theme in the history of French labor.

We shall test other differences, as well as some underlying similarities among the European socialist movements. We shall also observe the activities of the organization restored as the voice of world socialism, the Second Workingmen's International. Different contexts generated different movements. Nonetheless, European socialism demonstrated startlingly similar patterns of development. An inquiry into the reasons why constitutes an important objective of this book.

NOTES

[1] Oscar J. Hammen, "The Spectre of Communism in the 1840s," *Journal of the History of Ideas*, XIV (3) (June 1953), 404–420. In the early nineteenth century, use of the term *socialism* was limited to theory; *communism*, to revolutionaries seeking to implement it.

[2] Karl Marx, *Revolution and Counter-Revolution* (London: Allen & Unwin, 1891), pp. 4–5.

[3] Marx, *Address and Provisional Rules of the International Workingmen's Association* (London: Labour and Socialist International, 1924). George Lichtheim, *Marxism. An Historical and Critical Study* (New York: Praeger, 1965), pp. 103, 105.

[4] Marx, *Capital*, I (London: Sonnenschein and Co., 1908), p. xix.

[5] Boris I. Nicolaevsky, "Secret Societies and the First International," in Milorad M. Drachkovitch, ed., *The Revolutionary Internationals, 1864–1943* (Stanford: Stanford University Press, 1966).

[6] Henry Collins and C. Abramsky, *Karl Marx and the British Labour Movement: Years of the First International* (London: Macmillan; New York: St. Martin's Press, 1965), p. 288.

[7] Letter dated September 11, 1867. *Karl Marx and Friedrich Engels: Selected Correspondence, 1846–1895* (New York: International Publishers, 1942), p. 227.

[8] Donald C. Hodges, "Bakunin's Controversy with Marx . . . ,"*American Journal of Economics and Sociology* XIX (April 1960), 259–274.

[9] Max Nomad, "The Anarchist Tradition," in Drachkovitch, *Revolutionary Internationals,* p. 65.

[10] Lichtheim, *op. cit.,* p. 105. Much of the rest of this discussion is based on Lichtheim's account.

[11] Marx's letter to F. Domela-Nieuwenhuis dated February 22, 1881. Cited in Lichtheim, *op. cit.,* p. 121.

[12] Marx's letter to F. A. Sorge, dated November 5, 1880. Cited in Lichtheim, *op. cit.,* 113. Most present-day Marxists regard the Commune as a transitional revolution between those of the nineteenth and twentieth centuries. They see it as both the last *sans-culotte* insurrection and the first working-class uprising. Claude Willard, *Le Socialisme de la renaissance à nos jours* (Paris: Presses Universitaires de France, 1971), pp. 61, 63.

[13] Charles Morazé, *The Triumph of the Middle Classes* (Garden City, N.Y.: Doubleday, 1968), p. 28.

[14] The intensity of labor and the harshness of living conditions as factors

offsetting any increase in real wages was first pointed out by Marx in *Capital*. For an earlier period, but not earlier than that to which Marx refers, see Edward P. Thompson, *The Making of the English Working Class* (New York: Pantheon Books, 1966). See also Jürgen Kuczynski, *Labor Conditions in Western Europe, 1820–1935* (New York: International Publishers, 1937), pp. 30, 34–38.

[15] S. B. Saul, *The Myth of the Great Depression, 1873–1896* (London: Macmillan; New York: St. Martin's Press, 1969), p. 37.

[16] Max Beer, *The General History of Socialism and Social Struggles* (New York: Russell & Russell, 1957), pp. 121–122, and W. W. Rostow, *British Economy in the Nineteenth Century* (Oxford: Clarendon Press, 1948), Ch. 6, have related the development of socialism to the depression.

[17] The other two countries were Iceland and Luxembourg.

[18] Eric J. Hobsbawm, "Economic Fluctuations and Some Social Movements since 1800," *Economic History Review* V, 1 (1952), 3, 24.

[19] Saul, *op. cit.*, p. 30.

[20] Henry Pelling, *The Origins of the Labour Party, 1880–1900* (Oxford: Clarendon Press, 1965), pp. 7–8.

[21] Saul, *op. cit.*, p. 32.

[22] Karl Marx and Friedrich Engels, "Wage Labour and Capital," *Selected Works in Two Volumes* (Moscow: Foreign Languages Publishing House, 1955), I, p. 94. Both Marx and de Tocqueville cited and commented on by James C. Davies, "Toward a Theory of Revolution," *American Sociological Review* XXVII, 1 (February 1962), 5.

[23] Conventional theory suggests that prosperity leads to trade union economic action; depression to political and/or direct protest. See, for example, Henry Pelling, *American Labor* (Chicago: University of Chicago Press, 1960), p. 152, and Jürgen Kuczynski, *op. cit.*, pp. 34–38. A variation on this view is offered by David Brody, "The Emergence of Mass Production Unionism," in John Braeman, *et al.*, eds., *Change and Continuity in Twentieth Century America* (New York: Harper & Row, 1966), pp. 245, 249.

[24] In his 1884 letter to Karl Kautsky. Cited and elaborated on by Seymour Martin Lipset, "Socialism—Left and Right—East and West," *Confluence*, VII (Summer 1958), 173–176.

[25] Jacques Droz, *Le Socialisme démocratique, 1864–1960* (Paris: A. Colin, 1966), p. 86. The responses of British labor to changing economic conditions have been traced by W. A. McConagha, *Development of the Labor Movement in Great Britain, France, and Germany* (Chapel Hill: University of North Carolina Press, 1942).

[26] The relationship between the depression and Boulangism has been explored by the French historian Jacques Néré. A summary of his views in English may be found in his article, "The French Republic," in F. H. Hinsley, ed., *Material Progress and World-Wide Problems, 1870–1898*, Vol. XII of *The New Cambridge Modern History* (Cambridge: University Press, 1962), pp. 300–322.

[27] Selig Perlman, *A Theory of the Labor Movement* (New York: A. M. Kelley, 1966), pp. 299–300.

[28] Lichtheim, *op. cit.*, pp. 207–209.

²⁹ Gaston N. Rimlinger, "The Legitimization of Protest: A Comparative Study in Labor History," *Comparative Studies in Society and History* II (1959–1960), pp. 329–343. Jürgen Kuczynski, *The Rise of the Working Class* (London: Weidenfeld & Nicolson, 1967), pp. 146, 206–213. The following paragraphs are based on the former's discussion.

³⁰ Daniel Bell, "Socialism," in David L. Sills, ed., *International Encyclopedia of the Social Sciences* (New York: Macmillan, 1968), Vol. 15, p. 514.

SUGGESTED READING

THE MARXIST LEGACY

Isaiah Berlin. *Karl Marx: His Life and Environment*. London and New York: Oxford University Press, 1963.

Julius Braunthal. *History of the International*. Vol. I: 1864–1914. New York: Praeger, 1967.

E. H. Carr. *Michael Bakunin*. New York: Knopf, 1961.

E. H. Carr. *Studies in Revolution*. New York: Grosset & Dunlap, 1964.

David Caute. *The Left in Europe Since 1789*. New York and Toronto: McGraw-Hill, 1966.

G. D. H. Cole. *A History of Socialist Thought*. Vol. II: *Marxism and Anarchism*, 1850–1890. New York: St. Martin's Press, 1954.

Alexander Gray. *The Socialist Tradition*. London: Longmans, Green, 1946.

Elie Halévy. *Histoire du socialisme européen*. Paris: Gallimard, 1948.

Oscar J. Hammen. *The Red '48ers: Karl Marx and Friedrich Engels*. New York: Scribner's, 1969.

J. Hampden Jackson. *Marx, Proudhon, and European Socialism*. New York: Macmillan, 1962.

Harry W. Laidler. *History of Socialism*. New York: Crowell, 1968.

Carl Landauer. *European Socialism: A History of Ideas and Movements*. 2 vols. Berkeley: University of California Press, 1959.

George Lichtheim. *A Short History of Socialism*. New York: Praeger, 1970.

David McLellan. *Marx Before Marxism*. London: Penguin, 1972.

Karl Marx. *Selections from Capital, the Communist Manifesto, and Other Writings*. New York: Random House, 1932 (Modern Library ed.).

John Plamenatz. *German Marxism and Russian Communism*. New York: Harper & Row, 1965.

Bertram D. Wolfe. *Marxism: One Hundred Years in the Life of a Doctrine*. New York: Dial Press, 1964.

Irving M. Zeitlin. *Marxism: A Reexamination*. Princeton: Van Nostrand, 1967.

Centre National de la Recherche Scientifique. *La Première Internationale*. Paris: 1964.

LABOR AND SOCIALISM

H. L. Beales. "The Great Depression in Industry and Trade," *Economic History Review*, V (1934).

Asa Briggs and John Saville, eds. *Essays in Labour History*. London: Macmillan; New York: St. Martin's Press, 1960.

Walter Galenson, ed. *Comparative Labor Movements*. New York: Russell & Russell, 1952.

Royden Harrison. *Before the Socialists: Studies in Labour and Politics, 1861 to 1881*. London: Routledge & Kegan Paul; Toronto: University of Toronto Press, 1965.

Eric Hobsbawm. *Labouring Men. Studies in the History of Labour*. Garden City, N. Y.: Doubleday, 1967.

C. P. Kindleberger. *Economic Growth in France and Britain, 1851–1950*. New York: Simon & Schuster, 1969.

Annie Kriegel. *Le Pain et les roses. Jalons pour une histoire des socialismes*. Paris: Presses Universitaires de France, 1968.

David S. Landes. *The Unbound Prometheus*. London and New York: Cambridge University Press, 1969.

Frederic C. Lane, ed. *Enterprise and Secular Change. Readings in Economic History*. Homewood, Ill.: R. D. Irwin, 1953. Especially the essay by Marc Bloch, "Toward a Comparative History of European Societies."

Val Lorwin. "Reflections on the History of the French and American Labor Movements," *Journal of Economic History* XVII (1957).

Val Lorwin. "Working Class Politics and Economic Development in Europe," *American Historical Review*, 63 (1958).

Harvey Mitchell and Peter Stearns. *Workers and Protest. The European Labor Movement, the Working Classes and the Origins of Social Democracy, 1870–1914*. Itaska, Ill.: Peacock Publishers, 1971.

A. E. Musson. "The Great Depression in Britain, 1873–1896: A Reappraisal," *Journal of Economic History*, XIX (1959).

Adolf Sturmthal. *Unity and Diversity in European Labor*. Glencoe, Ill.: Free Press, 1953.

Sidney and Beatrice Webb. *The History of Trade Unionism*. London and New York: Longmans, Green, 1920.

TWO

The Rise

of Social Democracy

Socialism w a s
g i v e n political
e x p r e s s i o n
toward the end of the nineteenth
century. The collapse of the First International left the field to national
parties. The federative structure of the Second International only
furthered party development. Socialism spread throughout Europe
and in attracting the support of mass working populations expanded
in depth as well as in space. In the degree to which socialists found
their organizational machinery and personal freedom secure, they also
found themselves becoming integrated into the social and political life
of their respective countries. In coming to rely on existing legislative
procedures and hence adopting a piecemeal approach to winning stated
goals, socialism became increasingly "democratized." This happened
effectually in the nations of Western and Central Europe although to
different rhythms and with different styles. But where a party could not
openly recruit members, disseminate propaganda, or try to win political
power (as in tsarist Russia), its more militant members successfully overcame efforts to substitute reform for revolution.

BRITISH LABOUR

The Labour party indeed issued from the trade unions. Its appearance,
however, was late and its parentage mixed. Even if we discount the
part played here by ideologues, radicals, and politicians, it is better to
speak of the support given by labor to a political party rather than of
any initiative taken in its establishment. The affiliated trade unions
agreed to back the Labour Representation Committee (LRC), the
direct antecedent of the party. However, their agreement emerged
belatedly and only out of labor's awareness of the need for political

26

representation as a means to defend its economic interests. It is precisely in this fact that we find an explanation for much that stamped the history of the Labour party particularly in its early years. In Germany the reverse was true, trade unionism being largely the creation of the party, while in France there was continuing hostility and mutual distrust between parties and labor.

But in Britain, trade unionism preceded and helped create a viable socialist movement. Certainly, its development was influenced by earlier socialist organizations like the Social Democratic Federation (SDF), the Independent Labour party (ILP), and, to the extent that one wishes to consider it socialist, the Fabian Society. The first question to raise about the history of the British Labour party, however, concerns these organizations. Why was it that these first movements never won the large-scale support of labor which could have ensured their position as its political spokesmen?

THE SOCIAL DEMOCRATIC FEDERATION (SDF)

The early ties between the forces of organized labor and the SDF pointed to the likelihood of this support. Among its members were trade union leaders like Tom Mann and John Burns. Others who formed the federation in 1881 included such radical intellectuals as Belfort Bax; Marx's daughter, Eleanor Aveling; the poet, William Morris; and former members of the First International. All were grouped under the curious leadership of Henry Hyndman.

Hyndman himself may provide the best explanation for the inability of the group to attract widespread support. He was a composite of paradoxes—the grandson of a man who had made a fortune trafficking in slaves, the man who first read *Capital* while in the United States visiting his gold-mine investments, and a man whose private appearance never ceased to contrast with those of the people he sought to defend. The image that persists is that of the "gentleman, cricketer, and stockbroker, leading the toiling masses toward revolution in a top-hat and frock-coat, reinforced by that other stalwart of the SDF, the Countess of Warwick, in the special train which she ordered to take her home from the Federation conference."[1]

Nevertheless, it was Hyndman who gave the SDF its distinctly Marxist orientation, composed as it was of individuals inspired by the assorted teachings and memories of Chartism, positivism, and the single tax. Hyndman had visited Marx in the early 1880s, leaving the latter less than impressed. His understanding of Marxist doctrine was incomplete and oversimplified and yet he tried to impose it on others, a failing by no means unique in the socialist past. In this respect, he resembled

Jules Guesde, who introduced and popularized Marxism in France. Engels also disliked Hyndman and said that he had "managed to reduce the Marxist theory of development to a rigid orthodoxy."[2] His doctrinaire radicalism lacked revolutionary technique, and he was well-known for his authoritarian ways within the SDF.   Like the early years of Guesde's Workers party—also more of a sect than a party—intrigues gave way to schism and by 1888 Morris and Eleanor Aveling had broken away to form the rival Socialist League.

This is not to minimize the contribution of the SDF to the history of socialism in Britain.   Despite the opposition of Engels, Hyndman's sectarianism, and the continued schisms, the SDF endured as the chief repository of Marxism in the country.   It was to provide the largest contribution in membership to the British Communist party in 1920 and to school many future labor leaders, like George Lansbury and Ernest Bevin.

The SDF, however, never lived up to its hope of speaking for the English working classes.   Its ambition was wholly legitimate, given the trade union leader representation in its councils and the prestige it had won in union ranks for its support of the great London strikes of the 1880s. The "new unionism" of the unskilled workers had required help, and appreciated socialist efforts.   Indeed, it is difficult to dissociate the "new unionism" from the growth of socialism.   The industrial crises of the eighties were especially hard on the unskilled, and we have noted the leadership provided by Mann, Burns, and Keir Hardie. These men showed themselves willing to take more direct action in part because of their recognition of the class basis of organized labor.   The SDF held an identical outlook.   Hence everything pointed to its acceptance by labor. The SDF's—or Hyndman's—incomplete understanding of Marxist ideas led it to exaggerate reliance on political over economic action. Both the SDF and the Socialist League, despite their acceptance of labor leaders, remained scornful of trade unions, seeing in them competitors for working-class allegiance. Their revolutionary doctrine, moreover, was never accepted by British workers. Typical was the refusal by John Burns of Hyndman's request to fly the red flag. Although the SDF enlarged its organization, particularly in London, held demonstrations, and sent delegations to Parliament, it never returned a member to the House of Commons, never counted over 10,000 members, and never became a mass party.

Part of the problem lay in the inability of any of its members to recall any precedent for revolution in their lifetimes.   Here the situation differed from that in France.   We have seen that the task of socialism to win converts among British workers was at best slow and painstaking. Their tradition of reliance on their own means of self-defense discouraged political action. Moreover, the rejection of revolutionary solutions, even by the new unionists, is explained by the fact that British workers were not only repelled by SDF orthodoxy, but they were attracted to existing British prescriptions for social change. The utilitarian-tinged radicalism of Jeremy Bentham, Richard Cobden, John Bright, and the Chartists hindered any party advocating a labor-led violent social upheaval and a working-class dictatorship. The English radical tradition contained sufficient plans for social reform, and English labor came to support a mass party only when it became convinced that its interests needed defense in Parliament, which the Liberal party could not satisfy.

THE FABIAN SOCIETY

However important their contribution in other respects, current research indicates the Fabians did little to revise Marx or form a labor party. Marxism never managed to get implanted in England, and both Engels and the British Left had already rejected insurrection there. Fabians placed their political hopes in the "permeation" of existing organization, never quite believing in the formation of a new party.

Fabians drew inspiration from John Stuart Mill as well as from Robert Owen, John Ruskin, Henry George, Christian socialists, and Chartists. Their intentionally limited and well-educated membership (only 640 in 1893, under 3000 in 1914) aimed at working with existing state machinery and at persuading political parties to place social reform on their programs. Fabians encouraged its members to infiltrate other and larger organizations, a tactic wholly comprehensible for a tiny, London-based group. However, as Sydney Webb later admitted, it underestimated the trade unions as a political force. In gathering and making data available, and by applying arguments drawn from the social sciences, the society sought to implement its objectives by stressing benefits and not fairness. Fabians were bound to no program, but rather to what they called a *basis*, designed to create industrial democracy by means of improvements in administration and expansion of state power. This appropriately reflected the civil-servant mentality prevalent in the makeup of the organization. Both Sydney Webb and Sydney Oliver (later Secretary for India in a Labour government) came from the Colonial Office and revealed a professional faith in the usefulness of higher administration.

The *basis* stated flatly that the society worked for the "transfer to the community of such industrial capital as can be conveniently managed socially"; consequently it was not hard to subscribe to.[3] It even provided for "relief" to individuals undergoing expropriation. Although anti-Marxist and favoring the inevitable and progressive development of existing institutions, contemporaries still considered it as socialist. What theory there was, was stated by Mrs. Besant in the seventieth tract published by the society. Like the German visitor Eduard Bernstein, who frequented Fabian circles and would soon expound similar thoughts, she said: "There will never be a point at which society crosses from individualism to socialism. The change is ever going forward and our own society is well on the way to socialism."

Fabians saw their objective as one of "making socialism, not socialists," and envisioned the former as an extension of the state's powers. (Webb offered a list of state activities and called each an installment of socialism.) Only one of the Fabian essayists, Hubert Bland, suggested that "it is not so much what the state does as its purpose for doing it that is the test."[4] Given this approach, the Fabians gradually managed to make socialism respectable. Their political action was less significant. They tried to win over the Liberals and chose to remain separate from the ILP. Their initial vague republicanism also passed, and they resolved to defend existing institutions. Fabians did not succeed in convincing the masses. Some, like George Bernard Shaw, came to repudiate the masses and questioned the democracy that had allowed them to participate in affairs of state.

A recent inquiry by Professor Eric Hobsbawm into their activities has shed light on the politics practiced. He represents them as a new strata of salaried administrators, unaffiliated either with the profit system or with individual enterprise. Their socialism, he said, was the outcome of their reaction to Victorian ideas of laissez-faire and their anticipation of the need for state intervention. Their disenchantment with economic liberalism issued less from a vision of a changed society than from a desire for greater efficiency. The leadership called for a heavily modified capitalism, one that foreshadowed the welfare state by providing national planning and minimum standards, so bringing an end to pure individualism. In this context, their subsequent support of the state, even its imperialism, becomes more understandable.

Fabians reflected the rise of the salaried, professional, technical, and intellectual cadres of post-laissez-faire capitalism. Coming from the middle classes and assimilated socially and often financially with the wealthy, they resembled today's technocrats in preferring service well performed and socially useful as its own reward. Hence they conformed to the liberal-professional ideal, regardless of their position on private or public enterprise. Their part in the socialist and labor movement was accidental rather than essential. Thus, Fabianism was not so much part of a socialist revival in the 1880s as a middle-class reaction to the breakdown of Victorian certainties.[5]

Their role in that movement was that of anticipating and successfully establishing the principle of economic planning and long-term evolutionary programs in the Labour party. (This alone would serve to distinguish them from their continental equivalents.) Popular identification of Fabians as socialists no doubt furthered the socialist cause; however, in trying to make liberalism work, they were acting in the best liberal tradition.

THE INDEPENDENT LABOUR PARTY (ILP)

Tradition played a prominent part in keeping the forces of labor from violence. The growth of democratic institutions in the 1880s also provided the setting in which *gradualism* could flourish. Property qualifications for borough councillors were removed in 1882; electoral reform brought an end to corrupt voting practices the following year; and extension of the suffrage in 1884 practically made England a democracy. In 1885, before the establishment of any party, 11 candidates pledging themselves to further the interests of labor were elected to Parliament. The example then being set by Irish nationalist MPs, whose needed support required governments to look favorably on them, was to serve labor representatives in both British and French legislatures. But labor in England decided on a political organization of its own only when convinced that it could not rely on Liberals to return working-class candidates. Obstacles to political organization of labor were the reluctance of the Fabians to the formation of a separate party and the hostility of Hyndman, whose misguided orthodoxy led him to suspect democratic forms and reject cooperation with trade unions.

The former secretary of the SDF, H. H. Champion, who had broken with Hyndman, and the popular Keir Hardie were responsible for the formation of the first labor party and brought to an end the earlier policy of supporting labor candidates running on the Liberal ticket. Hence it was not from weak and divided socialist groups that the Independent Labour party emerged, but from elements of the new unionism's leadership determined to elect their own members of Parliament. Its program resembled the SDF in many ways, but it repudiated any call to revolution and even avoided use of the socialist label. Even so, Engels was delighted with the creation of a third *class* party. But his optimistic assessment of its strength proved premature. The party was not accepted by the SDF or by the Fabian Society and never really broadened its Scottish and northern English base. It did not perform as well as anticipated in the elections of 1895 when Hardie lost his seat, and lost members when it took an unpopular pacifist stand during the Boar War. Still, it was the first to seek and win trade union support as a political base, the first with a socialist program, the first to govern by means of an annual congress, and it was to act as a left-wing stimulus in the years to come.

THE BIRTH OF THE LABOUR PARTY

As important a reason as any for the limited growth of the ILP was the refusal of the powerful craft unions to extend their support. They preferred to continue cooperation with the Liberals. However, the reaction of employers in the 1890s to the sudden expansion of trade unionism at the end of the previous decade—expansion generated by industrial growth and concentration—prompted a change of heart. The attempts by employers to undermine the legal basis of working-class organization was easily and rightly interpreted as a paramount threat to the trade union movement. The growth of employers' federations, the resort to lockouts and wage reductions, imports of continental labor, the founding of a parliamentary pressure group in 1898, and the growing number of lawsuits (sometimes decided in the House of Lords) convinced even traditional unions of the need for political representation. The Trade Unions Congress in 1899 voted to create a Labour Representation Committee. This direct parent of the Labour party was supported by the railroad workers (because railroad legislation was discussed in Parliament) but fought by miners (who by virtue of their concentrated strength were able to organize so effectively as to force Liberals to accept their candidates). The leaders of the unskilled workers carried the day. The committee was founded to coordinate plans for political representation. It had no political program of its own, but the ILP won the job of secretary for its nominee, Ramsay MacDonald.

Labor in Britain had not followed the American example of rejecting affiliation with a nationally organized political party, but could not rely any longer on one of the existing parties. The Liberals had shown themselves too inflexible and were unable to represent working classes among their candidates. Their inability to do so could in large part be explained by the party structure. Candidates were chosen not by the central party organization but by local caucuses. The caucuses were composed of business and professional men and nonconformist ministers, because workingmen were unable to pay their own expenses as candidates. The Liberals' concern with the Irish question before the turn of the century had prevented them from taking up such reforms as social legislation and salaries for MPs. Trade union chiefs, who were ready to rely on political weapons and unable to have working-class candidates nominated, turned to the idea of a new party. MacDonald correctly noted: "We did not leave the Liberals. They kicked us out and slammed the door in our faces."[6] The remaining unions turned to the LRC after the Taff-Vale Decision of 1903. (It made unions financially responsible for damages caused by strikes and so jeopardized the right to organize.) There seemed no alternative but political action. Given these antecedents, doctrine could scarcely have been stressed. Trade union leaders did not want to impose a certain view of the world or to carry out a political revolution, but to win improvements.   Unlike continental parties not initially sharing this objective, the Labour party was to be spared prolonged struggle over the legitimacy of parliamentary tactics.

Founded to coordinate and not initiate political action, the LRC entered into a series of manoeuvers designed to reach electoral accord with Liberals.[7]   Still, it was this committee that became the Labour party.   Of its 12 members, 5 were socialists, although socialist groups contributed only 6 percent of its funds.   No socialist demands were formulated.

By the end of 1903 nearly all the trade unions, except miners' organizations, supported the committee.   In giving salaries to its MPs, it could exert greater discipline and act more like a party.   The LRC entered into an alliance with the Liberals to avoid competition in the 1906 election.   It proved enormously successful.   The committee won 29 seats in the great Liberal victory of that year, including the 7 won by the ILP.   All 29 candidates were of working-class origin, a feat probably unique in socialist history.   The name *Labour party* was adopted when the new Parliament convened.   The Trades Union Act it sponsored and saw passed repealed the Taff-Vale Decision.   The party increased its representation during the course of the legislative session when the miners' unions joined, and their 24 *lib-lab* representatives became part of the Labour delegation.

CONCLUSION

Unlike other European political groups claiming to represent the interests of labor, the Labour party was the creation of the trade unions (in France, trade unions were not granted legal standing until 1884).   Responsible for labor's ability to organize politically was the democratic structure of the nation. Revolutionary socialism, then, died in England long before the Russian Revolution of 1917.   The LRC considered the Marxist SDF a nuisance, and subsequent events strengthened its early aversion to doctrine.   The party's structure reflected its commitment to nonviolent solutions.   Until 1918 membership was indirect; the largest contingent, the unions, automatically enrolled their members.   Given its federated structure, the unions comprised the largest voting bloc at party conferences.   The policy set by these annual conferences was only morally binding on Labour MPs.   Advocates of a more rigid class orientation complained of this and could also point out that the absence of any theory allowed easy compromise within national and local governing bodies.[8]

Labour remained closely associated with the Liberals as the latter pursued their great social legislation program in the first decade of the

new century. As the party revealed its willingness to behave less as an opposition than as a pressure group (hardly surprising in view of its
origins), radicals in it grew dismayed. Additional concern was voiced
by workers, impatient for improvements and questioning unfulfilled
promises. Some began to envisage different, more revolutionary action.
When economic crises before World War I worsened conditions, discontented elements within the party, we shall see, were to be joined by
advocates of extraparliamentary action.

GERMAN ORTHODOXY AND REVISIONISM

After the repression of the Paris Commune and the forced exile of its
leaders, socialist propaganda and campaigning were most active in Germany. German socialists were long convinced of the primacy of political activity. The successful resistance to Bismarck's *antisocialist laws*
displayed by the newly formed Social Democratic party (SPD) stamped
it with a "heroic" image. Labor credited the party with their removal.

Unlike Britain, however, liberalism in Germany had not emerged
wholly intact. Throughout Europe, the period beginning with the close
of the Middle Ages was marked by the struggle of the commercial
classes against absolutism. Insofar as they were successful—and a chief
indication of success was the establishment of liberal institutions—modern
labor and socialist movements were enabled to work within parliamentary frameworks. In Britain, the liberal victory was assured in the
formative years of these movements. In Germany, Bismarck fought
liberalism to a draw. The greater the strength remaining to absolutism,
the greater was the need for labor to seek the democratic conditions in
which political power could be won. (That the reverse was also true
helps to account for the relative absence of political action on the part
of labor in the United States.) During the Second Reich, a great coalition based on a mutual desire for protection was formed between the
large landowners east of the Elbe River, who dominated the government in Prussia, and the forces of industry. Given the predominance of
Prussia in Germany, the rule of this coalition extended throughout the
Reich.

There were other differences between the German and British
models. In the former it was the party that aided the growth of the
unions, although the unions were to demand and win a position of
parity. German socialism at the outset was formally committed to
revolution, and although revolutionary theory survived, the need of the
party to press against a strongly structured state, to win electoral victories and to cater to the demands made on it by labor helped to
shape it as a reform movement.

LASSALLE

The Reichstag was far from democratic; however, it was elected by popular franchise.   If several competing socialist factions could unite, the winning of seats was possible.   The two largest groups were those founded by Ferdinand Lassalle, the General German Workers Association, and by Wilhelm Liebknecht and August Bebel, the League of German Workingmen's Associations.   Both were established in 1863.

Lassalle came from a wealthy merchant family.   He had a brilliant university career.   He was also a romantic who spent 12 years in 36 law courts defending the interests of a mistreated countess.   Like Marx, with whom he had worked on the *Neue Rheinische Zeitung* in 1848, he saw the need for an independent workers' party.   Unlike Marx he was willing to rely on the state to establish a regime of social justice, and to that end worked to strengthen it.   His efforts to have Prussia rather than Austria take the initiative in unifying Germany, and his struggle for universal suffrage against that state's reactionary *three class* voting system led to correspondence and conversations with Bismarck.   He was also prepared, like Louis Blanc, to rely on state-initiated producers' co-operatives.   Although killed in a duel shortly after founding the party, he helped to popularize socialism and give it a political identity.   He also helped to persuade socialists to show confidence in the state and in economic as well as political action.

LIEBKNECHT AND BEBEL

The other party was the work of the Marxists.   Liebknecht was an intellectual devoted to Marx, whom he had met while in exile in London after 1848.   Bebel was a self-educated workingman.   Both leaders disliked the statist orientation given to socialism by Lassalle and his successor, Johann von Schweitzer.   This prompted the decision to launch a separate party.   By 1868 they had managed to furnish their organization with a socialist program.   In 1869 they presided over the formation of the Social Democratic Workingmen's party at a congress in Eisenach.   Tactically, the disputes between the Lassalleans and Eisenachers centered on whether socialism should side with Bismark or with his liberal democratic opponents.

The unification of Germany in 1871, the beginning of economic depression, and shared persecution prompted a merger.   At Gotha in 1875, both parties accepted a program edited by Liebknecht to form the Social Democratic party. It accepted both the doctrine of the class struggle and the Lassallean view of the state as the framework in which socialism was to be won.   The program also provided a role for producers cooperatives.   Marx's criticisms from London that German workers would be diverted from their real task of overthrowing capitalism and the state associated with it made little impression on the leadership in its quest for unity. In the Reichstag election of 1877, the new party quickly demonstrated its strength by returning 12 deputies and amassing almost half a million votes, nearly as many as all other socialist party votes in the world.

THE "ANTISOCIALIST LAWS"

The response came in the form of Bismarck's antisocialist legislation, as well as his social welfare program, both undertaken in an effort to destroy the party. Mild by today's standards, the laws forbade meetings and the distribution of literature, leaving the Reichstag as the only forum for free speech. They were renewed every two years until Germany changed chancellors in 1890. Newspapers, however, were published abroad, like *Der Sozial-Demokrat* in Switzerland by Eduard Bernstein. The SPD vote grew progressively larger, reaching almost one and a half million in 1890.

During this "heroic" period, a quarrel over tactics arose within the party. Revolutionaries denounced its tepid response to state repression, while moderates pointed to its continual growth and electoral successes. Debate lead to a new program, adopted at the Erfurt Congress in 1891. Lassallean references to state-aided producers cooperatives were dropped, and a new declaration of principles contained such Marxist themes as the growing concentration of industry and the immiserization of the working class. It also predicted more frequent and extensive economic crises and a widening gulf between the classes. The solution lay in the social ownership of the means of production and in the international solidarity of the workers. The means consisted of reliance on political action.

The list of demands that followed aimed at furthering democratic procedures. Included were the franchise for women and the extension of universal suffrage in Prussia, the referendum, a progressive income tax, and the 8-hour working day. In stressing orthodoxy in principle and in naming reformist objectives, the Erfurt program established within the German party the dichotomy between theory and practice that led to widespread controversy. The party was already the oldest and the largest. Because of the prestige won by its successful opposition to Bismarck, it became a model in international socialism and its program a prototype for others.

VOLLMAR AND REFORMISM

It was logical that interested groups within the SPD should grasp the implications of these proposed reforms. Twice in 1891 the socialist representative in the Bavarian legislature, the aristocrat and former cavalry officer Georg von Vollmar, called for "opportunistic" reform and for an end to systematic opposition to the regime. When the German government professed concern with reforms after Bismarck's dismissal in 1890, he tried to bring to it socialist support. At Erfurt, Vollmar had championed gradualism in a series of critical speeches. It may be argued that the importance attached to the property-conscious and Catholic peasant of agrarian Bavaria, rather than to his counterpart in the industrialized north, helps to account for these signs of dissatisfaction with revolutionary Marxist theory and with intransigent political behavior. Although Vollmar's request for party acceptance of the Triple Alliance and military credits in the event of war could be ignored by the party leadership, his resolution favoring socialist support of private peasant ownership could not be. At the Frankfurt Congress of 1894, it was placed on the following year's agenda. With Karl Kautsky leading the opposition, the proposal was then defeated on the grounds that all private ownership was exploitive. Recognizing, however, that "agriculture has its peculiar laws . . . which must be studied and considered if the Social Democracy is to develop an extended operation in rural districts," a committee of inquiry was set up and authorized to publish its findings.[9]

Nor could the party ignore Vollmar's proposal for the nationalization of mortgages, extension of rural credit, and administrative decentralization. All these objectives enjoyed widespread rural support. The socialist delegation in the Bavarian legislature subsequently voted for a state budget that was more favorable to the interests of workers and small farmers. It was but one further step to formulate a demand for the full freedom of action of local socialist representatives. Especially desired was party acceptance of their refusal to follow the traditional tactic of automatically rejecting government budgets. The party, it was held, was not "a religous sect or a scientific school" and must concern itself with reality, "however disagreeable."[10] Hence, reformism—or the readiness to acknowledge that changed conditions could render revolutionary approaches unnecessary—was both proposed and practiced well before efforts were made to revise Marxist theory. When reformists began to receive the support of a newly vitalized labor movement, a breach was opened within the party.

SOCIALISM AND THE TRADE UNIONS

So-called *free unions* had been founded by working-class parties in the 1860s as recruitment agencies for political activity on the local level. (They stood in contrast to those founded by religious groups and the *Progressives.*) As the centralization of industry led to more centralized union organization, membership increased, but like the Bavarian socialists, trade unions found the revolutionary façade of the SPD a handicap in recruitment. So they stressed improvements in working conditions, and left socialist propaganda to the party, while the party leadership, in turn, remained indifferent to the unions. The semiannual subject index of its newspaper, *Die Neue Zeit*, contained no section on trade unions until the last half of 1897.

The era of prosperity beginning in 1895 favored trade union growth. Membership doubled betwen 1896 and 1900 to pass 600,000. By 1904, it had reached a million. The ratio between SPD voters and union members was changing in favor of the latter, and organized labor constituted an ever-increasing percentage of the party's votes. The nature of the union leadership was also evolving. It assumed more bureaucratic dimensions, with "dry and unimaginative accountant types" replacing the "merchant adventurer who deals in class struggles." The *two pillar theory* of German working-class activity emerged, calling on the unions to discharge the economic functions of labor, and on the party to discharge the political ones. This worked as long as there was no conflict of interest; however, when the party began to show signs of reverting to revolutionary approaches in 1905, the unions were to shed their neutrality and reveal themselves as "the most aggressive and powerful of the reformist forces."[11]

EDUARD BERNSTEIN AND REVISIONISM

It was in this atmosphere of increasing prosperity and greater real wages that *revisionism* emerged. It was the effort to equate theory with these reformist currents. It was also part of the reaction of philosophic idealism, particularly neo-Kantianism, to the mechanical determinism of ninetenth-centruy science. The work was undertaken by a leading party theoretician, Eduard Bernstein. Fabianism and what he was to call the "free air of London" had been encountered during his years of exile from Bismarck. It either provided the basis of his criticism or reinforced existing doubts about the validity of certain Marxist teachings, doubts generated during the 1870s. In any case, Bernstein returned to Germany a confirmed revisionist.

He published a series of articles between 1896 and 1898 entitled "Problems of Socialism." The ideas expressed were developed more thoroughly in his book, translated as *Evolutionary Socialism: A Criticism and Affirmation* (1899). Bernstein argued that although the SPD was reformist in practice, it had lost potential support by stubbornly remaining attached to revolutionary principles. Engels' death in 1896 had removed his inhibitions to speak out against "outdated dogma," and he urged the party to take advantage of the assistance that bourgeois liberalism could render.

In an attempt to distinguish the "pure science" of Marxism from "applied science," he systematically rejected those elements that constituted the core of Marxist theory. Marxist economics, he said, needed revision because it conflicted with reality. The labor theory of value failed to account for the value of services rendered and consequently required modification by the theory of marginal value. If capitalism was becoming increasingly concentrated and therefore producing more serious crises, Marxism failed to anticipate the ability of the system to check these tendencies. Nor could it account for the viability of small- and medium-sized industrial, commercial, and agricultural enterprises.

Marx's social analysis was similarly contradicted by circumstances. The class structure was not becoming increasingly polarized; the middle classes were thriving and a new class of technicians had emerged. The proletariat, on its part, was far from homogeneous. Marx's prediction of growing proletarian misery was belied by a rise in the standard of living for all classes in a period of general prosperity. How these and similar observations led Bernstein to doubt some underlying assumptions of Marxist thought (like historical materialism) need not detain us. What matters in our context is the implication of heresy in all these things. Bernstein rejected the notion of a dialectical class struggle leading to revolution and substituted the concept of linear evolutionary progress through reform.[12] He said that the revolutionary establishment of socialism was neither desirable nor possible. It would negate the very values socialism rested on and mean "the reckless devastation of productive forces, insane experimentalizing and aimless violence . . . carried out in the form of dictatorial revolutionary central power, supported by a terroristic dictatorship of revolutionary clubs."[13] (Bernstein had the Blanquist model in mind when writing these words; bolshevism was still an unknown phenomenon.)

If valid, these criticisms would necessitate a major reorientation in the policies of the SPD. For the party, we have seen, while pursuing piecemeal reform insisted on maintaining a revolutionary rhetoric which corresponded to its leaders' interpretation of orthodox Marxism. Specifically, it would be required to break out of its isolation, actively seek allegiances with bourgeois groups, and in every way act in accordance with the belief that socialism was to be attained not by violence but through successful reforms.

Bernstein urged the SPD to drop its façade of insurgency and appear as it in fact was: "a democratic socialist party of reform." It could then receive the support of liberals unable to accept Social Democracy's revolutionary propaganda. Was this support likely? Given conditions in Wilhelminian Germany, could democracy, much less socialism, be reached through parliamentary means? Bernstein's readiness to sanction a general strike in the event of restrictions placed on the suffrage revealed his doubts about the willingness of progressive elements in the bourgeoisie to move to their left or even actively defend the quasi-liberal status quo. Still, he hoped they could follow the example of English and French equivalents. Bernstein's critics, as might be expected, repeatedly reminded him that Germany was not England.

Pessimism was probably justified. The central issues in pre-1914 German politics were those of the tariff and the military. (Hence the coalition of east Elbian landowners, supported by an agrarian majority and industrialists chiefly in steel and coal.) This alliance between labor's bourgeois and aristocratic opponents originated in the 1860s. Impressed by Bismarck's successes, elements of the liberal Progressive party abandoned the struggle against Prussian authority. Consequently, socialist demands for free trade and the pursuit of a measured foreign policy could scarcely have been accepted by the majority in the Reichstag. On the other hand, revolution has been described as having had no chance of success in Germany, and "what small hope existed of establishing socialism in the foreseeable future depended on the triumph of revisionism."[14]

Regardless of the validity of Bernstein's considerations (and to return to our proper field of inquiry), revisionism was expanding within the German socialist movement. By 1897 it had acquired its own newspaper, the *Sozialistische Monatshefte,* which opposed Kautsky's *Neue Zeit.* A contingent of those committed to working for immediate reform within a state framework began to urge that the party add an imperialist plank to its platform. The acquisition of overseas markets was seen as a means of improving the material well-being of the German workingman. Some went so far as to suggest that approval be given to cartels in order to limit future economic crises and in this way organize capitalism. In arguing that the ground would thus be prepared for socialism, proponents of this latter belief were joined by more orthodox Marxists.

In England, there was little of Marxism to revise. Revisionism, or variations thereof, emerged mainly where Marxism had become more or less an official theology: in Germany, Austria, and later, Russia. In view of the SPD's leadership in international socialism and of the profundity of Bernstein's arguments, its appearance in Germany was most important. Paradoxically, however, the practical consequences of revisionism were of less significance in Germany than in France, where that country's socialist movement accepted the SPD's official repudiation of Bernstein's proposals. Revisionism provided theoretical justification for the reformism set forth in the Erfurt program. In so doing, it contributed to a growing schism within the party in Germany, implying that revolution would not occur and that there were alternatives to Marx. Insofar as Bernstein reflected European economic conditions since the mid-nineties, his ideas helped create an attitude that favored a gradualist program. His chief supporters were practical party men, especially SPD delegates from the south and trade union leaders. That is, like their British equivalents, they were professional people who happened to be socialists.

Because of that southern region's more liberal traditions, the SPD could participate in communal affairs and occupy local government posts in accordance with its electoral strength. The insulation there between society and Social Democrats was thinner.[15] What was true for Germany was true for international socialism. Reformism was strongest where liberal and democratic institutions were most firmly embedded. The converse was equally defensible, regardless of such individual exceptions as the Russian Plekhanov (as contrasted to Lenin), the English Hyndman, and the German Bernstein.

Toward the turn of the century, the prestigious Social Democratic party sought both reform and symbolic revolt. It refused to vote for government budgets or to salute the Kaiser, and these gestures were approved by SPD voters. The party took pride in being a socially defensive organization, in total opposition to society. It saw itself, in the words of the historian Peter Nettl, as an *inheritor* party. Its vote continued to climb. The party won over 10 percent of those cast in the Reichstag elections of 1887; over 19 percent in 1890; 27 percent in 1898, and 31 percent in 1903. Its numerical vote increased over this period of time from one and three quarters to over three million.

FRENCH REFORMISM

Hostility between trade unionists and socialists early emerged as a factor in the history of French labor. It helped to keep the socialist movement divided in the years to come. During the 1890s, however, most socialists (including Marxists) revealed their commitment to moderate or reformist tactics. They relied on the machinery for change made available by the Third Republic. This is the theme that we have to consider first. Although the French labor movement, heir to the anarchist tradition of Proudhon, differed from the German in opposing not only reformism but even political solutions, French socialism was becoming ever more reformist. The necessity of revolution was replaced by a view of peaceful and progressive change by means of democratic methods in a parliamentary framework.

JULES GUESDE AND MARXISM

Both economic and political forces had served to retard the development of the French socialist movement. First repression of the Left following the Commune and then economic depression of the 1880s undermined efforts at working-class organization. Trade unions and socialist groupings left fragmented and powerless grew timid and found themselves isolated. During its slow recovery, many within the socialist movement fell prey to the influence of Marxism. A number of returning emigrés abandoned Proudhonist and Blanquist sympathies, popular under the Second Empire, to adopt the new ideology. But the rapid growth of Marxism in France must be attributed primarily to the persistent efforts of its leading propagandist, Jules Guesde.

Guesde was born in Paris in 1845. A republican under the Empire, he supported the Commune, fled to Geneva after its destruction in 1871, and returned to France five years later. Frequent and intense contact with young Marxist intellectuals and much poring over Marxist classics persuaded him to repudiate a Bakuninist orientation acquired in Switzerland and Italy. What was absorbed most readily in Marx's writings were the political prescriptions set forth in the Communist Manifesto and in the analyses of the Commune. What was most readily vulgarized and taught was the insistence that there could be neither socialism nor socialization, and that no problem could be solved until the proletariat took power.

He founded *L'Egalité,* the first French Marxist newspaper, and in it repeatedly affirmed the tenets of class struggle. Impressed by the success of the German socialists in establishing a united party, Guesde favored the development of a workers' party in France. But he viewed it primarily as a means by which workers could be made class-conscious. At a national meeting of labor organizations held at Marseilles in October, 1879, those who advocated collectivism as the goal and political action as the means triumphed over delegates who supported economic and cooperative organization. The assembled delegates authorized the creation of a new party, the Federation of Socialist Workers, and with Marx's aid a minimum program was drafted in 1880. Historians of French socialism have exaggerated somewhat the extent of the collectivist victory, ignoring the concessions necessarily made to anarchists and Blanquists. Chief among these concessions was that which provided the party with a decentralized structure. The struggle to eliminate anarchist influence, for example, was to take over a decade and a half. Guesdism provided the most dynamic element in French socialism and was to leave a heritage claimed by both socialists and communists long after its disappearance as an independent force in the French workers' movement. For our purposes, it may be noted that other, more moderate socialists, Independents and Broussists, had long sought change through legal mechanisms. Not until Marxists pursued reformism after 1890 did this tactic become a significant factor in socialist history.

BROUSSE AND POSSIBILISM

However diminutive the socialist movement, reformist tendencies within it had appeared early in the Third Republic. The same resentment of Marxist authoritarianism that had cemented the anti-Marxist bloc in the First International reemerged among French socialists. Moreover, the restraints placed upon socialist propaganda and even on militant trade unionism after the Commune, as well as the successful consolidation of a parliamentary republic, all encouraged the appearance of an evolutionary, nonviolent approach.

The poor showing of Marxists in the 1881 legislative elections, in which they compiled only 60,000 votes, helped to arouse a reformist reaction. Resentment was expressed toward Marxist and German ideas by Paul Brousse, Benoît Malon, and others; conversely, emphasis was placed on local French tradition and needs. A faction within the federation, headed by Brousse, questioned the usefulness of revolutionary nomenclature if in practice it required programs that permitted recruitment of only "a handful of soldiers," produced "no effective results," and left threats "hanging in the air . . . and hands forever reaching." Brousse preferred to abandon what he called the "all at once" method favored by the party because, as he put it, it succeeded largely in being "nothing at all."[16] He sought instead to divide the ideal objective into several realistic stages and to formulate demands in such a way as to render them possible to fulfill. His "policy of possibilities" issued from his experiences on the Paris Municipal Council and rested on the suffrage that had sent him there. It relied on a decentralized structure and aimed at ever-widening public services beginning at the municipal level. Guesde complained that all this would *embourgeois* the party and dismissed Brousse and his supporters as "possibilists." When, however, they won a majority at the Saint-Etienne Congress of 1882, Guesdists broke away in the first of many schisms to rack French socialism and founded a separate Workers' party.

MALON AND INTEGRAL SOCIALISM

More momentous for reformism, from the standpoint both of theory and numbers of partisans, was a group of independent socialists who rejected affiliation with any faction. Corresponding to what one historian of the movement called "a peculiarly French temperament," Independents clustered about the important *Revue socialiste,* founded by Malon in 1885. Until his death in 1893, he provided reformists with intellectual inspiration. A former dyer and shepherd, and self-educated, he displayed an eclectic approach which drew on all socialist roots, Babeuf and Proudhon, as well as Marx. He denied that existing phenomena issued from economic causes alone and maintained that all who suffer (for whatever reasons) composed the socialist army. A newer, more integral form of socialism was therefore needed. It would transform society not only economically, but philosophically and morally; and Malon thus attached socialism to the humanitarian tradition. His ideas were rooted in the view of history held by Condorcet and Comte, as well as by Saint-Simon. Accordingly, he and his disciples stressed the French origins of socialist thought and saw Marxism as foreign to that tradition. Socialist legislation rather than revolution was held as the intention of integral socialism; the gathering of data was preferred to the threat of violence as a means; and the preservation of the republic that had given workers the vote was accepted as a concomitant.

Malon may thus be viewed as linking utopian socialists and Jean Jaurès, the future leader of the movement, in the development of French socialist thought; his influence may be compared with that of Mill on English radical thought. As Mill had translated Bentham's theories into a Victorian context, so the *integralists* translated the French socialism of the first half of the nineteenth century into the setting of the Third Republic and transformed the republicanism of 1789 into the drive for basic economic reform. Integral socialism set the moral tone for French social democracy for the next half century. The conversion of liberal deputies like Jaurès and Alexandre Millerand to socialism may be attributed to Malon and his associates, who persuaded them that in their new maturity socialists were agents of social development and "men of peace and prudence." Integral socialism gave the movement in France its first deputies, newspapers, review, and, ultimately, first minister.

As objectives of reformist socialism, Malon identified the enactment of social legislation and the nationalization of transportation, commerce, and finance. He pointed to the Commune as the motor of economic life and, like Brousse, reduced the role of the state to the administration of national public services. In praising the benefits of French democracy, integral socialists said that the Republic had necessarily to be maintained (although Malon's conception of socialism's role in matters of national defense was hazy). In asking for party unity, he wrote that socialists could not "devote themselves to internal revolution" while surrounded by "powerful and hostile monarchies" and situated "under the guns of the Triple Alliance." International socialist solidarity was defended, in part, as a means to promote simultaneous pressure on national parliaments for specific reforms and so prevent the nation unilaterally adopting them from being put at a competitive disadvantage.[17]

VAILLANT AND BLANQUISM

Before the elections of 1881 another socialist organization emerged and took on organizational shape. The Central Revolutionary Committee was composed of the followers of Auguste Blanqui, and they respected Marx. They remained more a movement than a party, advocating use of conspiratorial tactics in the style of 1848. In keeping with the Jacobin view that members of the proletariat were unable substantially to advance their own cause, a small group was to seize power on their behalf. Blanquists recognized as their chief Edouard Vaillant. Born in Vierzon in 1840 and educated in medicine, he became a friend of Blanqui and served on the Commune's executive committee. He benefited from the general amnesty of 1880 to return from exile. Four years later he was elected to the Paris Municipal Council. Although never relinquishing his revolutionary outlook, he showed his concern for the well-being of the workingman by fighting for such reforms as the establishment of a municipal labor committee and minimum standards in city contracts.

After the schism created by the Guesdist departure in 1882, Broussists founded a new party, abandoned the Marxist program adopted only two years before, and urged additional autonomy for individual socialists. The Guesdist Workers party, in turn, reaffirmed Marxism, reemphasized tight party discipline, and ultimately adopted the structure of the German Social Democratic party: sections at the base, regional federations above them, and a national congress at the summit. An executive council was established to administer party affairs between congresses, and the preponderant position on it by Guesde and his associates permitted them to stamp the party with their own imprint.

The strength of the Workers party lay in the industrialized regions in the north and center of the country, and in these areas among the metals industries and textile workers. Possibilists made a greater impact among the more skilled workers in the clothing and building trades, and were strong in Paris and western France. Brousse did not shrink from including bourgeois elements within party ranks and from calling for greater state intervention, particularly in the public services. By 1886 Possibilists had placed three candidates on the Paris Municipal Council, and Brousse was to become president of that body. The party grew concerned with winning additional victories and accordingly reduced the revolutionary aspects of its program.

The growing moderation of the Broussists created yet another schism. In 1890 a group of dissidents, led by the typographer Jean Allemane, accused the party of having moved too far from socialist principles and broke away. Except for Malon, Allemane held the distinction of being the only authentic workingman to play a leadership role in French socialism. Allemanists sought middle ground between what they regarded as the excessive centralization of the Guesdists and the extreme laxity of the Broussists. More antipolitical than either, they remained convinced that trade unions had a larger and more original part to play than most socialists were prepared to admit.   In 1891 they came out in favor of the general strike, and the teachings of Allemane were to become one of the roots of revolutionary syndicalism.

SOCIALISM AND THE FRENCH ECONOMY

The political impotence of French socialism in the early years of its formation was in large part the result of these incessant schisms.   One socialist sat in the 1881 legislature and only five in that elected in 1885. Competing for working-class support were Clemenceau's Radicals, with a program of social as well as political reforms. Factionalism, the implementation of the demand for political identity by these various tendencies, was perhaps the single greatest characteristic of the French socialist and labor movements. The explanation for its weakness, however, seems to be structural and psychological rather than ideological.

Steady if slow industrial growth had created a substantial working force in France.   Because of the unique structure of French industry, however, labor had not succeeded in organizing in defense of its interests. The French economy differed from that of other Western nations in that it retained its physiognomy of rural democracy.   Even in industrialized areas, aside from the northern and eastern departments where large-scale industry brought workers together and disciplined them (precisely the areas most heavily committed to Marxism), individual ownership and no great concentration of capital prevailed.   Of every 100 establishments, as late as the turn of the century, 70 contained only one or two workers, and 93 had fewer than 10 (the national average was 5.5), retaining thereby a markedly individual character. Even the thriving Department of the Seine (mainly Paris) still contained numerous small firms.[18]

A weakly concentrated capitalism helped to account for a correspondingly weak labor movement.   Strikes broke out largely in the mining, iron, and steel industries where concentration reached its peak. Workers, moreover, lacked a spirit of solidarity.   Many took the side of their employers in industrial conflicts.   In January, 1900, total trade union membership numbered only 491,000.   The corresponding figure in England reached 1.5 million.   In addition, the decentralized status of industry had solidly anchored within the worker a *petit bourgeois* ideal.   He did not feel himself radically removed from the small entrepreneur in whose shop or home he often worked, and who often earned little more than he did.   Thus at the end of the nineteenth century the working movement in France lacked unity and sufficient solidarity to present itself as a large and effective force.   One final observation, portentous of the future, is appropriate.   Trade unionists in Britain and Germany remained affiliated with socialists, while many but not all became independent of and hostile to their political champions in France. The reasons for the separation are varied and best discussed in a consideration of the chief consequence of this hostility—the development of revolutionary syndicalism.

It may have been the frustrations and sense of impotence issuing from the decentralized structure of French industry that caused socialist leaders to turn on each other, however much they disguised their attacks with ideological trappings.[19]   Structural analyses of the various factions are of little avail here because institutional frameworks, where they existed, did not prevent strong leaders from playing a dominant role. That these groups, even the Marxists before 1890, had relatively little structural organization and revolved around the personalities of their chiefs was best demonstrated by fact that the long party names were seldom used. Socialist parties, the sociologist Robert Michels wrote, "so often identified with a leader that they more or less officially used his name, as though to proclaim they were his property."[20] French groupings, we have seen, were very much referred to in terms of their leaders: Guesdists, Broussists, Allemanists, and soon, Jaurèssists. Party chiefs continued to exert preponderant influence after the establishment of institutional frameworks. This tendency was abetted by socialism's working-class clientele. Their natural realism allowed them to perceive the man behind the function and obey the individual not the title. Belief in institutions, according to the political scientist Maurice Duverger, depends on "certain abstract juridical culture and respect for forms and titles which belong to the middle class."[21]   Historical and political explanations also illuminate the divisions in French socialism. An historical revolutionary past, with different traditions of protest, and the freedom of expression offered by the Third Republic all worked against the early emergence of a united party.

REFORMISM

Thus, by the end of the 1880s reformists might best be described in terms of what distinguished them from Guesdists. The former tried to strike a balance between Marxism and those elements in French society found worthy of preservation. For reformists, it was through suffrage that they would implant socialism: by establishing public services, for the followers of Brousse; by transforming society not only economically but morally and philosophically, for the disciples of Malon. It may have been the gradualness of the approach that made for loose, almost nonexistent structures and permitted overtures to all interested parties. Confidence in anticipated election results prompted defense of the Republic against Boulangist opposition. Guesdism, on the contrary, was materialist in doctrine, small and increasingly disciplined in membership.

It made light of universal suffrage and the revolutionary potential of organized labor and expressed neutrality in regard to the defense of republican institutions.

However, the road to success had been indicated to the Marxists. By 1890 the Workers party had accepted the Republic and was concentrating on electing its candidates, a decision, as we have seen, in no way incompatible with the tactics set forth by Marx even in the 1848 *Manifesto*. The party program was made more attractive. It called for social legislation, a minimum wage, and free medical services. Guesdists began to win victories on municipal councils. By 1892 they had placed majorities on 26. Like Broussists and independent socialists, they soon found themselves absorbed by parliamentary activity. After his own election to the Chamber of Deputies in 1893, Guesde became infatuated with the benefits to be won at the ballot box. He began his definition of socialism as "social legislation in favor of labor." The state, he continued, would be pushed to socialize the means of production. When controlled by the workers, it would enable them to expropriate capitalist holdings. The immediate task was "to grasp as many reforms from the state as possible while awaiting the definitive transformation." Social legislation and the 8-hour day would breach the wall; the revolution would follow. The degree to which all this was compatible with Marxist thought is less important than the fact that Guesdists were behaving differently from before. The Workers party entered into alliances with other political groups and started to win legislative representation. French socialism thus began the large-scale involvement with reform that marked its history in the last decade of the century.

It required no great shift for moderates to continue their reformist tactics. A number of reasons, all related, explain the adoption of a reformist stand by Marxists. They came to realize that the likelihood of victory through an act of force had been overestimated. This misjudgment, in turn, issued from a superficial assimilation of Marxist doctrine that had led them first to underestimate the consequences of the vote, then to overestimate it, and consequently to expose themselves to accusations of dogmatism and sectarianism. Guesdist legislators tried to enact measures of social reform. The policy secured additional votes, but increasingly committed the party to work within a capitalist framework. The specific need to present the majority of Frenchmen, who in 1890 still worked on the land, with an attractive agricultural program may also be identified as a causal factor. Guesdists anticipated electoral advantages from alliances with progressive bourgeois groups, and their change of course soon became obvious.

Paul Lafargue, Guesde's chief lieutenant, was elected to the Chamber in 1891, the first Marxist to sit there. Marxists also joined the Socialist Union, a coalition of socialists and members of the Radical party organized by the Independent socialist, Alexandre Millerand, for the election of 1893. Almost 50 candidates running on socialist programs were returned. Allied with Radicals, they became a force to be reckoned with.

The architect of the socialist success and the movement's most formidable parliamentary personality was the lawyer Millerand. A Radical associated with Clemenceau, he came under Malon's influence and was converted to socialism in 1891. Also from the Radicals, but more important for the future of socialism in France, came Jean Jaurès. He was born into a bourgeois family in Castres, and excelled at the renowned École Normale, where he specialized in philosophy. He was elected to the 1885 Chamber and was drawn into socialism by the school's librarian, Lucien Herr. The latter convinced him that it was not necessary to be a Guesdist or a Blanquist in order to be a socialist. Jaurès was to put into practice the idealism introduced into French socialism by Malon and was to remain the movement's uncontested leader until his death in 1914.

Socialists formed a tightly knit minority in the Chamber of 1893–1898. Allied with Radicals, they overturned governments deemed insufficiently progressive and also helped to oust a conservative president of the Republic. More positively, socialist deputies adopted and defended positions that earlier would have been seen as inconceivable. The first all-Radical ministry of Léon Bourgeois, with a program headed by separation of church and state and a progressive income tax, deliberately sought socialist support. Socialists approved the day-to-day requests of the government and prevented its fall by voting even to retain the repressive legislation enacted in the wake of previous anarchist attacks.

Every socialist faction, save the revolutionary Allemanists, approved of Millerand's Saint-Mandé speech in May, 1896. In setting forth the minimum criteria permitting a candidate to receive socialist support, it embodied the reformist standpoint. As a legislator, Guesde submitted bills calling for the establishment of grievance machinery and labor councils. He hailed the Socialist Union and said there was no need of theoretical accord for republican defense.

In regard to foreign affairs, Guesde's consistent view of war as the natural outcome of bourgeois conflict and his denunciation of insurrectional means to prevent it were compatible with growing patriotic feeling on the part of reformists. France was to be defended by its proletariat. Accordingly, even the forthcoming alliance with tsarist Russia (for socialists the most reactionary regime in Europe) was endorsed. The Eleventh Annual Workers Party Congress, held in October, 1893, asked only that a distinction be made between sailors and officers at the impending visit of a Russian squadron. The executive council of the party (and *français* was now firmly added to *Parti ouvrier*) in a in a declaration addressed to the workers of France said that it was "calumny" to maintain that socialists had no country. Internationalism in no way implied national degradation or sacrifice. On the contrary, nations constituted the "necessary step towards humanity," and the success of the "French proletariat's historic mission" required "a great and strong France." The Marxist proclamation ended with: "France attacked will have no more ardent defenders than socialists of the Workers party."

Revolutionary Blanquists also defended the Franco-Russian alliance. Vaillant described it as a measure to keep the peace. If socialist criticism of the pact developed later in the decade, much of it stemmed from fears that a total commitment to Russia might be contrary to French national interests. Closer to home, Guesdists defended the Republic during the Panama scandal. For the elections of 1898 the Workers party asked labor to reaffirm its faith in this "necessary instrument of [its] emancipation." Both in domestic and foreign affairs the reformism of French socialists appeared complete. Few could anticipate a new surge of militancy at the end of the century, one strengthened by the pressure of revolutionary syndicalism.

SOCIALISM IN RUSSIA

The pattern of socialist development in Germany and France, or variations thereof, appeared elsewhere. The many small groups that had emerged at the time of the First International began to congeal into national units. Most were based on the German example. Dutch socialists adopted the Gotha program in 1882, but a dozen years of struggle against the anarchists took place before the Social Democrat party was founded in 1894. The constitution approved by the Belgian Workers party, founded in 1885, was similarly designed, although Proudhonist influence remained substantial in the party for some time. And ethnic differences between Flemish- and French-speaking segments of the population encouraged a more decentralized structure and greater reliance on local government. The parties formed in Austria and Switzerland also looked to the German experience. Kautsky drafted a revolutionary Marxist program for the newly founded Austrian Social Democratic party early in 1889. We shall see, however, that in order to give expression to the major ethnic groups within the Austrian Empire, its highly centralized structure was transformed into a loose federation within a decade.

The Italian and Spanish movements (countries more economically underdeveloped and with workers subject to stronger anarchist influence) resembled the French pattern and shared its propensity toward doctrinal discord. Still, in Italy, after the deaths of Mazzini (1872) and Garibaldi (1882) and an extension of the franchise in 1882, anarchists were expelled from the party in the early nineties. Reformism appeared to carry the field. In Spain, Marxism never managed to repress the anarchist-dominated trade union movement. Nowhere else was organized labor sufficiently developed to introduce socialism and prevail in working-class politics.

The other great exception, although of a totally different order, was that of Russia. After the assassination of Tsar Alexander II in 1881, the autocracy stifling Russian political life only intensified. There seemed no chance for the emergence of legal mechanisms to bring about social change. Consequently, there seemed to be little possibility of a political party devoted to the interests of labor. Opposition leaders were forced into exile. A different brand of socialism was to be required, but not until the 1905 Revolution would bolshevism be considered a possible prototype.

Amidst a variety of prescriptions for social change considered by a creative if powerless intelligentsia, two views may be identified as predominant. One aimed at a populist solution (*narodnichestvo*). Its adherents pointed to the socialist character of indigenous institutions, and saw no need to follow Western examples. The other sought to imitate the West and specifically to struggle for a bourgeois revolution in order to create the liberal society that alone, it believed, could make socialism a reality. The complicating factor in the history of Russian socialism is that power was ultimately won by those who rejected both a populist approach and the establishment of bourgeois democracy.

Populists (*narodniks*) offered a Russian revolutionary plan which proposed to bypass capitalism and reorganize society on the basis of the *mir*, or village collective holdings. Populism constituted the dominant radical tradition before socialism. Its advocates saw in the peasant commune the seeds of future cooperative society and hoped to avoid a harsh and disruptive capitalism. In contrast to the Bakuninists, Peter Lavrov called for a nonterrorist means to the same agrarian socialism. Lavrov had been an artillery colonel and mathematics professor in the Military Academy. His political views led to his arrest and exile. Published in 1868–1869, his *Historical Letters* specified a program of propaganda and education to be carried out among the peasants. These essays animated the Russian populist movement.

Young people, many educated abroad and exposed to the teachings of Alexander Herzen and Bakunin, had already sensed a debt owed to the masses. They idealized the peasantry and saw in it a source of wisdom. Roused by Bakunin's appeal in the spring of 1873, hundreds moved to the countryside. They wanted to live there, to teach and to learn, but were rejected and reported by the suspicious farmers. And a hostile government opposed even these efforts. Disillusioned with populist idealism, many turned to insurrection. Early revolutionaries pinned their hopes on the assassination of the worst government officials. A number were attempted. The most notable was that of Alexander II by the organization known as the *People's Will*. The government responded with greater and more effective repression. Other revolutionary Marxists living in exile attacked all populist alternatives.[22]

PLEKHANOV

One such group, with a wholly Marxist program, was founded in Geneva in 1883. G. V. Plekhanov, who had translated several works of Marx and Engels into Russian, was a key figure. The son of a minor landowner, he had shown sympathy for the peasant and as a student had become involved in revolutionary activity. He came to reject the populism which taught that capitalism in Russia was accidental and not at all necessary as an agent of change. In contrast, he considered the peasantry as hopelessly retrograde and incapable of revolution. Only the working class generated by a triumphant capitalism and allowed to express itself by means of bourgeois-liberal institutions could achieve a socialist society. Among his associates were Vera Zasulich, who had been acquitted in a sensational jury trial after an attempted assassination of the chief of Saint Petersburg police, and Paul Axelrod, who was influenced by Lassalle and by the German Social Democratic party organization. The group, known as the Emancipation of Labor, broke with populists and denied that an indigenous socialism based on existing peasant collectivization could be attained. Following Plekhanov's lead, its members rejected individual heroics and doubted that peasants could take the initiative in the drive for social reorganization. They preferred to base their analyses on history and science.

As a propaganda organization, the group helped to create the first Marxist circles within Russia. It attacked the *narodniks* and attempted to prepare Russia for a Marxist socialist revolution. However, it enjoyed little visible success. In addition to the handicaps attendant on any party working in exile, it was burdened by a clannish organization (Plekhanov's personality discouraged recruitment) and financial problems. The stress placed on doctrinal purity earned it the scorn of sympathetic but critical socialists abroad who preferred an action-oriented approach. Still, aside from a few short-lived groups within Russia, it was the only Marxist organization in the 1880s, in the period between the decline of populism and rise of Marxism.[23]

Populism survived under vastly modified form in groupings founded near the turn of the century. It received national identity in 1901 as the Socialist Revolutionary party (SR) (and, it might be argued, by the Bolsheviks themselves, insofar as Lenin tactically accepted the need for alliance with the peasants). Socialist Revolutionaries observed the teachings of Herzen and Bakunin, rejected bourgeois revolution, and sought an extension—in the form of nationalization (but with cultivation left to the individual peasant family)—of the socialist elements already founded on common use of the soil owned by the village. The SRs won the support of various intellectuals, civil servants, and students. Opposed was the Social Democratic Labor party (SD) founded at Minsk in 1898. Because Social Democratic leaders were arrested shortly afterwards, the theoretical modifications and tactics were provided by Lenin from abroad. Vladimir Illyitch Ulianov was born in 1870 into a family of civil servants. He turned to revolutionary agitation after the execution of an older brother for terroristic conspiracy. He read Marx and organized a socialist group in Samara, where he practiced law. Lenin was arrested and sent to Siberia in 1895. Not until 1900 did he return; he was again arrested, and shortly after left Russia to live in exile.

ECONOMISM

Russian Social Democrats constituted a small group of intellectuals and students. They had few contacts with workers. Workers, on their part, were untrained in trade union organization. The industrialization carried out by the regime and the economic prosperity of the mid-nineties were responsible for a surge of working-class activity. Labor's demands were largely economic: reduced hours, higher wages, and improved conditions. Socialists took advantage of this discontent to increase their propaganda and aid strikes, and so win greater influence. They led the Moscow and St. Petersburg strikes in 1895 and a textile strike the following year. These acts on behalf of labor gave rise to currents within socialism at about the turn of the century known as *economism*. Insofar as its proponents held that the struggle for the immediate economic needs of the workers took precedence over political demands for the abolition of the tsarist and capitalist regimes, it roughly corresponded to Western reformism.

Notoriety was given to these ideas by the decision to allow the legal publication of Marxist literature. The government had eased restrictions on Marxist-oriented publications as part of its effort to destroy what it regarded as the greater enemy, populism. The economist, Peter Struve, published an attack on populism, urging a strictly scientific and determinist Marxist method and predicating societal change and the fulfillment of working-class objectives on a bourgeois victory and its accompanying industrial and liberal growth. Consequently, some Marxists relegated a workers' revolution to a remote future; it was necessary first to follow the Western example and strive for a liberal and democratic

state. Critics, especially Lenin, could point out that while socialists elsewhere sought the destruction of capitalism, those in Russia wanted to
promote its growth. His opponents, in turn, could retort that they were
simply following the prescriptions set forth by Marx.

It should be said that Marx could hardly be held responsible for all
the tactics subsequently drawn from his writings. It was perhaps natural
for him to be cited by those who argued that Russia must submit to the
inevitable growth of capitalism. However, he had postulated no law
which said that Russia had to match the Western experience, unless, of
course, Russian industrialization took place along Western lines.[24]

A disciple of Eduard Bernstein, S. N. Prokopovitch, distinguished
political efforts, best left to the liberal bourgeoisie, from labor's struggle
for economic improvement. Hence the insistence by economism that
labor could achieve its objectives without recourse to any party established on its behalf. The political appearance of the proletariat, it argued, was premature. Workers were still too weak, and political intervention would serve only to frighten the middle classes and drive them
to support the government.

It was to counter this approach that Lenin, in exile, founded the
journal *Iskra* (Spark) and in 1902 published *What Is To Be Done?*
Both newspaper and brochure took the position that workers were to
play a directing role in bringing forth the conditions of their own
emancipation. Specifically, political organization was required. Political and economic power, he argued, could not be separated, and the
struggle to win both must be fought along class lines by a class party.
Necessary was a professional revolutionary organization acting as an
avant-garde for the working class.

His analysis did in fact correspond to changing realities. The great
wave of strikes had petered out at the turn of the century. Political
issues were once more paramount, and within five years a revolution was
to break out. Lenin's writings elicited a change in strategy by his party.
In insisting that socialism would have to be imposed on the working
class by the party, he planted the seeds of dictatorship in the Russian
movement. In any event, these debates left the realm of theory when
Social Democrats split on the question of reorganizing along the lines
he laid down.

THE SECOND INTERNATIONAL

Even in those parties in which it was assumed that the reorganization
of society on socialist bases required revolutionary action, political imperatives made for the acceptance of democratic forms and generated
a willingness to work for change within existing state frameworks.

Revisionists in Germany wanted to give this approach theoretical expression. In Russia, during a period of mounting industrialization and relative prosperity, a roughly similar tendency might be detected. Before considering the reaction to these events, we must ask whether parallel tendencies were felt within the organization that arose in 1889 to further mutual socialist objectives, the Second Workingmen's International. We shall see that given its federated structure, it could hardly have been otherwise.

The Marxist legacy was uncertain, perhaps necessarily so, about the road to power. It insisted only on political rather than economic means. Marx was in no way dogmatic about the socialist future and appeared willing to let tactics reflect circumstances. After the failures of 1848, and aware of the extent to which existing regimes had profited by improvements in military proficiency, he was prepared to recognize the durability of bourgeois control. An age of revolutionary upheaval, he admitted, had come to an end. Although revolution was never ruled out, Marx estimated that under some progressive regimes socialism might be achieved without recourse to violence. The "revolution" here meant the complete reorganization of society that would follow the socialist conquest of power. Insofar as the SPD's Erfurt program served socialism as a prototype, it continued the ambiguity. Its statement of principles implied a catastrophic base, but it omitted any reference to revolution; and the specific reforms listed were all readily attainable through parliamentary procedures. Hence the question remained: Was the political action prescribed for workers to be revolutionary or parliamentary, or both; and if the last, how were the two approaches related?

Marx died in 1883. Engels survived him by over a decade and displayed even greater tactical flexibility.

One can envisage that the old society could peacefully grow into the new one in countries where the representatives of the people concentrate all power in themselves, where one can do, constitutionally, whatever one pleases, so long as the majority of the people give their support, in democratic republics such as France and America, or in monarchies like England where the dynasty is powerless against the will of the people. But in Germany, where the Government is almost omnipotent and the Reichstag and other representative bodies for all practical purposes powerless, to proclaim anything like this in Germany would be to remove the fig leaf from absolutism and use it to conceal one's own nakedness.[25]

In almost his last work, the introduction to Marx's *Class Struggles in France*, Engels had nothing but praise for the SDP and its 2 million voters. He pointed to the military improvements that had taken place since 1848, like the greater troop mobility made possible by improvements in transportation and the increase in firepower offered by the breech-loading rifle. In advancing the capabilities of the regular army, these changes all worked to the advantage of those defending the status quo. They rendered the days of the barricades over. Engels did not reject revolution, especially where the vote did not exist (precisely the passages struck from German editions by Social Democratic editors fearful of legal reprisals). But in arguing that national legislatures might contain socialist majorities and that they could ensure victory for the working class, he had accepted gradualist tactics. An overall assessment of the Second International suggests that the spokesmen for international socialism were no less committed to parliamentary procedures.

Marx and Engels were responsible for the delay in reviving the International. They estimated that necessary requisites were strong national (meaning Marxist) parties and the elimination of hostile socialist systems whose rivalry would once more be disastrous. In point of fact, Marxism emerged triumphant in only two parties, the German and the Austrian, by the time the Second International was founded. Equally paradoxical was that while the founders of Marxism feared the peculiarities of British and French socialists, the most formidable opposition came from the anarchists.

ANARCHISM

The early years of the Second International, as was the case with the last years of the First, were marked by the battles fought against anarchists. For our purposes they may be regarded as those who rejected all compromise with parliamentary forms and viewed the existence of the state as incompatible with individual liberty. Depending on the sect involved, anarchists sought to destroy it, or to work for as much decentralization as possible. We need not focus on the theoretical debates, but should estimate their consequences for international socialism. Members of the Second International were all too aware of the clash between the exponents of political and economic action (between Marxists and Bakuninists) that did so much to break up its predecessor. Anarchists were fought successfully at the International's early congresses, the delegates to which went on record as expressing preference for political solutions. The effort to proscribe anarchists and repudiate the reliance placed on their chief weapon, the general strike, was the great battle fought out in the first decade in the life of the Second International.

Anarchism flourished where the state was most economically retarded and repressive, largely in areas bordering the Mediterranean and in Eastern Europe. Some but not all of its practitioners advocated the use of terror. Arguments for the expulsion of anarchists were heard at the International's first congress, in Paris, in 1889. They were revived at Brussels two years later, and a majority warned against "inopportune" use of strikes and boycotts. At Zurich, in 1893, it was acknowledged that parliamentary action was the "means *par excellence* by which [workers] can attain their emancipation." Accordingly, they were urged to struggle for the establishment and defense of the suffrage and other democratic procedures.[26] The delegates also decided to bar anarchists from future congresses. Those not recognizing the necessity of political action (the model of German Social Democracy was paramount) were not to come. This decision, and its extension to syndicalists at the London congress of 1896, marked for all practical purposes an end to anarchism as a major international movement and so was of major importance in the history of socialism. Soon *anarchist* came to include all who rejected the Marxist evaluation of a political party. Like the word *Trotskyite* at a later date, it became a term of general abuse. Although the decision taken at London did not mean, as anarchists rightly pointed out, that the International was committed to reformism, it tacitly recognized that in practice labor was to pursue its aims by legal and largely political means, and that reformism had stamped international socialism with its imprint.

Why was it necessary to prohibit *syndicalists* (the French word for trade unionists) along with anarchists? The answer lies in a tactical decision taken by anarchists to infiltrate the ranks of labor. This approach had been urged by Peter Kropotkin, Elisée Reclus, and other anarchists critical of total recourse to acts of terror, to "propaganda by the deed," which had resulted in numerous bombings and assassinations in the 'nineties. They warned that continued reliance on sporadic acts of violence would isolate and destroy the movement. As an alternative and as a means by which anarchists could find a new base for mass support and produce something other than a series of ineffectual and isolated protests, they suggested the penetration and control of the trade unions. Anarchism would then be brought back to direct contact with the workers, who in turn could become agents of revolutionary action. By 1896 the process was well under way, especially in France where a new labor federation, that of the Labor Exchanges, had been established the year before. Consequently, many anarchists with union credentials had come to London and had aroused socialist hostility. Despite the decision to exclude its practitioners from organized socialism, revolutionary syndicalism was to survive as a gadfly on the socialist left. We shall have occasion to return to it when discussing a departure from the practices that marked socialism in the 1890s.

In addition to its struggle against anarchism, the Second International applied what it regarded as a second lesson learned from the experiences of its predecessor. Unlike the First, it refused to impose a centralized structure. It was rather a federation of parties and other national groupings, and they were granted considerable autonomy. Nor were its members overly concerned with organizational matters. In the last years of the nineteenth century international socialism was permeated by a millenarianism that suggests an analogy with early Christianity. The excesses of an ever more concentrated capitalism and the astonishing growth of the French and German parties generated feelings of imminent victory. The days of capitalism were numbered and the last crisis at hand. The first congresses of the Second International were preoccupied with preparing workers for the ultimate assault. At the SPD's Erfurt Congress, Bebel had unabashedly told the assembled delegates: "I am convinced that the fulfillment of our aims is so close, that there are few in this hall who will not live to see the day."[27]

By the turn of the century, however, it was apparent that revolution was not impending. Capitalism had proven more stable than expected. National parties were seen as most useful when acting within their respective political frameworks. Socialists heard proposals to have the International authorize the establishment of permanent executive institutions. In 1904 they created an executive committee and a salaried secretariat. The pattern of SPD structure prevailed, however, and ultimate responsibility continued to rest in international congresses. Because it remained a loosed federation of autonomous parties, the International reflected the problems and predispositions of its members.

One other decision was portentous of the future. At the time the International was established, the delegates decided to have member parties organize a May Day celebration in the form of a one day cessation of work. The date had been suggested by the American Federation of Labor. Nearly every party implemented the resolution, and the bloody repression of French workers at Fourmies in 1891 testified to the passions unleashed. But the German Social Democratic party refused to declare a compulsory holiday for labor. It feared the loss of its vote and argued that the act was contrary to the emphasis placed on political action.

Its anarchist opposition overcome, the International was to turn to the problems attendant on the role of socialism in the modern parliamentary state: participation in government, imperialism, and peace and war. The extension of the franchise widened the gap between member parties in western and eastern Europe. Conflicts between social democrats and revolutionaries were to destroy the International in the crucible of war.

CONCLUSION

A survey of Europe's leading socialist parties before the end of the nineteenth century reveals that most had rejected catastrophic solutions in practice and that some were attempting to do so in theory. This is not to say that Marxism had been renounced. On the contrary, such concepts as a materialist interpretation of history, the class struggle, growing concentration of industry, and a collectivist goal by now connoted socialist thinking. Gradualists found no incompatibility between reliance on parliamentary machinery and collectivization (to take the most prominent Marxist theme). Socialism possessed an individualist ideal, to assure everyone the "integral development of his personality," or, as we should say, an equal opportunity to reach his potential. It could be attained only by society's readiness to make available those things necessary to provide an individual with personal security and adequate means of development; that is, society's readiness to appropriate property. In view of the impossibility of allocating equal shares, property was to be owned and put to use by the collectivity.

Socialism, however, was not only a reaction to social injustice; but for the Marxist, the scientifically determined and historically fashioned form that society must take. It was the very issue of the capitalist regime and the concentration of ownership created by that regime. The socialist recognized this growing concentration and sought to put it at the disposal of society. In no other way, it was clear, could the masses be rendered the ownership of the means of production. Hence collectivization was held not as a deterrent to, but the very condition of individualism. Not collectivism, but the initial reliance on revolutionary means to attain it was being abandoned by reformists.

Responsible for the shift in tactics was the growth of liberal and democratic institutions, particularly the right of association and the extension of the suffrage. While trade unions would defend the worker's professional interests, political rather than corporative action could make his ultimate emancipation a reality. Hence the emphasis placed on winning public power. If, for example, within the French movement a Jaurès never ruled out revolution, in 1898 he was describing democracy as "the largest and most solid terrain on which the working class can stand . . . the bed rock that the reactionary bourgeoisie cannot dissolve without opening fissures in the earth and throwing itself into them."[28] Moreover, the mass party began to develop a structural and bureaucratic organization, as well as a variety of ancillary institutions. It was natural to think in terms of ensuring their preservation, and this reenforced the moderation practiced by an already prudent leadership.

The repudiation of violence took several forms, but this much seems clear: revolutionaries found themselves increasingly on the defensive and were required to vindicate their commitment to insurrection. Revolutionary sentiment flourished chiefly in countries like Russia, where the failure of populism and the absence of any constitutional framework could scarcely permit a parliamentary approach. Like their English counterparts, the question for Russian socialists was not one of revising Marx. Unlike them, it was rather one of how literally his prescriptions were to be taken: of deciding whether to work for the growth of a bourgeois and democratic state in order to bring into existence the necessary agent of change, a proletariat, or to rely instead on violent or economic alternatives. Regardless of the many real differences between British Fabianism, French reformism, German revisionism, and Russian economism, they had enough in common to suggest the universality of an evolutionary approach. It must also be said that a revolutionary minority never ceased denouncing what it regarded as excessive reliance on the caprices of a bourgeois state. In view of the state's persistent unwillingness to vote a socialist majority into office, that minority was to see its ranks swelled with disillusioned reformists in a resurgence of revolutionary sentiment early in the new century.

NOTES

[1] The portrait was by Eric Hobsbawm, *Labouring Men* (London: Weidenfeld and Nicolson, 1964), p. 233. It was fashioned from information contained in Chuscichi Tsuzuki, *H. M. Hyndman and British Socialism* (London: Oxford University Press, 1961).

[2] For Hyndman as propagandist see Thelma H. McCormack, "The Motivation and Role of a Propagandist," *Social Forces* XXX (May 1962), 388–394. Engels letter to Sorge is cited in Henry Pelling, *Origins of the Labour Party* (Oxford: Clarendon Press, 1965), p. 216. Engels was also to criticize Jules Guesde for refusing to cooperate with French Radicals.

[3] Reproduced as the second appendix to Edward R. Pease, *History of the Fabian Society* (London: F. Cass, 1963).

[4] *Fabian Essays in Socialism* (London: Turnstile, 1962), pp. 247–248.

[5] See Eric Hobsbawm's essay, "The Fabians Reconsidered," in his *Labouring Men*, pp. 250–271. I have relied on his account for this and the next paragraph.

[6] Henry Pelling, *A Short History of the Labour Party* (London: Macmillan; New York: St. Martin's Press, 1965), p. 224. Also his *Origins of the Labour Party*, p. 165.

[7] Ralph Miliband, *Parliamentary Socialism* (London: Allen & Unwin, 1961), p. 15.

[8] *Ibid.*, p. 32.

[9] Reproduced in R. C. K. Ensor, ed., *Modern Socialism* (New York: Harper & Row, 1908), pp. 220–228.

[10] *Ibid.*

[11] Carl Schorske, *German Social Democracy, 1905–1917* (New York: Wiley, 1965), pp. 12, 16.

[12] Eduard Bernstein, *Evolutionary Socialism: A Criticism and Affirmation* (New York: Schocken, 1961), pp. 155, 200–224.

[13] Cited in Milorad M. Drachkovitch, *De Karl Marx à Léon Blum* (Geneva: Droz, 1954), pp. 149–150.

[14] The first view was expressed by George Lichtheim, *Marxism, op. cit.,* pp. 286–289; the second by Klaus Epstein, "Three American Studies of German Socialism," *World Politics* XII (July 1959), 634. Also see Peter Gay, *The Dilemma of Democratic Socialism* (New York: Columbia University Press, 1952), pp. 141–148, 226.

[15] Peter Nettl, "The German Social Democratic Party as a Political Model," *Past and Present* XXX (April 1965), 68–69.

[16] *Le Proletaire,* November 19, 1881. Cited in L. Derfler, "Reformism and Jules Guesde: 1891–1900," *International Review of Social History* XII (1967), Part I, 66–80. I have reproduced portions of my article for this section.

[17] Harold R. Weinstein, *Jean Jaurès: A Study of Patriotism in the French Socialist Movement* (New York: Columbia University Press, 1936), p. 28.

[18] Of the 575,000 industrial establishments in France in 1896, 534,000 had fewer than 10 workers. J. H. Clapham, *The Economic Development of France and Germany, 1815–1914* (Cambridge: University Press, 1963), pp. 258–259.

[19] Georges Lefranc, *Le Mouvement socialiste sous la IIIe République* (Paris: 1963), p. 65.

[20] Robert Michels, "Some Reflections on the Sociological Character of Political Parties," *American Political Science Review* (November 1927), p. 754.

[21] Maurice Duverger, *Political Parties* (New York: Wiley, 1959), p. 179. For subsequent citations, see Derfler above.

[22] Grégoire Alexinsky, "Le Mouvement socialiste en Russie du XIXe siècle," *Revue Historique* 222 (1959), 88–112.

[23] Samuel H. Baron, "The First Decade of Russian Marxism," *American Slavic and East European Review* XIV (1955), 316–319, 326–327.

[24] Oscar J. Hammen, "Marx and the Agrarian Question," *American Historical Review* LXXVII (1972), 702.

[25] Friedrich Engels, *Die Neue Zeit,* vol. XX, 1 (1901–1902). Cited in Julius Braunthal, *The International, I, 1864–1914* (London: Nelson, 1966), pp. 266–267.

[26] Patricia Van der Esch, *La Deuxième Internationale, 1889–1923* (Paris: Bibliothèque de l'histoire économique et sociale, 1951), p. 76.

[27] Braunthal, *op. cit.,* p. 196.

[28] Jean Jaurès, "Le Socialisme français," *Cosmopolis* (January 1898), p. 125.

SUGGESTED READING

BRITISH LABOUR

Max Beer. *A History of British Socialism,* 2 vols. London: Allen & Unwin, 1953.

C. F. Brand. *The British Labour Party*. Stanford: Stanford University Press, 1964.

G. D. H. Cole. *British Working Class Politics, 1832–1914*. London: Routledge, 1941.

Margaret I. Cole. *The Story of Fabian Socialism*. London: Heinemann, 1961.

Fabian Essays. (First published 1889). London: Constable, 1949.

Emrys Hughes. *Keir Hardie*. London: Allen & Unwin, 1956.

A. M. McBriar. *Fabian Socialism and English Politics, 1884–1918*. New York and Cambridge: Cambridge University Press, 1962.

Philip P. Poirer. *Advent of the Labor Party*. London: Allen & Unwin, 1958.

Beatrice Webb. *My Apprenticeship*. New York and London: Longmans, Green, 1926 ed.

GERMAN REVISIONISM

Pierre Angel. *Eduard Bernstein et l'evolution du socialisme allemand*. Paris: Didier, 1961.

Georg Eckert, ed. *Wilhelm Liebknecht. Briefwechsel mit Karl Marx und Friedrich Engels*. The Hague: Mouton, 1963.

Ferdinand Lassalle. *Romantic Revolutionary*. Westport, Conn.: Greenwood, 1947.

Vernon L. Lidtke. *The Outlawed Party. Social Democracy in Germany, 1878–1890*. Princeton: Princeton University Press, 1966.

Karl Marx. *Critique of the Gotha Program*. New York: International Publishers, 1970 ed.

Franz Mehring. *Geschichte der deutschen Sozialdemokratie*. Stuttgart: Dietz, 1919.

Roger P. Morgan. *The German Social Democrats and the First International, 1864–1872*. Cambridge: University Press, 1965.

G. A. Ritter. *Die Arbeiterbewegung im Wilhelminischen Reich*. Berlin: Colloquium Verlag, 1959.

G. Roth. *The Social Democrats in Imperial Germany*. Totawa, N.J.: Bedminster Press, 1963.

FRENCH REFORMISM

Edouard Dolléans. *Histoire du mouvement ouvrier*, vol. 2. Paris: A. Colin, 1936.

Maurice Dommanget. *Edouard Vaillant, un grand socialiste, 1840–1914*. Paris: La Table Ronde, 1956.

Harvey Goldberg. *The Life of Jean Jaurès*. Madison: University of Wisconsin Press, 1962.

Carl Landauer. "The Guesdists and the Small Farmer: Early Erosion of French Marxism," *International Review of Social History* VI (1961).

Carl Landauer. "The Origins of Reformist Socialism in France," *International Review of Social History* XII (1967).

Aaron Noland. *The Founding of the French Socialist Party.* Cambridge, Mass.: Harvard University Press, 1956.

David Stafford. *From Anarchism to Reformism: A Study of the Political Activities of Paul Brousse. . . .* Toronto: University of Toronto Press, 1971.

Jacques Vidal. *Le Mouvement ouvrier française de la Commune à la Guerre mondiale.* Paris: Bureau d'éditions, 1934.

Claude Willard. *Les Guesdistes. Le Mouvement socialiste en France (1893–1905).* Paris: Éditions sociales, 1965.

SOCIALISM IN RUSSIA

Samuel H. Baron. *Plekhanov: The Father of Russian Marxism.* London: Routledge & Kegan Paul, 1963; Stanford: Stanford University Press, 1966.

Leopold H. Haimson. *The Russian Marxists and the Origins of Bolshevism.* Cambridge, Mass.: Harvard University Press, 1955.

John Keep. *The Rise of Social Democracy in Russia.* Oxford: Clarendon Press, 1963.

Richard Kindersley. *The First Russian Revisionists: A Study of "Legal Marxism" in Russia.* Oxford: Clarendon Press, 1962.

Evgeny Lampert. *Sons Against Fathers: Studies in Russian Radicalism and Revolution.* Oxford: Clarendon Press, 1965.

Theodore H. Von Laue. *Why Lenin? Why Stalin? A Reappraisal of the Russian Revolution, 1903–1930.* Philadelphia: Lippincott, 1966.

THE SECOND INTERNATIONAL

G. Haupt. *La Deuxième Internationale. Étude critique des sources. Essai bibliothèque.* Paris and the Hague: Mouton, 1964.

James Joll. *The Anarchists.* New York: Grosset & Dunlap, 1966 ed.

James Joll. *The Second International, 1889–1914.* New York: Harper & Row, 1966.

George Woodcock. *Anarchism.* Cleveland: World Publishing Co.– Meridian Books, 1962.

THREE

The Return

to Marxist Orthodoxy

Gradualists correctly assessed their defeat at the Second International's Amsterdam Congress in 1904 as meaning the imposition of German Marxist orthodoxy on international socialism and as the revival of a significant and militant left wing within its member parties. They also ascribed a resurgence of economic solutions to revolutionary trade unions displaying a readiness to resort to such direct action as general strikes and sabotage.

The turn away from the reformism practiced during the late 1880s and 1890s was in part the result of a rigid class structure (allowing for limited mobility), lack of continuing electoral successes, and a sustained economic upswing causing prices to rise faster than wages. Particularly in Britain, the economic picture was further clouded by short-term depressions during the first decade of the century. Parliamentarianism, moreover, particularly socialist participation in government, pointed to further diminution of class consciousness and provided powerful justification for the revolutionary minority that had refused to cooperate. There was growing discontent between militant veterans, strong in party councils, and their more politically attuned representatives in national and local legislatures. It was a Frenchman who pointed out that there was more in common between two deputies, one of whom was revolutionary, than between two revolutionaries, one of whom was a deputy. But the sentiment could be subscribed to by observers elsewhere.

The return to a more militant socialist stand took different forms. In Germany it issued both from defeats of revisionists through attacks from the center and from the resurgence of the revolutionary left. In France the dissident factions founded a new party based on the class-struggle concept, which ended previous electoral and parliamentary cooperation with progressive bourgeois parties. Disenchantment with the slow progress of political action also induced a revolutionary syndicalist response. Similar discontent in Britain generated greater militancy within the parliamentary Labour party and also produced new economic proposals in the form of *guild socialism*. In Russia, revolutionaries managed to impose their objectives and methods of organization on their less-militant colleagues. Although no cause-and-effect relationship need be inferred, large-scale revolution broke out in 1905, and the Russian example reinforced the militant response elsewhere. Reformism, however, resurfaced—seemingly stronger than before—before the outbreak of World War I, its advocates placing a premium on ensuring means of national defense.

THE DEFEAT OF REVISIONISM

In view of the predominant role played by the SPD in international socialism, its internal battle between the orthodox and revisionist positions is significant. Revisionists, including the members of the Bavarian delegation in the Reichstag and party bureaucrats like Gustav Noske, Philipp Scheidemann, and Friedrich Ebert, thought of party organization almost as an end in itself; revisionists also included trade union officials like Karl Legien, who were concerned with improving working conditions and impatient with ideological distinctions.

THE DRESDEN CONGRESS

The issue was debated at the party's Hannover Congress in 1899, and spokesman for the orthodox position was Karl Kautsky. Relying on statistical evidence, he systematically demolished revisionist arguments. He demonstrated that there had been relative if not absolute pauperization of the working class. He asked whether it was useful to destroy the revolutionary ideal of the proletariat. In pointing to the political structure of Germany, where the bourgeoisie cooperated with the forces of authoritarianism, he answered his own question. He was able, moreover, to point to counterrevolutionary threats. The Saxon parliament had recently abolished the equal vote; the Junkers were threatening to deport SPD leaders; and the year before, the Kaiser proposed legislation making incitement to strike a criminal offense. Revisionism was condemned at Hannover, again at Lubeck in 1901, and at Dresden in 1903.

THE REVOLUTIONARY LEFT

Led by Rosa Luxemburg and Karl Liebknecht, the German radical Left was adamant in its opposition to revisionism. The decision of the parliamentary leader of the French socialists, Alexandre Millerand, to join a bourgeois government of "republican defense" provided an event for additional opposition. Luxemburg rejected arguments that the Millerand case was exceptional. All exceptions endangered the class-struggle concept, and socialism must sustain its opposition for as long as a bourgeois society remained. She stressed the importance of theory and asserted that party activity had no meaning without it. "Wage slavery," she pointed out, was based not on any existing legislation but on the very nature of the economy. It constituted one of the basic conditions of capitalist domination which could never be altered by legal reform. Capitalist rule itself was extralegal; hence revolution and not reform was necessary.[1] A neo-Marxist movement was to emerge among the generation of socialists born 1870–1880 and centered in central and eastern Europe. Rudolf Hilferding (1876–1942), Otto Bauer (1881–1938), Lenin (1870–1924), Leon Trotsky (1879–1940), Karl Radek (1885–1941), and Rosa Luxemburg (1870–1919) all agreed on the need to upgrade the importance of theory, using tactics only as its executive arm. They also sensed the importance of new problems, particularly the role of nationalism in working-class society.

German revisionism, it has been argued, failed not only because liberalism failed, but because of the prevailing economic and military situation. The tariff issue was central. Revisionists were seen as identifying free trade with democracy, supporting amicable relations with Britain, and working for general European peace. Because it threatened the protectionist coalition of landowners and industrialists, this program had no chance of success in the Reichstag. Because of the predominance in government of the military classes, furthermore, militant socialists doubted that Germany could evolve along liberal lines without revolution. Some revisionists eventually came to support this stand in their readiness to consider a general strike in 1913 as a means of winning constitutional reform.[2]

At its Dresden Congress in 1903, the SPD approved a resolution reaffirming the orthodox conception of the class struggle. This act decisively defeated the revisionist movement within its ranks. At the same time, a revolutionary period may be said to have opened in Germany. A series of strikes coincided with mounting agitation for suffrage reform in Prussia. In January 1905, news came of the Russian Revolution. It appeared as justification of the radical position and, for the movement, settled the problem of relations between the SPD and society at large. The party returned to its self-imposed isolation with a vengeance. Revisionists had wanted to bring the SPD and society at large closer together. Defenders of the established Marxist position sought to continue the separation. But radicals also urged social organization and action, although of a totally different nature than did the revisionists. Luxemburg returned from Russia in 1906. On the basis of these experiences, she challenged the notion that success depended on strong organization, a full treasury, and prudent leadership. The revolution in Russia, she said, had created the necessary organization. Trade unionism, as had been the case in Germany itself, would grow fastest when reacting to a hostile government.[3]

By 1910 this left-wing opposition was accusing the SPD leadership of blocking and dampening suffrage agitation and of failing to recognize and respond to revolutionary situations with appropriate weapons —that is, of detaching itself from both friends and enemies. Like revisionists, radicals wanted the party to end its isolation, although not by expanding its parliamentary activities, but by offering leadership to the masses when they developed revolutionary potential. Organization and action were seen as complementary and as furthering each other's growth.

This debate was illustrated by German Socialist response to the general strike. A nationwide refusal to work had been given theoretical expression by the Frenchman Georges Sorel, but like all orthodox Marxist organizations, the SPD fought off the idea as irrational and romantic regardless of any revolutionary fervor it might create within working-class ranks. Because of radical pressure, however, arguments for the strike received a sympathetic hearing at the party's Bremen Congress in 1904. When the Congress at Jena was convoked a year later, the Russian Revolution had broken out and widespread strikes had taken place in the Ruhr. Bebel now advocated reliance on the general strike as a defensive measure in the event that the suffrage and right of association were jeopardized. He also considered it a means by which the franchise might be extended in Prussia.

This victory of the revolutionaries proved short-lived. Not only did revisionists like Bernstein fear risking the very existence of the party (in his 1905 pamphlet, *The General Strike*), but trade union chiefs rejected what they considered a political strike. Accordingly, in secret negotiations held before the 1906 Mannheim Congress, between union chiefs like Karl Legien and socialists like Bebel, it was decided that the party would pursue no policy opposed by the trade unions. Overcoming Kautsky's opposition, the SPD recognized the strength of the trade unions by granting them parity. There would be no more question of a general strike, and revolutionary sentiment was relegated to symbolic rather than significant expressions—refusal to vote on the budget or to salute the Kaiser by the party's Reichstag delegation.

Even so, spokesmen for revolution were not stifled. Luxemburg and others went on criticizing the concern shown by the leadership for the party's structure and organizational agencies. In continuing to place their faith in the revolutionary spontaneity of the masses, they were to get the chance to test their views in the revolution that followed

Germany's defeat in World War I. But in turning to questions of nationalism and imperialism in the years immediately preceding the war, the SPD was to reveal its renewed commitment to the existent state.

THE UNIFICATION OF FRENCH SOCIALISM

The revolutionary surge implicit in the defeat of revisionism and in the development of the SPD's militant left wing had minor tactical consequences in Germany. It enormously influenced socialism in France, for the Dresden Resolution was adopted by the Second International in 1904 and it was made the sine qua non of a newly unified French party.

Why was a majority of French socialists prepared to abandon the reformist tactics followed since the early nineties? In part the answer rests on the premium placed on unity and on the disappointing results of the 1898 election. Guesde had hoped to see over 100 socialist deputies returned and anticipated a majority in the not-too-distant future. In fact, the movement had not substantially increased its representation, and both he and Jaurès were defeated. It would appear that one characteristic of the "deradicalization" process was the optimism that the successes initially won by recourse to moderate means must necessarily continue, making disillusion all the greater when they did not.[4] When it became clear that France was not about to vote socialist, a renewed response by the party's revolutionary left wing was to be anticipated. That militant socialists received additional support was due, above all else, to the Millerand case. The controversy generated by the participation of a socialist in the government embroiled French and European socialism at the turn of the century. It helped to account for a revolutionary outburst in both socialism and syndicalism, permitted militant socialists to unify the party on pretty much their own terms, and was to stamp subsequent European socialist history with its imprint.

THE MILLERAND CASE

The existence of a multiparty system in France made it unlikely that any one of them would win a majority. Consequently, governments tended to be coalitions of different personalities brought together to reflect a common approach to politics or to provide a solution to a pressing problem. The problem in 1899 was the Dreyfus affair and the threat to the regime seen as coming from the Army and the Church. At first inclined to regard the affair as another bourgeois quarrel—here a rich army officer condemned by his peers—most socialists at first followed the example of aloofness set in the Boulanger and Panama affairs. By 1898–1899, however, many came to accept the analysis made by Jaurès. Once convinced of Dreyfus' innocence, he viewed the affair not as a simple struggle over the guilt of an officer, but one between the progressive elements in the nation and the organized forces of re-action. Years of parliamentary participation and countless appeals to achieve goals by legal means now bore fruit. Socialists identified them-selves with the Third Republic and rallied to preserve it.

To ensure himself of left-wing support, Premier René Waldeck-Rousseau, designated in June, 1901, selected Millerand as his Minister of Commerce. Initially making no objection on grounds of principle, socialists were infuriated to learn of the similar participation of a reactionary general who had crushed the Paris Commune 30 years before. After a period of moral repugnance, militant socialists found doctrinal justification to reject the presence of a socialist in govern-ment as marking a retreat from the class-struggle concept. They argued that socialists in bourgeois governments (and ultimately in a left-wing parliamentary coalition) would weaken working-class militancy and force the party to support nonsocialist programs. Their case was strengthened by Millerand's support of the ministry's domestic and foreign policies. Defenders of participation pointed to the measures of social reform that were being taken as a logical extension of the reformist tactics previously practiced. Prominent among the *ministe-rialists* were the socialist deputies, and the larger issue may be identi-fied as the hostility between *militants* and veterans in party councils on the one hand, and the socialists elected to national and local legis-latures on the other—a conflict by no means limited to French so-cialism.[5]

The turmoil aroused by the Dreyfus affair and the threat seen in a clerico-military reaction prompted renewed concern over socialist unity. Thanks in large part to Jaurès' efforts, socialist groupings held a general congress in December, 1899. In debating *ministériellisme,* the delegates voted an ambiguous resolution neither approving nor condemning it. Most held the event as unique and estimated that there had been no united party to judge. To avoid a possible Marxist departure, however, they went on record as affirming in principle that the class struggle prohibited the entry of a socialist into a non-socialist government.

UNITY—ON A REVOLUTIONARY BASIS

It was with relief that they turned to the question of unity. The newly created French Socialist party (PSF) was to be a federation, not a fusion of existing groups, and based on the reformist principles set forth at Saint-Mandé. This unity proved ephemeral; reformist and revolutionary socialists split over the Millerand case and the issue of subjecting socialist deputies to party control. Guesdists walked out of the congress held in 1900, and Blanquists, the following year of 1901. Together they formed the basis of the rival revolutionary Socialist party of France. Independents and Broussists continued to support participation and greater freedom for deputies. The gap widened. Antiministerialists on one occasion censured deputies supporting the government, while the resentful deputies justified their behavior in terms of the long-run benefits they said would accrue to socialism. Reformists and revolutionaries were once again opposed.

The revolutionary Socialist party of France (PSDF) disclaimed proposals for social reform and gave secondary consideration to amassing a large popular vote. Prereformist tactics were once more pursued. Elections best served propaganda purposes. In those of 1902, reformist socialists won 600,000 votes and 37 parliamentary seats. Revolutionaries compiled a respectable 400,000 votes, but by rejecting electoral alliances, gathered only 14 seats.

This division came to an end with the Second International's acceptance of the German Social Democratic party's condemnation of revisionism. Its Amsterdam Congress in 1904 adopted the SPD's Dresden Resolution, which rejected any attempt "to blur evergrowing class distinctions." It dashed any hopes that might have remained of continuing the policy of participation in government and also prohibited electoral and parliamentary cooperation with other left-wing parties. An earlier congress, held in Paris in 1900, had accepted the compromise resolution of Karl Kautsky. It had condemned in principle the appearance of a single socialist in a bourgeois cabinet, but recognized its usefulness in exceptional circumstances. The issue was then held as one of tactics and to be determined by individual socialist parties.

THE SECOND INTERNATIONAL TURNS TO ITS LEFT

THE DEBATE OVER PARTICIPATION

The socialist world had followed events in France closely. As might be expected, the particular reaction to socialist participation in government reflected and extended the attitude towards tactics previously adopted. In England, pragmatic Fabians at once applauded Millerand's entry. More surprising was the approval of the Marxist Social Democratic Federation (SDF). Hyndman, who professed to follow French events closely, wrote that it was the "duty of every French socialist" to support the government against reaction. In Germany, revisionists like Bernstein and Vollmar approved. In the center, Kautsky, as we have seen, was ambivalent. If largely opposed to ministerial participation, he doubted that violence was still necessary for the socialist conquest of power. Yet the issue under consideration was less than vital, and a socialist in government might create an illusion of force. Socialists had to remember they were still very much in the minority.

Radicals like Liebknecht and Luxemburg went further than Guesde and Vaillant in opposing participation. For Luxemburg the importance of the case could not be minimized. It was "a question of the whole sum of political and economic problems, of principles and tactics which represent the very heart of the socialist struggle." She acknowledged that government participation was the logical consequence of parliamentary participation. But if socialism was to be introduced only after the destruction of capitalism, and if socialists worked toward that end, then participation was self-defeating. Socialists can sit in a parliament, she said, but not in a government, for the latter only executes laws and cannot introduce principles. The socialist in government, if an enemy of the present order, must either be in constant opposition to his colleagues (an untenable position), or he must fulfill his functions—that is, not act as a socialist within the limits of government action. The experience, she concluded, can only be prejudicial to the principle of the class struggle. Emile Vandervelde, speaking for Belgian socialism, held similar reservations. Aside from "exceptional cases," he was absolutely opposed to participation because the disadvantages outweighed the advantages and because it was better to give unconditional support to progressive bourgeois governments than to compromise oneself by sharing power.[6]

In reply to a questionnaire distributed by French reformist socialists, 29 leading figures in the socialist world, from Victor Adler to Emile Vandervelde, were asked their views. Twenty-seven gave unqualified approval for the socialist proletariat to intervene in bourgeois quarrels, either "to defend political liberty," or, as in the Dreyfus affair, "for the sake of humanity," and to do so without jeopardizing the principle of the class struggle. On the principle of participation, however, 12 replies were largely affirmative, 17 largely negative. The most adamant rejections came from those areas where the likelihood of a socialist getting to power was remote and where it was difficult even to contemplate the prospect.[7]

The impact of the Millerand case on French and international socialism, and their ultimate repudiation of ministerial participation, was enormous. It was to inspire a renewed reliance on revolutionary tactics and to alienate the reformists who refused to agree. One's attitude toward *ministerialism* came to serve as a test of one's commitment to socialism, and that attitude had to be negative. Lenin regarded *Millerandism* as the chief threat to socialist success.[8] He later denounced socialists who joined governments during World War I as guilty of deliberate treason, and he was to make *antiministerialism* a test of eligibility for joining the Third International.

THE AMSTERDAM CONGRESS

The issue was fought out at Amsterdam, and the chief protagonists were Jaurès and Bebel. The former tried to demonstrate that the structure of French socialism was unique, benefiting from a democratic republic. When at the SPD's Jena Congress in 1906, Bebel questioned the usefulness of the general strike as an offensive weapon, he argued that conditions in Russia, where the tactic might be useful, were so abnormal that they served no useful example.[9] Obviously he had rejected the right of Jaurès to say the same thing at Amsterdam. In adopting this resolution, international socialism sanctioned the defeat both of German revisionism and French reformism.

Delegates to the Amsterdam Congress insisted on the unification of socialism in France. The two parties thereupon established a joint unification committee that called for withdrawing the French Socialist party from the left-wing parliamentary coalition. Socialist deputies were to revert to a policy of intransigent opposition and to limit their activities to the defense of working-class interests. The new party was to be distinctly revolutionary, although some measures of social amelioration might be pursued. The goal envisaged was the total collectivization of society, and was to be reached by irreducible opposition to the established bourgeois order and the state that represented it. Socialists were to reject every means of maintaining the government, including military credits, secret funds, and the budget itself. The unity that was realized, then, was of an entirely different order than that called for at Saint-Mandé. The accent was placed on the international organization of the proletariat and on class action; the basic texts omitted references to the nation and to the legal conquest of power.

For the sake of unity, Jaurès and a majority of reformists agreed to these terms. In 1905, the unified socialist party or the French section of the Workers International (SFIO) was born. Aristide Briand, a former anarchist who had called for the general strike but was now a reformist spokesman, summed up the resentment of the minority within the SFIO. He regarded the conditions set forth at Amsterdam as the triumph of German Marxism over the democratic traditions of French socialism. In the opinion of the dissidents, the price paid by Jaurès for unity was too high.[10] That the return to revolution proved incomplete and that tacit acceptance of reformist tactics soon reemerged could not easily have been anticipated. Like its German and international equivalents, the French socialist movement turned to the left early in the twentieth century, and elements of this reestablished Marxism were to endure in practice as well as in theory throughout the Third Republic. Aside from sending representatives to a national coalition government in the early years of World War I, socialists were not to participate until Léon Blum formed a Popular Front cabinet in 1936.

THE LABOUR LEFT

It is inexact to say that British socialism underwent experiences parallel to those of its counterparts in Western and Central Europe. If there was little Marxism to revise, there was little to revive. Still, within the Labour party, there were those disillusioned with the parliamentary approach. The opposition came largely from its most radical component, the ILP. A challenge also came from outside the party, from people anxious to forego political solutions in favor of economic ones.

Labour's parliamentary delegation did not grow. The miners' representatives who swelled its ranks in 1906 had simply switched their allegiance from the Liberals, but understandably continued to support that party's extensive social legislation program. Liberals needed the help of Labour, particularly after they lost their absolute majority in 1910. Labour candidates entered into electoral pacts and, if successful, acknowledged the debt owed to Liberals. These first Labour MPs also accepted (and with gratitude) Liberal tutelage in acquiring parliamentry skills and party discipline.

However, the Labour left wing saw in these very things justification of their fears that the party's representatives in Parliament were becoming opportunist. The Left was active in party councils. The latter consequently showed the same suspicion toward parliamentary socialists as socialist party councils on the continent. It was decided in conference that the party had the right to give binding instructions to its delegation in the House of Commons. In 1910 four members of the ILP's National Council published a pamphlet, "Let Us Reform the Labour Party." It condemned the "suicidal" reformism displayed by the MPs; it had "reduced the whole Movement to acute anemia or rabid melancholy."[11] The Council criticized the Labour party leadership for abandoning the original ILP position and urged it to combat "both capitalist parties."

The Labour party was defended at ILP congresses by Ramsay

MacDonald, chief of the faction seeking compromise. His "argument from democracy" held the necessity of defending democratic institutions, for they alone gave minority parties like Labour a national hearing. He averred that the objective "ought not to be to form a Socialist party, but a party that will journey to socialism."[12] These views were opposed by George Lansbury, who represented the workers of east London. But neither he nor other labor leaders offered any significant theory or plans for social reconstruction. Labor's ideological weakness was taken advantage of by Hyndman, who in 1911 gathered malcontents into a British socialist party. His SDF provided the chief source of strength.

Further opposition came from within the ranks of organized labor. Militant trade unionists did not see Liberal social legislation as meeting working-class goals. They accused Liberals of regarding Labour as an accessory designed to keep workers tranquil. More concerned with rising prices—hence reductions in real wages—and with ensuring continued employment, they began to question the commitment to political solutions. The hostility between labor and its parliamentary spokesmen was revealed in the former's successful efforts in returning an ILP candidate in 1907, Victor Grayson, despite Labour's refusal to accept him. More serious was an attack from the Right by trade union leader W. V. Osborne, who belonged to the Liberal party. He brought suit against the practice of having unions grant financial aid to Labour candidates, and the judgment was confirmed in the House of Lords. The decision threatened the entire financial structure of the party.

The disappointing results of the 1910 election generated more disillusionment. Only 43 Labour candidates were returned. Even this small contingent was far from unified. For example, while a majority supported the Liberals' social insurance legislation of 1911, some condemned the idea of any workers' contributions. In any event, they regarded the law as wholly inadequate. Personality conflicts exacerbated existing divisions. Keir Hardie retained considerable support, but was not skillful in Parliament. He was successfully fought by MacDonald, who was clever and charming but lacked conviction and insight. Arthur Henderson was an excellent trade union administrator, but more of a liberal than a socialist. Opponents of the Labour-Liberal alliance rallied to Hyndman's new Socialist party. Those who remained, particularly individual sections and personalities within the ILP, continued to oppose the moderation practiced by the Labour MPs. Their opposition accounted for the decision of a stormy party conference in 1914 to approve a resolution reminding the parliamentarians of the party's more socialist objectives. Not until after World War I, however, would a formal commitment to socialism be made.

REVOLUTIONARIES IN RUSSIA

Was there a similar resurgence of revolution in Russian socialism? The pattern, of course, differs insofar as there are few alternatives to revolution in an authoritarian state. Yet we have seen that the phenomena of *legal Marxism* and *economism,* in the degree to which they sought to further liberal growth rather than work for proletarian insurrection, were analogous to the reformism practiced in the West. Correspondingly, the impetus given to the adoption of more violent approaches by the Revolution of 1905 and the development of a theory of action by Lenin and the Bolsheviks may be taken as the Russian equivalent to the harder line sought in Western socialism.

BOLSHEVISM

The split between the two wings of the Marxist party in Russia was not based on theoretical issues debated at the turn of the century. Whether to admit the necessity of allowing a liberal bourgeoisie to develop democratic institutions or to bypass capitalism and rely on the revolutionary potential of the proletariat proved less divisive than the question of party organization and structure. In his antieconomist tract *What Is To Be Done?* published in 1902, Lenin argued that a socialist party was not merely the sum of its agreeing members. It was a disciplined (hence authoritarian) group of professional revolutionaries acting on behalf of the working class. This Jacobinlike "vanguard" was the logical consequence drawn from the failure of populism. It held the masses incapable of revolutionary creativity, doubted the effectiveness of revolutionary spontaneity, and maintained that revolution could be achieved only by a "conscious minority" drawn from the intelligentsia and requiring conspiratorial organization.

Paul Axelrod, Julius Martov, and others denied the need for centralization, and called for a continuation of the open recruitment then practiced. At the second Social Democratic congress, held in Brussels and London in 1903, Lenin at first found himself in a minority. Together with his colleagues on the newspaper *Iskra,* however, he managed to have the party reject the demand for autonomy made by the Jewish Bund. (It had preferred, as had other ethnic and national organizations in the party, to maintain its separate identity.) The departure of these delegates gave him the majority necessary to win approval of his organizational proposals.

Bolsheviks pursued their hardened line in the years that followed. In his *Two Tactics of Social Democracy* (1905), Lenin condemned reformism as weakening the forces of revolution. The proletariat, he said, was to be something more than a "bourgeois auxiliary." He prescribed an alliance with the peasantry in an effort to isolate the middle classes. This advocacy of a revived populist policy may have constituted Lenin's most significant contribution to Russian socialism. Mensheviks, on the other hand, (the minority rejecting the party's organizational statutes) considered themselves the legitimate heirs of Marxist thought.

In criticizing Kantian idealism, Lenin developed a philosophical basis for this thought. From the standpoint of tactics he urged that a middle position be taken between those who repudiated any legislative participation, chiefly intellectuals dismayed by the failure of the 1905 Revolution, and those willing to cooperate with the state in hopes of advancing the growth of liberal institutions. In 1912, to combat what he viewed as right- and left-wing deviationism, he founded a separate Bolshevik party. The newspaper *Pravda* was set up and published in Krakow to further propaganda.

Russian social democracy was further divided by the views of Trotsky, then living in Vienna. He agreed that revolutionary movements must destroy first the remnants of feudalism, and then capitalism. However, he argued that the movements could be "telescoped," that one revolution could follow on the other. He said, furthermore, that once successful, revolutionaries in Russia must work for revolution elsewhere to avoid being crushed by a hostile capitalist world. This doctrine of *permanent revolution* may be considered his greatest theoretical contribution. In the summer of 1912, Trotsky tried to win the leadership of all the socialist forces holding objections to Lenin's centralized party structure. These forces included Mensheviks, national minority groupings, and the Jewish Bund. It was to deal with this factionalism that the Second International agreed to discuss Russian socialism at its Vienna Congress, scheduled for 1914. It was never to meet. Placed in perspective, however, Lenin and bolshevism played a small part in international socialism before World War I. Few expected a successful socialist revolution in Russia.

SOCIAL REVOLUTIONARIES

The refusal of Bolsheviks to follow the Western example of promoting bourgeois liberalism as a condition of socialism was shared, although in an entirely different way, by the other great revolutionary party in Russia, the Socialist Revolutionaries (SR). The party's basic program was composed almost in its entirety by V. M. Chernov. It was adopted at its first congress, held in Finland in 1906. The program remained essentially the same through the SR's victory in the election of 1917. Displaying the populist bias of its membership, it vaguely called for *socialization* of the land, carried out by uncompensated expropriation and redistribution on the basis of use. Politically, the party supported republican forms, but insisted on administrative decentralization. How extensive land reform was to be accomplished without a considerably strengthened state was never satisfactorily explained. The party also promised to implement the federative principle with regard to the national minorities living in Russia. Only in its list of "maximum objectives" was industry discussed; the collectivist principle was to be extended to all aspects of the private economy only after its application to the land. Based as it was on the peasants' collectivist and revolutionary potential, Socialist Revolutionaries offered more a statement of policy than a program for action.[13]

Perhaps the chief point that should be made about this period of Russian socialism was the awareness of most that the strategies adopted must necessarily be revolutionary. This supports the observation that regardless of its common Marxist heritage, the shape taken by a socialist organization reflected the conditions set by the regime it was intended to combat. Bolshevism maintained its total hostility both to the regime and to its liberal opponents because Lenin was convinced of the hopelessness of cooperating with the middle classes in common parliamentary efforts. Russian capitalism, he estimated, was the product of state endeavors, not natural growth, and its close association with the forces of authority cast doubts on its readiness to fight for liberal reforms. But in teaching that workers were to rely on their own resources, either directly or in support of a vanguard operating on their behalf, Russian socialism became the most radical in Europe. In the West, the most radical opposition to the capitalist state came no longer from socialists, but from syndicalists.

THE REJECTION OF POLITICS

REVOLUTIONARY SYNDICALISM

The endorsement of the movement's revolutionary bases by the newly unified French socialist party was matched, or rather, preceded by an expression of similar sentiment within organized labor. Disenchanted with middle-class intellectuals presuming to speak in defense of its interests, weary of Marxists hostile to economic approaches, and reflecting the decentralized status of industry in France and southern Europe, numerous labor leaders displayed their readiness to follow the paths laid out by Proudhon and Bakunin and abandon political solutions. We have seen how anarchists, on their part, began infiltrating and winning control of trade unions in order to find a new base for mass support. The apparent willingness of even a government containing a socialist to countenance armed repression of strikes had heightened labor's distrust of politics. The General Confederation of Labor (CGT) relentlessly condemned government bills designed to enlarge trade union rights and add to industrial legislation. It viewed these efforts as part of a larger scheme to tame working-class fervor and make organized labor an adjunct of government. Industrial conciliation bills were similarly seen as traps, intended to defuse militant minorities within the unions.

Syndicalism, then, was a reflection of a weak labor tradition and a decentralized economy. It was also a reaction to socialism's apparent incompetence and willingness to shelter ambitious politicians making use of working-class aspirations. The nation had, in fact, demonstrated little social conscience. A factory act of 1848 limited the male worker's day to 12 hours, and administrative difficulties made a shorter day for women and children virtually unenforceable in mixed workshops of men, women, and children. Trade unions were granted legal recognition in 1884, but employers found themselves responsible for labor accidents only in 1898. The middle and farming classes still comprised a majority in a country that was only begining to experience large-scale industrial growth. They combined forces to retard social legislation and so keep down taxes. The hostility of employing firms, small in size and often family owned, and their ability to organize industrywide associations retarded union growth and increased industrial tension.

The socialist contingent in the French Assembly was unable to enact legislation consonant with its strength. In part the explanation for its failure to do so rested on the fact that by the late nineties the economy had emerged from its depressed state and had begun the great upward swing lasting through World War I. Real wages rose steadily in the decade before the war, though not as fast as in the previous decade (gaining perhaps 6 percent between 1900 and 1915). Profit-taking, however, rose even faster. Corporate income was 24 percent higher in 1909 (a recession year) than in 1901, and workers were aware of the extent to which their employers were making money. Moreover, the accompanying rise in prices, if not great enough to offset monetary wage increases, was acutely felt within the average household.[14]

A more immediate explanation for the French case, however, was that despite socialism's mounting reliance on evolutionary tactics before the end of the century, it was impossible to minimize the fear raised by the prospect of collectivism and the ferocity of the bourgeois response to it. The fear at this time of socialism and anarchism, the two being invariably confused, was one of the dominant characteristics of French political life. It is in this context that the paucity of social legislation becomes understandable. When workers' gains failed to match increases in general living standards, disillusioned elements within labor tired of political action and reverted to the violence urged by the most militant among them. With its strength increased by fusion in 1902 with the rival Federation of Labor Exchanges, the CGT moved away from politics. In adopting revolutionary syndicalism, elements within organized labor were prepared to find solutions outside the legally constituted framework.

Revolutionary syndicalists looked to insurrection as the outcome of class war. Their spokesman was the dedicated and deformed Fernand Pelloutier, the CGT national secretary. His ideas about syndicalism's intended role also endowed it with an ideology. Pelloutier looked to the trade union (*syndicat*) as the nucleous around which production, to take place at the communal level, was to be organized. Representatives would be sent to regional, and ultimately national, labor councils; the latter would replace legislative assemblies and other political bodies, and so create a new society, based for the first time on the single most important function of society, its labor.

Revolutionary syndicalism was the product of labor itself. Trade union chiefs were not led to it by the writings of Georges Sorel and other theoreticians who sought to give the movement philosophical expression. A former engineer and now economic theorist, Sorel had developed concepts that were largely impractical. They were intended to serve as myths designed to put workers in a state of combat-readiness to change societal forms. He saw the proletariat as possessing a reservoir of unconscious moral forces and prescribed working-class violence as a means by which a decadent society could be made virtuous. One such "myth" was the general strike, the simultaneous stoppage of work that would sound the knell for capitalist society. These ideas may best be studied as part of the antirationalist response in the intellectual history of the period. For our purposes, it is sufficient to note that syndicalists were rejecting political means to achieve working-class emancipation and insisting on more revolutionary approaches, including strikes, sabotage, and violence. At its Amiens Congress in 1906, the CGT repudiated all affiliation with political groupings.

In France, this revolutionary outlook was to endure until the outbreak of war in 1914. It reemerged in the widespread disillusion with the war and in the hopes aroused by Bolshevik success. Syndicalist discontent accounted for the great wave of strikes that washed over the country, strikes broken by the repressive action of the Clemenceau and Briand ministries before the war and by the Millerand Ministry immediately after it. Clemenceau (1906–1909) did not hesitate to use troops. Briand (1910) resorted to the ingenious device of mobilizing striking railroad workers and so subjecting them to military discipline. The antimilitarism of most syndicalists was a logical outgrowth of their hatred of the established order. The army was held as the clearest manifestation of state power; hence the efforts to convince recruits that they were the dupes of the ruling classes. In all of these things there was a marked reversal of the legal procedures previously relied upon, and a rejection of the state, once held worthy of defense.

Admittedly, these views were those of a minority. Most French workers, like their equivalents everywhere, held traditionally limited goals. They showed themselves willing to negotiate and readily accepted compromise, particularly with an increase in the use of collective bargaining procedures. Current research has revealed that syndicalism was in large measure limited to labor leaders, and that their revolutionary tradition had intellectual and political causes. Their attempts to convert most workers were unsuccessful.[15] Even so, the fact remains that in repudiating political avenues to social change, the organizations speaking for labor were behaving differently from before.

Syndicalism prevailed in Latin Europe. In France and Italy it seemed related to economic retardation. In Spain the movement found strength in even the most advanced regions of a generally retarded economy. Here it encountered anarchism in its classic form, total rejection of the state. Conceivably, there was an unconscious longing to substitute a new faith for that once placed in the now conservative and hostile Church. The strong separatist feelings in Catalonia and the desire for political autonomy explain in part the perpetuation of anarcho-syndicalist sentiment there. The outbreak of a general strike, however, in one of the most industrialized countries on earth—England in 1926—renders easy generalization impossible.

The failure of these attempts showed that economic action alone was not to be relied upon. A variant of syndicalism emerged in North America, where it found support among the miners and loggers in the western United States. If similar to European movements in some respects, the International Workers of the World (IWW), however, was very much a native product and wholly compatible with the strong individualism displayed by workers in these occupations. It was no more successful than its European counterparts, and probably a lot less so. The most important consequence of revolutionary syndicalism, in all its manifestations, was the contempt for political action left in its wake. French trade union officials, for example, were long prohibited from taking parliamentary seats. This hindered the formation of alliances between unions and political parties, even in parliamentary democracies where they were possible and necessary. Long unable to cooperate, each was to suffer.

GUILD SOCIALISM

A related antipolitical response by labor, one that emphasized even more strongly the role of the laborer-producer in the new social order, was the development of guild socialism in England. Apparently responsible were the same economic preconditions that contributed to a revival of militancy in British socialism. Greater use of bank deposits, cartellization, protectionism, and large-scale gold production all helped to generate long-term inflation. Depressions and accompanying unemployment followed both the Boer and Russo-Japanese wars. Growing German competition and industrial self-sufficiency in the dominions shrank traditional export markets. The same low growth rate (and falling prices) that plagued the economy in the late 1870s and 1880s returned between 1901 and 1910.[16] Finally, as we have seen, there was mounting discontent with the Labour party's parliamentary representatives and criticism of the party as a Liberal appendage.

This dissatisfaction was expressed in a number of ways. James Connolly, who helped develop the Irish socialist movement, was converted to syndicalism by his experiences with the IWW while in the United States. In his book, *Socialism Made Easy* (1905) he spoke of constructing an industrial republic within the shell of the political state, so that once organized, the former could break out of its confines and replace the latter. Tom Mann, the former secretary of the ILP, had returned from Australia and France. He began to publish *The Industrial Syndicalist* in 1910 and taught that only if workers displayed their strength in their places of employment could hopes of emancpation be realized. He called for revolutionary syndicalism in Wales and preferred more open hostility by workers toward their employers. Like their companions in France, many within this new labor Left wanted to reemphasize the class-struggle concept. Their views were adapted to English conditions by the contributors to another review, *New Age*: A. J. Penty, the architect and designer of garden cities, whose book *Restoration of the Guild System* (1906) was seminal; A. R. Orage, editor of the review; S. G. Hobson, who formulated much of guild socialist theory; and G. D. H. Cole, who did much to popularize it. For the latter, guild socialism was, in an English setting, "essentially parallel to syndicalism in France." That it was also a compromise between syndicalism and socialism was revealed by its intention to retain the state, although a truncated one. In contrast to syndicalist theory, if not practice, guild socialism was markedly nonmilitant.

Briefly, workers could win economic power only by acquiring control over the distribution of labor. Reflecting its intellectual origins, particularly the *medieval socialism* of William Morris and John Ruskin, it would entrust production to a number of guilds, each holding a monopoly, while representatives of each trade would be sent to a central *guild congress*. Consumers' interests would be represented in parliament, which would set production goals and priorities. The state's role was to be that of supreme arbiter in case of conflict between the two.

Self-governing, the guilds were to establish their own working conditions. Like revolutionary syndicalism, and reacting to the administrative socialism called for by Fabians, guild socialists displayed their hostility to state bureaucracy. They saw the state not as an instrument to be used but only one more association. Workers' organizations rather than state socialism provided the solution. These notions of class struggle and industrial democracy were given expression and defended in George Lansbury's *Daily Herald,* founded in 1911, while the *Daily Citizen,* the newspaper speaking for the parliamentary group, warned against "dangerous innovations."

British workers, in contrast to those presuming to speak for them, responded to what they regarded as the inadequacies of the party set up to defend their interests. They did so in a manner parallel to that of their French counterparts. Great strikes broke out in the half decade before World War I began. They originated not only in the demand for salary increases but in the intensification of labor to which workers were subjected and in the progressive withdrawal of privileges long held by the most skilled among them. These strikes were often accompanied by violence. They also demonstrated concern with such objectives as labor's participation in managerial decisions. The strikes of the dockers and railroad workers in 1911, the miners in 1912, and working-class agitation in Ireland the following year have collectively come to be known as the *great unrest* in the history of British labor. A significant consequence was an increase in trade union strength, from two million members in 1904 to over four million in 1913. They also promoted vertical, or industrial organization (the association of workers in similar industries, regardless of the jobs they held). In 1914 a triple alliance of railroad, transport workers, and miners was created, and it anticipated negotiating collective contracts with employers in these areas. War broke out, however, before it could do so.

The subsequent history of the impact made on general socialist thought by syndicalism and guild socialism need not detain us. Aside from Spain, whose syndicalist movement became the most important in the world until crushed by Franco, advocates of economic action reached the peak of their influence in the years preceding 1914. After that, as G. D. H. Cole was to admit, growing expertise was required as technology advanced and hence made it more difficult for the average worker to make the judgments required. Moreover, with the recognition of the relative weakness of the trade union movements throughout the world came a greater awareness of the need to rely on political action. Even so, demands for greater working-class control in decisions affecting labor was a product of the syndicalist experience. So were new and different socialist proposals for social reorganization. The schemes for nationalization advanced by the Fabians in 1920 now called for the control of state-owned industries by national boards containing a majority of working-class representation.

CONCLUSION

Our concern with these champions of economic action was to see them as symptomatic of working-class discontent with socialism, an unhappiness shared by left-wing socialists. In Russia, it was natural for socialists to accept greater reliance on revolution. In Germany, we have witnessed the party's resumption of an orthodox Marxist stand and the revival of a more militant stand by radicals within it. In England and in France, much of the explanation for a renewed revolutionary response may be cast in general and not in specific terms. Higher prices coupled with occasional unemployment and disappointment in parliamentary results contributed to having workers and socialists forget their minority position. The left wing of both movements voiced greater skepticism about the usefulness of legislative and even political action. Labor's complaints were by no means unjustified. Its early parliamentary representatives lacked meaningful legislative programs and included opportunists concerned with furthering their own careers. Reliance on state machinery, however, was momentarily dropped, not destroyed. For in grappling with the new and related problems of national defense and overseas expansion, socialism was once more to reveal its commitment to the preservation of the regime making party life possible. On the other hand, the militancy displayed before 1914 made it difficult for socialists again to neglect their principles or their clients. But allegiance to both was to prove contradictory, and this loyalty became a mixed blessing when, in a later age, fresh departures would be required.

NOTES

[1] J. P. Nettl, *Rosa Luxemburg*, 2 vols. (London and New York: Oxford University Press, 1966), p. 209.

[2] George Lichtheim, *Marxism* (New York: Praeger, 1965), pp. 286–287. Carl Schorske, *German Social Democracy* (New York: Wiley, 1965), p. 274.

[3] Nettl, *Luxemburg*, pp. 309–310.

[4] For a theoretical discussion of this "deradicalization" process, see Robert C. Tucker, *The Marxian Revolutionary Idea. Essays on Marxist Thought and Its Impact on Radical Movements* (New York: Norton, 1969), pp. 172–198.

[5] Leslie Derfler, "Le Cas Millerand. Une nouvelle interprétation," *Revue d'histoire moderne et contemporaine* (April–June 1963).

84 SOCIALISM SINCE MARX

[6] Hyndman's response in *Justice*, September 2, 1889. Cited in C. Tsu-zuki, *H. M. Hyndman and British Socialism* (London and New York: Oxford University Press, 1961), p. 124. For the Fabians and Kautsky, see the summary in *Revue politique et parlementaire*, October 10, 1889, pp. 150–160. For Liebknecht, *Vorwärts*, July 27, 1899. Luxemburg's article, "Sozial Reform oder Revolution," appeared in the *Leipziger Volkszeitung*, July 6, 1899, translated as "Une question de tactique," in *Le Mouvement socialiste* (August 1899), pp. 132–137. Vandervelde cited in *La Petite République*, October 10, 1899.

[7] The replies were first published in the XIth *Cahiers de la Quinzaine*, 1st series, 1899, and reproduced in Jean-Jacques Fiechter, *Le Socialisme français: de l'affaire Dreyfus à la grande guerre* (Geneva: Droz, 1965), pp. 69–75.

[8] Lenin, "Social Democracy and the Provisional Revolutionary Government," and "On the Provisional Revolutionary Government," *Collected Works*, VIII (January–July 1905); 2nd rev. ed. (Moscow: Progress Publishers, 1965), pp. 82, 471. Participation for purposes of infiltration, however, came to be recognized as a useful tactic by communists.

[9] Schorske, *op. cit.*, p. 44.

[10] Eugène Fournière, *La Crise socialiste* (Paris: E. Fasquelle, 1908), p. 73. James Joll, *The Second International* (New York: Harper & Row, 1966), pp. 104–105.

[11] Ralph Miliband, *Parliamentary Socialism* (London: Allen & Unwin, 1961), p. 29.

[12] Ramsay MacDonald, *Socialism and Society* (London: Independent Labour Party, 1905). See Ch. 6.

[13] Oliver H. Radkey, "An Alternative to Bolshevism: The Program of Social Revolutionism," *Journal of Modern History* XXV (March 1953), pp. 25–39.

[14] Peter N. Stearns, *Revolutionary Syndicalism and French Labor. A Cause Without Rebels* (New Brunswick: Rutgers University Press, 1971), pp. 17–18.

[15] *Ibid.*, pp. 102–103. It is not clear, however, why labor leaders were so out of touch with their rank and file.

[16] S. B. Saul, *The Myth of the Great Depression* (London: Macmillan; New York: St. Martin's Press, 1969), p. 53.

SUGGESTED READING

Margaret Cole. *The Life of G. D. H. Cole.* New York: St. Martin's Press, 1971.

George Dangerfield. *The Strange Death of Liberal England, 1910–1914.* New York: G. P. Putnam's Sons, 1961.

Israel Getzler. *Martov. A Political Biography of a Russian Social Democrat.* Cambridge: University Press, 1967.

S. T. Glass. *The Responsible Society: The Ideas of the English Guild Socialists*. London: Longmans, Green, 1966.

Jean Maitron. *Histoire du mouvement anarchist en France, 1880–1914*. Paris: Société Universitaire d'Éditions et de Librairie, 1955.

Michelle Perrot and Annie Kriegel. *Le Socialisme français et le pouvoir*. Paris: Études et documentation Internationale, 1966.

F. F. Riddley. *Revolutionary Syndicalism in France. The Direct Action of Its Time*. Cambridge: University Press, 1970.

Georges Sorel. *Reflections on Violence*. Glencoe, Ill.: Free Press, 1950.

Bertram Wolfe. *Three Who Made a Revolution: A Biographical History*. New York: Dial Press, 1964.

FOUR

Socialism

and Nationalism

Although t h e
p a r t i e s they
founded w e r e
presumed to be nationwide, socialists
had never debated nationalism. Here,
too, the Marxist legacy was ambigu-
ous. Marx recognized nations as historical entities. Workers, he wrote,
sought their control not their destruction. Social democrats could
point to his defense of free Poland (in the program drafted for the
First International's Geneva Congress of 1866) and to his oft-repeated
claims that Germans had every right to defend themselves against
imperialist aggression both from Napoleonic France and tsarist Russia. On the other hand, he formulated no theory and set forth no guidelines for nationality problems. For Marx, the question was secondary;
its solution lay in progressive economic development. In working to
unify the peoples of the earth, industrialization would lead inexorably
to the decline of the nation-state:

In every country the proletariat is in the presence of a single and same
interest, of a single and sole enemy, of a single and sole struggle. . . . National
peculiarities and antagonisms among peoples are progressively being effaced
with the development of the bourgeoisie's commercial freedom, the world
market, the uniformization of industrial production and the conditions of
life that correspond to it.[1]

No doubt socialists held an internationalist ideal. At the outbreak
of the Franco-Prussian war, and considering themselves as having been
attacked, 3 of the 5 German Social Democrats in the North German
Parliament voted in favor of war credits. (Bebel and Liebknecht supported neither Bismarck nor Napoleon III). After the overthrow of the
Second Empire, however, they refused to support the war effort and
protested the annexation of Alsace-Lorraine. Most French socialists did
not distinguish between General Boulanger and his bourgeois opposition, led by Jules Ferry, in the election campaign of 1889. They remained aloof during the Panama scandal and, as we have seen, initially

refused to involve themselves in the Dreyfus affair. The policy statement issued by the Second International in 1891 constituted the orthodox socialist position. An American Jewish group had asked about the socialist response to anti-Semitism. The resolution voted by the Brussels Congress subordinated "antagonisms or struggles of race and nationality [to] the class struggle between proletarians of all races and capitalists of all races." It merely condemned anti-Semitic and, we may infer, nationalist agitation as "one of the manoeuvres by which the capitalist class and reactionary governments try to make the socialist movement deviate and to divide the workers."[2]

NATIONALISM AND SOCIALISM IN CENTRAL EUROPE

NATIONAL AND AUSTRIAN SOCIALISM

National feeling first appeared as a major divisive force among socialists in Austria-Hungary. The Hapsburg Empire contained a variety of ethnic groups, although since 1867 executive power was shared by German-speaking Austrians and the Hungarian monarchy. Viennese workers were aware of the lower salaries and living standards in Slavic lands, and fears of widespread immigration created tension in the capital. Similarly, Germans in Prague were uneasy at seeing themselves displaced by Czechs. Predictably, the socialist party scheduled a debate on the matter.

The Austrian Social Democratic party was organized in 1874 and followed a pattern resembling that in Germany. By 1889 a program was adopted stressing the conquest of political power. Much of the credit belonged to Victor Adler, to be the long-time leader of Austrian socialism. He was descended from a wealthy family of Jewish merchants and had studied medicine and psychiatry. Strongly affected by the misery of the workers he saw in Vienna, he turned to politics instead. Adler met Bebel, later Engels, and became a Marxist. He held enormous prestige and respect, and his ability to find and apply compromises kept the party together and furthered its growth.

Hostility between centralizers and separatists among Austrian socialists was heightened by undeniable airs of superiority on the part of the Germans within the group. As self-proclaimed representatives of a higher culture, they insisted on retaining the German language for official use. Pressure for greater autonomy came from nationalist movements like the Young Czechs, which sought to reestablish a Bohemian state. To avoid conflict and possible fragmentation, the party in 1897 adopted a new federal structure. It provided for the representation of the six chief national groups: Germans, Czechs, Poles,

Ruthenians, Italians, and Slovenes. Under the umbrella of a common executive, each was given autonomy.

More independence was granted when Austrian socialists approved a complex resolution offered at the party's Brünn Congress two years later. It marked a compromise between proponents of dismemberment and those wishing to preserve national coherence. The nationalities question was to be solved within the confines of the existent state. Rejected were classical solutions in which each nationality was allotted territory, with minorities asked to leave or accept assimilation. A federative or multinational state was considered unsuitable for the Empire, in which a single community might contain a number of ethnic groups. The congress preferred to regard the state as an association of persons. Each socialist, regardless of residence, was to settle upon his nationality, as he did his religion. No one group, neither Germans nor Hungarians, could enjoy special privileges. This decision and the debates from which it issued marked the beginnings of theoretical concern with national problems for European socialists.

Much of the credit for the Brünn resolution went to the jurist Karl Renner. Of Moravian origins, he was very much aware of the issues involved. In having responsibility for political and economic matters fall on a central administration, he separated them from cultural questions, which became the province of regional autonomous bodies. Renner developed his views in several important books published after the turn of the century. He was strongly patriotic during World War I and was to serve as president of the Austrian Republic after 1945. Otto Bauer agreed that dissolution of the Empire was not necessary and that national antagonisms, insofar as they divided the workers and diverted them from economic and social questions, only served bourgeois interests.[3]

However, the matter was not put to rest. Czech socialists remained hostile to a common executive. They reproached the Germans in the Austrian party with monopolizing the trade union leadership, and their complaints were debated at the International's Stuttgart (1907) and Copenhagen (1910) congresses. At Copenhagen they pointed out that the ratio of Czech socialiasts to the total Czech population was greater than that for German socialists in Austria. But their demand for a position of parity for their own language was quashed. A minority of Czech socialists estimated that they had nothing to hope for from the International. They refused to accept its rejection of a separate party. By 1911 Czech and German-speaking socialists were competing in a general election. It was apparent that national feeling ran strongest in what Adler called the *Little International* of Austro-Hungarian socialism.[4]

POLISH SOCIALISTS AND THE SPD

Similar tendencies were to be observed on the part of Polish socialists vis-à-vis the German Social Democratic party. Three million Poles lived in Germany, and the SPD leadership held conflicting views about their future. Wilhelm Liebknecht and others took a pre-1848 position in calling for a free Poland. They saw it as the most democratic solution and one that would also serve as the best guarantee against Russian expansion. However, the party did not grant Polish socialists autonomy. It preferred to retain one Social Democratic organization while making sure that the "Polish comrades" enjoyed equal rights. Still, there was little opposition from his compatriots when Bebel said that "a good comrade who only knows German is much more useful than a Pole incompetently speaking Polish." The SPD disavowed the independent Polish Socialist party founded in 1892.[5]

Few defended this decision more arduously than the most illustrious Polish member of the SPD, Rosa Luxemburg. She too preferred that her countrymen work within the larger German party framework. Like Marx, she disclaimed all questions of nationality. Her experiences in Polish socialism convinced her that if socialists got involved with them, they would waste time with local quarrels and exhaust themselves. Luxemburg backed up her feelings with empirically based arguments. Her thesis on "The Industrial Development of Poland," her articles, and her speeches before German and international congresses aimed at demonstrating that the Polish bourgeoisie was tied to Russian capitalism and not serious about Polish emancipation. Only the combined efforts of all the proletarians subordinate to Russian rule could reestablish Polish liberty.

The influence of French utopians, Russian nihilists, and Bakuninists helped establish socialism in the Balkans during the 1870s. At the outset, socialist objectives and national independence were related. Socialists participated in the Bosnian-Herzegovinian uprising against Turkey in 1875. The Bulgarian Social Democratic party (founded in 1891) split over the question of national independence in 1903. The faction comparable to reformists in the West, the *broads,* was prepared to acknowledge the importance of national sentiment. The *narrows,* on the other hand, preferred to focus on issues relating exclusively to the class-struggle concept.

The question of nationalities was resolved neither in large multinational parties like the German and Austrian nor, for that matter, in the Second International. The theoretical struggle it unleashed in the Hapsburg Empire continued until the coming of war. Luxemburg's position was rejected by Lenin. Disturbed by what he regarded as Renner's excessive influence on Russian socialists, he sent the young

Stalin to Vienna to study the problem. In a series of articles, published in 1913 as *Marxism and the National Question,* Stalin first criticized Austrian socialists for placing too much stress on maintaining ethnic identities. He then took issue with the solutions proposed. A nation was not an association entered into voluntarily. It was more deeply rooted. On the other hand, Stalin condemned the Austrians for having divided the party and trade union movement. He concluded that socialists ought to recognize the strength of national feeling and support attempts to achieve independence if in so doing the cause of revolution were furthered. Lenin elaborated on this last conclusion and argued that national struggles in certain regimes can in fact contribute to world revolutionary strategy. Not all, however, were useful; he especially denounced the alleged chauvinism and national "separatism" of the Jewish Bund, and each had to be weighed for its value.

NATIONALISM AND SOCIALISM

All parties seeking social change, but particularly those relying on existing government machinery, were caught up in this dilemma. If interested in winning reforms, was it not necessary to defend the state capable of providing them? The reconciliation of class interests (which transcended national boundaries) with national interests was not new to revolutionaries. Jacobins found little incompatibility between patriotism and, if not international socialism, then international social change. Bismarck's social legislation aimed at promoting national objectives. (Indeed, the term *national socialism* was first used in Germany in 1895. It was then applied to Austrian Social Democrats who preferred a federation of national units to a central party.) On the other hand, as a nation industrialized, it necessarily withdrew from unbridled policies of laissez-faire. The natural corollary to the socialization of the nation was what E. H. Carr called the "nationalization of socialism."[6]

The right to national self-defense was early accepted by socialists. Marx and the general council of the First International agreed with Liebknecht and Bebel on Napolean III's aggression in the early months of the Franco-Prussian war and approved German measures of retaliation. We have seen that only after the establishment of a provisional republican government in France and the disclosure of Prussian territorial aims did German socialists vote against continuing war credits. Socialist attitudes on imperialism and war were the two most heavily debated issues by international socialists in the years before 1914. That the closest of correlations may be found between reformism, on the one part, and national and imperialist feelings, on the other, will scarcely cause surprise.

FABIANS AND THE EMPIRE

Fabians long stressed independent rather than international action as a guide for British working-class politics. As early as 1897, in the appendix to their *Industrial Democracy*, the Webbs suggested that socialists be flexible so that "each community may therefore work out its salvation in the way it thinks best." The society opposed continued reliance on free trade as dangerous to British prosperity. To formulate and express the Fabian attitude toward empire, and particularly the society's stand on the Boer War, was the task assigned to George Bernard Shaw. His pamphlet, *Fabians and the Empire*, was the first fully developed statement made by the society on foreign and imperial matters. Because it incorporated the detailed critical suggestions of some 150 Fabians, it can be considered the view of the majority.[7]

Shaw said that the world had evolved "far beyond the primitive political economy of the founders of the United States and the Anti-Corn Law League." Most relevant was the new stage reached by international development. The only question was whether Great Britain was to be "the nucleus of one of the world empires of the future or whether it should stupidly lose its colonies and be reduced to a tiny pair of islands in the North Sea." In presenting an early argument from civilization, Shaw maintained that small states like the Boer Republic were

anachronistic in the new world of the twentieth century. . . . A Great Power, consciously or unconsciously, must govern in the interests of civilization as a whole; and it is not to those interests that such mighty forces as goldfields, and the formidable arguments that can be built on them, should be wielded irresponsibly by small communities of frontiersmen.

Fabians were not to view the British Empire from any "narrow" vantage point of the working class—or any other class in the "national community." They were concerned with the effective social organization of the whole Empire and its "rescue from the strife of classes and private interest." It was in Great Britain's national interest to keep it intact. Shaw recognized the need for reform. Required was an overhaul of the consular system in order to take full advantage of trade doors opened by British arms. Also needed were military reforms to better defend imperial possessions. Like all socialists, Fabians called for the creation of a reserve militia and even specified training procedures. Noteworthy is the fact that these military suggestions came at a time when both the Liberal and Conservative parties opposed all forms of compulsory military service.

Not all socialists supported the Boer War. Hardie and MacDonald opposed it, while Hyndman was patriotic and imperialist. His pro-French sympathies led him to urge naval preparation for war with

Germany. In the December 31, 1898 issue of *Justice* he said that England required a great navy to protect her imports, and that "our existence as a nation of free men depends on our supremacy at sea."[8] His big-navy stand was to cost him the presidency of the British Socialist party in 1913. The bureau of the International was disturbed by these divisions among English socialists, but war intervened before it could recommend steps for a united party.

The Labour party itself never really took a stand on foreign policy issues and rearmament.[9] Most Labour MPs and a Liberal minority opposed the government's determination to keep ahead of Germany in naval construction. The party could argue that on ideological grounds Russia, with whom an entente had been reached in 1907, was as much an enemy as Germany. More traditionally, it criticized military spending as a social waste. Socialists in the party placed faith in the Second International, whose most important member was Germany, to keep the peace. (The SPD in 1910 had rejected as "impractical" Keir Hardie's proposal that the International recommend a general strike in the event of war. This was conveniently ignored.) The trade union bloc left foreign affairs to the Labour MPs. Unless working-class interests were clearly affected, it remained unconcerned. Labour's ambivalence about rearmament issued in part from its awareness that military expenditures meant jobs, a consideration not lost on MPs representing shipbuilding districts. The patriotism displayed by many Labour members in Parliament fanned the antipathy of the party's left wing toward the reformism and opportunism practiced. However, the attitude toward war of a labor party lacking any ideological basis may not be terribly illustrative. More suitable is an examination of the views on these matters held by French and German socialists.

REFORMISM AND NATIONALISM IN FRANCE

The acceptance of reformism by collectivists in France meant greater socialist support for the Third Republic, in foreign as well as in domestic affairs. Given their faith in the virtues of universal suffrage, it was natural for them to endorse the regime that promoted its exercise from threats both within and outside of France. Moreover, reformist socialists found no incompatibility between the internationalism they preached and the primacy of French interests they defended. What better way, they declaimed, to guarantee the success of international socialism than to have France take the lead in its expansion! What surer way to jeopardize that success than to weaken the one country that had introduced the principles of liberty and equality to Europe! Furthermore, for many socialists, as for most Frenchmen, the defeat of 1871 and the loss of the two provinces had never been forgotten.

French financial and diplomatic activity (and obstinacy on the part of Bismarck's successors) led to an entente between France and Russia in 1891 and to an alliance two years late. Reformists asked for and won socialist support for the Franco-Russian alliance. The question was a particularly thorny one for socialists. Although internationalist in outlook, many supported the Republic's efforts to find allies. Russia, on the other hand, an authoritarian state with a long history of anti-revolutionary activity, was anathema to the Left.

In seeking socialist support for the alliance, reformists like Mille-rand pointed to Engels' "prophetic" letter of September, 1870 warning against a German seizure of Alsace-Lorraine. As the defeated power, France could not set the example of disarmament. The disturbance of the European peace, Millerand told a socialist gathering in 1893, depended not on her but on a king's volition. Regardless of the socialists' deep-rooted resentment, the Russian alliance could further national security, and they owed their first loyalty to France. Accordingly, he also asked them to accept the twofold responsibility of universal compulsory military service and the burdens of a budget of war. On the condition, said Millerand, that the alliance was to be a contract among equals, and that French interests were not to be subordinated to Russia, socialists, along with their fellow Frenchmen, supported it.[10]

French socialists accepted this position, however grudgingly. It was defended in the reformist Saint-Mandé speech, subscribed to by nearly all of them. It guided their thinking on foreign affairs until a wave of militant internationalism swept over the far Left in 1904–1905. Marxists did not object. In foreign relations, Guesde's consistent view of war as the natural outcome of bourgeois conflict and his denunciation of insurrectional means to prevent it were compatible with growing national feeling on the part of reformists. France was to be defended by its proletariat. As was mentioned earlier, an alliance with Tsarist Russia was affirmed at the Eleventh Annual Congress of the Workers party, held October, 1892. The only qualification set forth at this meeting was that requiring Russians debarking at Toulon to be distinguished as officers or sailors. This represented a throwback from the socialist egalitarian tradition and showed that the leaders of the Workers party, or *Parti ouvrier,* were growing progressively more patriotic. "France attacked," said its manifesto, "will have no more ardent defenders than socialists of the Workers party."[11]

In London, Engels noted the Guesdists' progressive incorporation of patriotism into French Marxist thought and approved. He called it "very rational," and said that "international union can exist only between *nations (sic),* whose existence, autonomy, and independence as to internal affairs is therefore included in the very term of internationality." Electoral considerations also prompted the Marxists. They were aware of the reluctance of French voters to turn the keys of national security over to internationalist-minded socialists. Guesde was to complete the fusion of patriotism and socialism. In the France of 1789, he wrote, no one said, "Down with Picardy." To support the Second International today, one did not need to denounce France. "If Frenchmen then did not cease to be Normans," he went on, "socialists today do not cease being Frenchmen. Those who seek to distinguish between the two are playing into the hands of the bourgeoisie."[12]

The Franco-Russian alliance was also defended by Blanquists. Even Vaillant felt that such an alliance would promote peace. The degree to which even militant socialists thought in terms of French interests was revealed at the Workers party's Montlucon Congress in 1898. Tsar Nicholas II had proposed universal disarmament, a long-standing socialist goal. But the cautious Guesdists were caught up in the election campaign of that year and rejected the proposal for use in their platform.[13]

During the remainder of the decade, socialists in the Chamber of Deputies continued to support the alliance. What criticism they made was of the government's refusal to divulge the terms. They feared that France would be compelled to support Russian territorial ambitions in Asia. Socialist spokesmen, also afraid that the alliance might work to prevent the return of Alsace-Lorraine, protested against proposed French participation at ceremonies scheduled for the opening of Germany's Kiel Canal. The Alsatian senator, Scheurer-Kestner, observed that socialists seemed more concerned with the lost provinces than most Frenchmen. If Alsatians regarded the "moment of justice" as imminent, he wrote, the "great majority of the population feared a disaster."[14]

Socialist concern for national security can be explained in the context of reformism and by the pressure of electoral considerations. Was the same concern shown after the adoption of a harder line by the newly unified party in 1905? If momentarily muted, it reemerged well before the outbreak of World War I. Despite the imposition of orthodox Marxist doctrine, the reformism of the nineties, with notable exceptions like ministerial participation, once more prevailed. Jaurès was able to synthesize diverse sentiments and redirect the movement into democratic channels. The lack of unity among militant socialists also helped. Their disagreements, with the issue of participation finally resolved, quickly resurfaced. Indeed, revolutionary syndicalists and socialists sympathetic to syndicalism saw the SFIO as a reformist party scarcely differing from the progressive bourgeois elements with which it was once more willing to cooperate.[15] Even the socialist leadership acted sufficiently reformist to discredit references to the 1890s as an aberration in the history of French socialism. Guesde pursued the dictates of his rigid orthodoxy and Vaillant continued to demonstrate his concern for the workingman, revealing an evergrowing political pragmatism. Both, as they had a decade before, began to lead their respective federations, the Nord and the Seine, the two most powerful socialist groups in France, back to reformism. They were followed, in turn, by younger party chiefs like the militant Jean Longuet and Pierre Renaudel, as well as the more moderate Albert Milhaud and Albert Thomas.

The history teacher and militant socialist Gustave Hervé spoke for the most pacifist elements within the party. He was noted for an article, especially for a phrase pulled out of context, which deplored the carnage of Napoleonic battle by referring to the "flag in a dung-heap." In 1906, Hervé proposed recourse to the general strike and armed insurgence in the event that war broke out. At the SFIO's Limoges Congress of that year, Guesde condemned both pacifism and revolution. In replying to the militant stand taken by the CGT earlier in the year, he startled newspapermen when he warned of the "danger of exaggerated internationalism" and spoke in terms of "national duty." The French proletariat could best serve socialism by completing a revolution in France, for it was responsible to the proletariat everywhere for its own bourgeoisie. At the party's Nancy gathering the following year, he denounced any recourse to the general strike in case of war. If carried out, Guesde argued, the winning power would be the nation with the fewest socialists, and those in France had necessarily to support their country. Vaillant and Jaurès, in separating themselves from Hervé and in acknowledging the requirements of national self-defense, came to support the strike as the only tactic with any chance of success in preventing war. Vaillant overcame the opposition of Hervé and the uncompromising advocates of insurrection in 1909. At home, socialists agreed once more to electoral and parliamentary alliances with progressive middle-class parties.[16]

The nationalist revival in France that preceded the onslaught of World War I was supported by shipbuilders and munitions makers. However, it differed from that which had marked the anti-Dreyfusards. The new nationalism was not anti-Semitic, but determined in what it regarded as its duty to the country.[17] Socialists like Jaurès sought a compromise between Guesde, who would make no effort to stop war, and Hervé, who denied that the nation had any right to socialist support. For Jaurès, the working class was the heir to the national tradition, and socialists made the best patriots. The state was not to be destroyed, but conquered from within. His approach to military self-preparedness was a carefully thought-out plan for a citizen militia as a substitute for a standing army. He led socialists to struggle, unsuccessfully, against extension of conscription to three years in 1913.

Socialists in France wanted to stave off impending war, but when it came, the great majority, like all of its Western counterparts, resolutely supported the government. At the end of the first month of fighting in 1914, Guesde, Marcel Sembat, and soon Vaillant joined the conservatives Jules Méline and Denys Cochin in a "sacred union" coalition government. In giving its approval, the SFIO joined those socialists like Aristide Briand, René Viviani, and Alexandre Zévaès, who had refused to associate with the unified party under the terms set forth at Amsterdam and had organized a separate Republican-Socialist party. This group, however, took an increasingly patriotic stand. It ultimately dropped its socialist character, even before the war began. As the war progressed, the main party was to refashion it.

THE SPD AND IMPERIALISM

The German Social Democratic vote for war credits on August 4, 1914 evoked enormous surprise throughout Europe. Enough is now known about the history of the party to suggest that it would have been more astonishing if its Reichstag delegation had voted any differently. Still, this most orthodox of parties at least in theory had repeatedly beaten back attempts to revise doctrine. Because it lacked any Jacobin and Blanquist tradition to help reconcile nationalism and socialism, the experience of the SPD may be more useful than even that of the unified French socialist party.

There was no single tradition, in regard to patriotism, in the German socialist past. Lassalle was the proponent of a strong state. Bebel and Liebknecht condemned Prussian territorial ambitions in 1871. The early Social Democrats were sympathetic to republican France. However, some, like Vollmar, feared the desire for *revanche* and a possible Russian alliance. Even as doctrinaire a Marxist as Kautsky echoed the need for national resistance when he defended military training and called on loyal socialists to register their patriotism.[18]

The colonial expansion of the 1890s, together with the birth of a navy in 1898 and the Moroccan Crisis of 1905, revealed both increased German activity abroad and conflict within the party. Imperialism and socialist attitudes toward it became a major issue. The SPD officially opposed all activities of the capitalist state, including its colonialist policies. The reasons were varied. Heavier taxes levied to support overseas expansion fell (given the injustice of extant fiscal policy) most heavily on workers. Cheap labor exploited abroad would compete with German workers and result in low wages and possible unemployment at home. Forced acquisition of markets would postpone capitalist crises, and so preserve the status quo. Revulsion generated by imperialist practices added moral fervor to theoretical hostility. Nevertheless, by 1912 imperialism was sanctioned by two groups within the party. The most important support came from revisionists on the Right.

Radicals, in addition, argued in favor of imperialism—that it was a necessary stage in capitalist growth and, accordingly, should not be opposed.[19]

Revisionists maintained that in a thriving capitalist economy the workers' lot would continue to improve. Hence it was in their own interests to further economic growth. As the world economy developed, moreover, free trade would be replaced by protectionism, and to compete successfully, the state required working-class support. As on so many other occasions, socialist-imperialists were able to back their arguments with occasional Marxist texts. Marx had sanctioned British rule in India as causing a social revolution. He had urged the Prussians to take Schleswig-Holstein and had called for war against Russia. His advocacy, however, in each case was based not on any desire to improve working-class living standards (as socialist-imperialists wanted) but to arouse processes that would quicken socialist revolution by bringing economic and social progress.

Bernstein wanted to modify the party's anticolonialist stand. He invoked humanitarian concerns and also said that it was not necessary to renounce German interests because English, French, or Russian chauvinists might be displeased. Not only could the German worker identify himself with his country, but socialism would be easier to achieve if his country were a wealthy one. The worker who voted for state and local councils, he said, was "the fellow owner of the common property of the nation; whose children it educates in common, whose health it protects, whom it secures against injury; [he] has a fatherland without ceasing on that account to be a citizen of the world." Bernstein denied that any state or nation had an absolute right to any part of earth. The earth itself belonged to humanity, and a "higher" civilization possessed superior rights with regard to the use of its raw materials.

It must be added that Bernstein never gave blanket endorsement to German imperialism. The nation, he was all too aware, was not a democracy, and he found a naval program unnecessary. What he wanted was a reappraisal of his party's absolute antiimperialism, which condemned the quest for colonies as nothing more than avarice for marketplaces. Together with other revisionists, Bernstein found the uncompromising hostility of Kautsky, George Ledebour, and Parvus (Alexander Helfand) "useless" and "unrealistic." His approval of imperialism was qualified, but it was condemned along with his revisionism.

The SPD's antimilitaristic stand also generated conflict. Opposed to all arms expansion, the party in 1905 supported mass demonstrations against the government's foreign policy during the Moroccan Crisis. Still, Social Democratic leadership criticized as futile and visionary Karl Liebknecht's proposal to foment pacifist propaganda among recruits. Together with Kurt Eisner, Liebknecht was vigorously attacked by

Bebel at Mannheim in 1906. It was at this congress too that Bebel, like Guesde, condemned any recourse to the *Massenstreik* in the event of war. He also maintained, both here and at Essen the following year, that it would be hopeless. The nation, then fully armed, would only impose martial law, resort to military justice, and so crush the strike. Right-wingers in the party went further. The Reichstag deputy from Chemnitz, Gustav Noske, told the Essen Congress that in the event of war socialists, like other Germans, would do their duty. He told the Reichstag the same year that the SPD would work to safeguard German independence. Bebel's blanket rejection of the general strike had revealed that he was making no absolute distinction between a war of aggression and a war of defense. The Center was sliding to the right, and radicals in the party became embittered.[20]

In 1907 the SPD's Reichstag delegation voted against appropriations for a German venture in Southwest Africa. Chancellor Bernhard von Bülow took the opportunity to dissolve the legislature and call for a new election. He ran a nationalist-oriented campaign for his bloc of parties and in so doing branded the SPD as traitorous. The party suffered the worst setback in its history. Although it slightly increased its vote, it lost almost half its seats. The defeat drove home the importance of foreign-policy issues to the leadership. The party, it was felt, had underestimated the appeal of imperialism and nationalism to the masses. The fact that only one debate was held on foreign affairs (at Mainz in 1900) had revealed the preponderancy of domestic issues. The SPD, therefore, loudly proclaimed its patriotism. If Bebel continued to censure the harsh treatment accorded recruits, he also did so on the grounds that it would impair the fighting qualities of the army. His position was becoming indistinguishable from that of the Right.

Party behavior became more contradictory. It voted in 1907 for an inheritance tax to make the rich pay their share. The purpose of the tax, however, was to offset deficits caused by large naval expenditures. German delegates to the Second International's Stuttgart Congress, we shall see, lustily condemned war. However, they rejected any action beyond protest designed to prevent it. Still officially anticolonialist, the party's criticism became more muted after 1907. Economic arguments were the kind resorted to—colonies were not worth the price paid for them. German socialists exerted pressure and had the same Stuttgart Congress adopt an ambiguous resolution on imperialism. It held that while the popular benefits of colonialism had been greatly exaggerated, capitalism could still serve as a civilizing agent. Earlier congresses had condemned imperialism without qualification. The debate and its outcome showed how international socialism had abandoned revolution; it showed, too, that the German party was the leader of socialist conservative forces.[21]

The SPD executive shrugged off radical criticism and grew even more circumspect. After von Bülow's fall and the decomposition of his "bloc" in 1909, elements within the party allied themselves with liberal bourgeois groups. The SPD organized agitation against Prussia's three-class voting system, but rejected a general strike (considered self-defeating) to support this agitation. It joined with the trade unions in attacking the SPD youth leagues, then centers of antimilitary agitation, on the pretext they had to be brought into the regular party organization. In the summer of 1911 a German gunboat steamed into Agadir Harbor to prevent the French acquisition of Morocco. The party leadership decided to ignore the incident; it hoped it was not serious enough to bring about war, and socialist agitation might prove harmful in the general election scheduled for the following year. Bebel overcame the objections of Rosa Luxemburg, who wanted to arouse popular aversion to the government. He was determined to focus on domestic issues. The election of 1912 indeed proved a great socialist victory. The party gathered a third of the votes cast and won 110 seats in the Reichstag. However, the victory had required an electoral alliance with the Progressive party, which meant further watering down of historic SPD positions. In 1898 the party had opposed every increase in the standing army and navy. In 1903 it opposed every military bill requiring additional taxes. In 1912 it opposed only those bills providing for indirect taxes on consumer goods.[22]

Radicals won a victory of sorts at the Chemnitz Congress of 1912. One of the more notorious socialist-imperialists, Karl Hildebrand, was expelled. The debate, however, had revealed a distinct anti-British bias. German industry must be supported and British expansion limited. Socialist-imperialists used the same arguments as their bourgeois counterparts to justify overseas expansion: economic need and cultural superiority. They added the benefits that would accrue to workers and thus ease the transition to socialism. They were doubtless sincere, but their premises were just as faulty. Historical research has demonstrated that imperialist nations did not trade as much as had been anticipated with their colonies and that these colonies were not particularly profitable. Clearly, socialists could share the same misconceptions as the middle classes.

The defeat of the socialist-imperialists was hardly decisive. The Right retreated to an older nationalist position, while the Left and Center voted antiimperialist, antichauvinist resolutions as a matter of convenience. At its Jena Congress in 1913, the party for the first time approved the vote of its parliamentary section for military taxes. The government had agreed to raise the funds by direct taxes on property rather than by indirect ones that lay most heavily on the poor. In ensuring that the burden would be distributed more equitably, and arguing that the budget was bound to be passed in any event, the SPD approved the tax, justifying its decision with references to the familiar Marxist texts approving German action against imperial France and tsarist Russia. This vote foreshadowed that for war credits a year later. The importance of the socialist-imperialists and nationalists lay not in their numbers, which were few, but in the fact that they were tolerated by the rest of the party. In this, too, may be found the origins of socialist support for the war and for German expansion as a wartime objective.

More symbolically significant was the SPD's decision to disavow the minority within it unwilling to show proper respect for the Kaiser. These socialists, as a matter of principle, refused to rise during his speech closing the Reichstag. To avoid embarrassing their less militant colleagues, they usually absented themselves. Early in 1914 militant socialists wanted to have the full party delegation express its disapproval of the regime by remaining seated. They were outvoted. The relevant resolution stated:

We must express rational ideas in a rational way, not with manifestations utterly inconsistent with rational thought. . . . There are no longer any Social Democrats who still believe that the task confronting us today is the forcible overthrow of our present form of government. . . .[23]

We may conclude that three groups of opinion prevailed within the SPD from the time of the Erfurt program to the outbreak of World War I: an openly revisionist and patriotic Right, a radical and internationalist-minded Left, and a compromising Center anxious to maintain organizational coherence and to increase the party's political representation. The Center, constituting the great majority, appeared to lean toward the Left ideologically, but in practice it played down the role of armed proletarian uprising and was closer to the Right. Between 1906 and 1913 the Center, because of the growth of the trade unions and party prosperity, moved even nearer to the Right. On the issues of national defense and collective opposition to war, the party had taken an openly patriotic position, leading to the schism of 1917 and the acceptance by the Left of the Communist International.

IMPERIALISM AND THE INTERNATIONAL

Not until its Paris Congress of 1900 did the International discuss colonial questions. Once again, it reflected the divisions of its national sections. Aware of the struggles within British Labour over the Boer War and among German Social Democrats over imperialist expansion, the International vaguely went on record as anticolonialist on largely humanitarian grounds. The resolution at Amsterdam (1904) remained tenuous, in spite of Hyndman's attack on British overseas administrative policies. Between 1905 and 1910, Franco-German conflict over Morocco, mounting awareness of the brutalities of colonialism, and the turn to the left by workers' and socialist movements prompted greater interest in imperialism. An extensive debate took place at Stuttgart (1907). Many French delegates had made known their opposition to their government's Moroccan policy. Belgian socialists had learned of King Leopold II's intention to give his private domain in the Congo to the nation. Some wanted its internationalization; others favored the state's acceptance if placed under full parliamentary control. Most preferred to abandon it. These alternatives were all presented at Stuttgart, and a resolution offered by Kautsky was narrowly voted. It simply required socialist parties to combat all forms of colonial exploitation. The debate revealed the International's inability to appreciate the role of the underdeveloped world in global revolutionary strategy. Ultimately, anticolonial sentiment triumphed at International congresses. Like antireformism, however, it received greatest support from socialists in countries where colonial problems were not pressing.

ITALIAN SOCIALISTS AND COLONIAL WARS

Perhaps the sharpest divisions over imperialism appeared in the Italian Socialist party (PSI). It dated from 1892, and like others in Latin Europe had to contend with syndicalist demands for direct action. Still, it was able to return 32 deputies by 1900. During the first 20 years of its existence, the story was one of repeated purges and schisms. They revealed the diverse shades of feeling within the party and the inability of the majority in the center to mold socialism into an effective political force. A decade before World War I broke out, the party might be described as an unwieldy agglomeration incorporating the entire Italian Left. It ranged from syndicalists under Arturo Labriola to orthodox Marxists led by Constantin Lazzari and Enrico Fermi (who, if revolutionary by inclination, worked for party unity) to reformists like Filippo Turati. Furthest to the Right stood those opposed to revolution in any form, particularly Léonidas Bissolati and Ivanoe Bonomi.

Beginning in 1904, the party moved toward its right. Two events were responsible: a general strike and the entry of Catholics into Italian political life. Premier Giovanni Giolitti fought the strike begun in September by Labriola's syndicalists. Giolitti dominated Italian politics from 1892 until Mussolini's seizure of power, and his skillful if devious use of compromise and concession enabled him to control extremist groups within the legislature. The tactics used were illustrative of his political style. He allowed the strike, based in Milan and the industrial north, to play itself out; then he dissolved the legislature and called for new elections (in the hope that public irritation over seemingly futile strikes would result in fewer socialist members). At the same time, Pius

X relaxed the prohibition against Catholic participation in elections. The PSI consequently lost 6 of its 33 seats and at once embarked on a more conservative course.

Socialism also reflected the relative prosperity of the early years of the new century. The national debt was lowered, greater social expenditures were made, and industry benefited from a series of favorable trade agreements. Giolitti legally permitted workers to strike, and in 1906 the General Confederation of Labor (CGL) was founded. At its Florence Congress of 1908 and overcoming radical opposition, the party reconsidered the advisability of calling for immediate and violent revolution. Under Turati's guidance, Labriola and the syndicalists were ousted. The PSI became more attractive to the CGL membership and was in a better position to compete for the Catholic vote. It appeared set on a policy of closer cooperation with the government.

Hostility between militant socialists and reformists intensified at the time of the war in Tripoli of 1911. In September, Italy went to war with Turkey in an effort to acquire the Libyan capital. Socialists were violently divided over which course of action to take. Turati favored a colonial policy and support of the government's war efforts. Radicals in the party reacted strongly. They reached a position of ascendancy at the Reggio Emilia Congress of July, 1912. At their demand—particularly that of the militant Benito Mussolini—Bissolati and Bonomi were expelled. Sixteen deputies thereupon formed a new reformist party, while Mussolini assumed the editorship of the main party's newspaper, *Avanti*. The PSI took an increasingly negative stand on parliamentary alliances. The future founder of the Italian Communist party, Amadeo Bordiga, credited Mussolini with laying the foundations of the radicalism in the party that was to culminate in the formation of the PCI in 1921.[24]

THE INTERNATIONAL AND THE COMING OF WORLD WAR I

Unlike that of imperialism, the question of war and the means of preventing it had preoccupied the Second International since its founding in 1889. However, the issue remained an academic one until 1904 when two member nations, Japan and Russia, had gone to war with each other. Despite their anxiety to find preventive measures, the delegates could not reach agreement on those proposed. The tactic most often discussed, we have seen, was the general strike. It was debated and rejected (because of ideological differences and doubts about its effectiveness) at the Brussels and Zurich gatherings in 1891 and 1893 respectively.

A successful general strike in Belgium together with the Russian Revolution of 1905 revived faith in the general strike.[25] Its defenders included revolutionaries like Lenin, Luxemburg, and Liebknecht; anarchists; syndicalists; most French delegates; and such British socialists as Henderson, Hardie, and MacDonald. At both the Stuttgart and Copenhagen Congresses this coalition introduced resolutions favoring its use as the most promising way to prevent conflict from expanding into war. It was easier to agree that war was the product of capitalism and would disappear when the latter was replaced by socialism. Three proposals were put before the delegates assembled at Stuttgart. Hervé called for the general strike and insurrection after war was declared. Vaillant and Jaurès took a roughly similar stand, with greater emphasis on the strike. The German delegation agreed on the need for opposition, but wanted no specific steps to be listed. Bebel argued that to appeal for desertion would mean the end of the SPD. Socialists of each country, he said, must be left to act in the way they think best. A compromise text was ultimately voted. It asked only that all socialists, in the event of a declaration of war, work for its prompt end. Thanks to Lenin and Luxemburg, however, the last sentence was expanded. Socialists were also urged to do everything possible in order to take advantage of the crisis "to agitate and arouse the people and thereby quicken the fall of capitalist domination."

The conservative German delegation, then, had feared repression of its party. Like Guesde, Bebel maintained that the nation with the best organized proletariat would be the one defeated. He also pointed out some very real practical difficulties. To be successful, the strike required the cooperation of the trade unions, particularly the socialist unions. But unionized workers comprised a minority of the total labor force, and those under socialist auspices, a smaller minority yet. The CGT numbered 600,000 in a total French labor force of 7 million (about 8 percent). In Germany, 23 percent of unionized workers belonged to nonsocialist trade unions.[26]

To overcome this lack of numerical strength and to meet the growing threat of war, Vaillant and Keir Hardie proposed a modified resolution at the International's Copenhagen Congress in 1910. It envisaged the prevention of war by use of the general strike, but "in industries which supply war with its implements: arms, munitions, transportation, and mines." However, Karl Legien and other trade union chiefs doubted it would work. Key industries such as railroads in Germany were precisely the ones not controlled by socialist unions. Critics also pointed to the absence of connecting links among the unions that would enable them to coordinate their action. (The International Federation of Trade Unions experienced the same failings as its sister organization: a lack of any means of enforcing its decisions and a preponderant German influence.) The Vaillant-Hardie resolution was tabled. The International's Bureau was to examine it and refer it to the Vienna Congress scheduled for 1914. It never met.[27]

Concern over the Balkan Wars prompted the International to call for an extraordinary congress. It was held in Basle in December, 1912, and was marked by great optimism and stirring demonstrations. Especially memorable was Jaurès' speech in the city's cathedral. The congress demanded the creation of an all-inclusive Balkan Federation and asked the proletariat of every involved nation to exert pressure on their governments in order to keep them out of Balkan affairs. Despite the insistence of Hardie and Vaillant, no plans were formulated in the eventuality of war. By this time, Jaurès had dropped any remaining reservations about the general strike; he was determined to do everything possible to stop the war he felt was sure to come. Even so, he made it clear that French socialists would be justified in resisting German aggression. Bebel feared a Russian attack. These apprehensions, if understandable, only weakened the International's will to act. In any case, legislative protest would probably have been useless, for the inability of socialists to exert any real influence on their respective governments was only too clear. France and Germany had pursued their Moroccan policies regardless of left-wing opposition.

SOCIALISM IN 1914

On the eve of World War I, socialism was nonetheless the single most important political force on the continent and was gaining strength in England. In Germany, the SPD was the largest party in the Reichstag. It contained over a million members, had won almost 4.5 million votes (30 percent), and held 110 seats (40 percent). The French SFIO had received 1.4 million votes and held 76 seats (13 percent). There were socialist parties in 20 European countries, although only in about half a dozen outside of Europe. If they so chose, socialists could occupy government posts. The PSI in Italy had refused invitations to serve in government posts extended to Turati in 1903 and to Bissolati in 1911. As leader of the strongest Danish party, the socialist Thornwald Stauning was asked by the king to form a government in 1913. The Swedish party decided to join the government in 1914 to defend the rights of parliament against royal prerogative.[28]

The emergence of socialism as a political force had changed the very nature of politics. It introduced the modern mass party. Previously, parties tended to be collections of notables; they would henceforth contain a mass membership, machinery for recruitment, a party press, and seek to be all-encompassing. Socialist parties already concerned themselves with working-class lives to the extent of providing everything from social club to consumer cooperative. In Germany, a veritable labor culture had developed. "A working-class child, SPD model, could begin life in a socialist crèche, join a socialist youth movement, go to a socialist summer camp, hike with the socialist *Wandervögel*, sing in a workers' chorus, and be buried by a socialist burial society in a socialist cemetery." The SPD possessed 91 daily newspapers with over one and a half million subscribers. It enjoyed an income of 1.47 million marks and saw 12,232 representatives elected at all levels of government.[29]

Other parties served as variations on that in Germany. Socialists in Italy found it necessary to overcome revolutionary anarchism and democratic Mazzinianism. The presence of diverse ethnic groups in the Austrian empire required a federative approach. Scandinavian socialism followed the English pattern of reformism and close affiliation with the trade unions. One constant was that as the suffrage widened, the socialist vote, and hence representation in legislative bodies, increased. Another was the enormous amount of suspicion and fear aroused by socialist initiatives within the middle class. With more retarded industrial development in Latin Europe, we find a greater separation between socialists and trade unionists, with a correspondingly greater mistrust of the former by the latter. Finally, socialists could do useful work in national legislatures in the degree to which democratic institutions were effective. Regardless of its political plurality, the SPD was to play no role in fashioning national policy until the advent of the Weimar Republic.

SOCIALIST PARTY STRUCTURE

Whether of parliamentary origins, as in France, or of labor origins, as in Britain, working-class parties tended to distrust their legislative representatives and tried to subject them to closer party control. Hence the power of the party executive and its resolution to impose discipline. Another determinant of party structure was the understandable wish, in the absence of any other means of financial support, to recruit as members as large a percentage of the masses as possible. Most important was the egalitarian longing to make the party as democratic and representative of its membership as possible. Consequently, caucuses were replaced by branches, and avenues were kept open between them and higher policy-making bodies. For a party with trade union antecedents, a special difficulty arose over the question of membership. Not until 1918 could individuals join the British Labour party.

Despite sincere efforts to erect and maintain a democratic structure, bureaucratic and oligarchical tendencies soon emerged.[30] By 1914 the SPD had some 3000 permanent officials, one for every 250 members. Institutional framework, moreover, did not prevent strong leaders from playing a predominant role. Individual leaders enjoyed great personal power and prestige. In the words of the political scientist Maurice Duverger, some were "very authoritarian and very imbued with their personal power and not much inclined to dilute it." These groups and parties revolved about the personalities of their chiefs—the names Lassalle, Stauning, Branting, Guesde, and Jaurès most readily come to mind.

Despite such efforts to ensure democratic control through collective executives, annual congresses, and disciplinary committees, socialist parties like trade unions were authoritative and hierarchical if not authoritarian. Moreover, a small nucleus of what the French call *militants* attended party functions faithfully and elected and furnished leaders. The yearly congress, which in theory subjected the executive to the delegates of the entire party membership, often proved no check at all. Many members were too poor or indolent to send delegates, and these annual gatherings were not necessarily representative.

Perhaps the single most compelling characteristic of organized socialism, from the standpoint of modern European history, was the gulf that separated the party (as represented by its executive) from its parliamentary delegation. In theory the latter was subject to party control and its members responsible to their local federations or branches. In practice socialist legislators regarded themselves as responsible primarily to their constituents, invariably less radical. Of major importance here was the type of voting system used. Greater party control could be exercised in large constituencies and with list voting. Then the resources made available by the party often determined whether a candidate was successful. Conversely, in small, single-member constituencies a socialist could appeal to a relatively small number of voters and so find himself able to ignore party attempts to impose discipline. As a result, conflict widened between militant party councils and reformist-minded, compromise-seeking legislators. The independence of socialist politicians from their parties, or, put another way, their greater dependence on their constituencies, accounted for much of the nationalism and reformism practiced. If alliances were made, either electoral or parliamentary, socialist members of parliament became more moderate still. For it is a political fact of life that a coalition is seldom more radical than its most conservative member.

These considerations are important for the history of socialism. The German party may once more serve as our example. The Reichstag delegation, at the least, won a disproportionate share of power within the SPD in the years before World War I, although no provision was ever made for it to play any special role. Consequently, on August 4, 1914, it ceased being what Peter Nettl called an "inheritor party," became a pressure group (Lenin's "stinking corpse"), and during the war sought concessions for its clients, the German workers. (Admittedly, the workers were then no less patriotic, and probably more so, than the deputies.) Together with other labor parties in Europe, the SPD was competing for rewards instead of working to "inherit" them long before 1914.[31] Disastrous for socialism was the fact that after the war, and under pressure from communists on their left, this tendency was to be strengthened and perpetuated.

NOTES

[1] Cited in Annie Kriegel, *Le pain et les roses. Jalons pour une histoire des socialismes* (Paris: Presses Universitaires de France, 1968), pp. 81–82.

[2] Cited in James Joll, *The Second International* (New York: Harper & Row, 1966), p. 68.

[3] Jacques Droz, *Le Socialisme démocratique, 1864–1960* (Paris: A. Colin, 1966), pp. 105–106. Charles A. Gulick, *Austria from Habsburg to Hitler*, 2 vols. (Berkeley: University of California Press, 1948), pp. 1369–1370.

[4] Kriegel, *op. cit.,* p. 87.

[5] *Ibid.,* pp. 85–86.

[6] E. H. Carr, *Nationalism and After* (New York: Macmillan, 1945), p. 19.

[7] G. B. Shaw, *Fabianism and the Empire* (London: G. Richards, 1900). Cited in Bernard Semmel, *Imperialism and Social Reform: English Social Imperial Thought, 1895–1914* (London, Allen & Unwin, 1960), p. 70.

[8] C. Tsuzuki, *H. M. Hyndman and British Socialism* (London and New York: Oxford University Press, 1961), p. 198.

[9] Henry Pelling, *A Short History of the Labour Party* (London: Macmillan; New York: St. Martin's Press, 1965), p. 28.

[10] Text in *La Revue socialiste* (October 1893), pp. 499–503.

[11] Cited in L. Derfler, "Reformism and Jules Guesde: 1891–1904," *International Review of Social History* XII (1967), Part I, 70.

[12] Engels letter to Laura Lafargue dated June 20, 1893. Friedrich Engels, Paul et Laura Lafargue, *Correspondence,* 3 vol., III, *1891–1895* (Paris: Éditions sociales, 1959), p. 284. Guesde's preface to J. Vingtras, *Socialisme et patriotisme* (Lille, 1900).

[13] Maurice Dommanget, *Edouard Vaillant* (Paris: La Table ronde, 1966), p. 222.

[14] Bibliothèque Nationale, Division of Manuscripts, N. A. fr. 12711, A. Scheurer-Kestner, "Souvenirs d'un républicain alsacien," vol. VIII, "1896–1898," p. 167.

[15] *Le Mouvement socialiste* (May–June 1906), p. 188; April 15, 1906, pp. 377–389.

[16] Alexandre Zévaès, *Histoire du socialisme et du communisme en France de 1871–1947* (Paris: Éditions France-Empire, 1947), pp. 331–332.

[17] Eugen Weber, *The Nationalist Revival in France, 1905–1914* (Berkeley: University of California Press, 1959), p. 9.

[18] Sinclair Armstrong, "The Internationalism of the Early Social Demo-

crats," *American Historical Review* 47 (1942), pp. 249–254. G. Roth, *The Social Democrats in Imperial Germany* (Totawa, N.J.: Bedminster Press, 1963), pp. 96–100. A. Joseph Berlau, *The German Social Democratic Party, 1914–1921* (New York: Columbia University Press, 1949), p. 47.

[19] Abraham Ascher, "Imperialism within German Social Democracy prior to 1914," *Journal of Central European Affairs* XX No. 4 (January 1961), 397. My next three paragraphs are based on this article.

[20] Carl Schorske, *German Social Democracy, 1907–1917* (Cambridge, Mass.: Harvard University Press, 1955), pp. 69–75. Charles Andler, *La Décomposition politique du socialisme allemand, 1914–1919* (Paris: Éditions Bossard, 1919), p. 14.

[21] Ascher, *op. cit.*, pp. 403–404. William Maehl, "Triumph of Nationalism in the German Socialist Party on the Eve of the First World War," *Journal of Modern History* XXIV (1952), pp. 28–29.

[22] Schorske, *op. cit.*, pp. 227–228.

[23] *Vorwärts*, July 2, 1914. Cited in William E. Walling, *The Socialism of Today* (New York: Holt, Rinehart & Winston, 1916), pp. 55–56.

[24] Fulvio Bellini, "The Italian Communist Party: Pt. I: The Transformation of a Party, 1921–1945," *Problems of Communism* V (January–February, 1956), 37. Droz, *op. cit.*, p. 138.

[25] Joll, *op. cit.*, p. 127.

[26] *Ibid.*, pp. 131–133. J. Braunthal, *History of the International*, I, *1864–1914* (New York: Praeger, 1967), p. 301.

[27] Joll, *op. cit.*, pp. 128–130.

[28] R. C. K. Ensor, *Modern Socialism* (New York: Harper & Row, 1904), pp. 25–26. Braunthal, *op. cit.*, p. 273.

[29] The quotation is that of Daniel Bell, "Socialism," *International Encyclopedia of the Social Sciences* (New York: Macmillan, 1968), vol. 15, p. 511. Figures from Franz Osterroth, ed., *Chronik der Sozialistisherin Bewegung Deutschlands* (Berlin: Dietz, 1956), p. 62.

[30] Maurice Duverger, *Political Parties* (New York: Wiley, 1959), p. 154. See also Robert Michels, *Political Parties* (Glencoe, Ill.: Free Press, 1958).

[31] Peter Nettl, "The German Social Democratic Party as a Political Model," *Past and Present* XXX (April 1965), pp. 85–86.

SUGGESTED READING

Franz Borkenau. *Socialism, National or International*. London: Routledge, 1942.

Milorad Drachkovitch. *Les Socialistes allemandes et français et le problème de la guerre, 1870–1914*. Geneva: Droz, 1953.

Jacques Droz. "Der Nationalismus der Linken und der Nationalismus der Rechten in Frankreich (1871–1914)," *Historische Zeitschrift* 210, February 1970.

R. A. Kann. *The Multinational Empire. Nationalism and National*

Reform in the Habsburg Monarchy, 1848–1918. 2 vol. New York: Columbia University Press, 1950.

Lenore O'Boyle. "Theories of Social Imperialism," *Foreign Affairs,* XXVIII (January 1950).

Hans Wehler. *Sozialdemokratie und Nationalstaat. Die deutsche Sozialdemokratie und die Nationalitäten fragen in Deutschland von Karl Marx bis zum Ausbruch des Ersten Weltkrieges.* Würzburg: Holzner, 1962.

FIVE

Socialism

and Communism

Mounting disen-
chantment with
World War I re-
awakened the militant tradition in
Western European socialism. The
November Revolution of 1917 in
Russia not only stimulated revolution but was welcomed because of
already existing revolutionary fervor. The greatest schism to be experienced by socialism—that generated by the questions of nationalism
versus internationalism and insurrection versus reform—was reflected in
this prewar situation. This was not resolved, in part because agreement
on a theoretical level could not be reached. The domestic reformism
practiced by socialists through democratic and parliamentary institutions was never accepted by a militant minority. World War I provided
the conditions in which this minority could grow and become a majority, in at least the French and Italian parties. By setting a successful
example, the Bolshevik revolution furthered the process, but this tended
to push democratic socialists further toward the center in support of
existing institutions. Their commitment to democracy became so strong
that socialists could readily be identified by their hostility to "communist dictatorship." Hence, in spite of the many real changes brought
about by the war, the prewar divisions within socialism remained largely
unresolved.

The Second International was discontinued when it failed to
prevent the outbreak of war. (Its successor, the Labor and Socialist International, was to remain a federation of autonomous parties.) The
parties of which its predecessor was composed were convinced of the
war's defensive character and supportive of their respective governments. Hence on the same day, almost at the same hour, socialists in
both the French Chamber of Deputies and the German Reichstag
voted war credits, and the Belgian party authorized Vandervelde to
enter a war cabinet.

SOCIALISTS AND WORLD WAR I

Most parliamentary socialists responded to the outbreak of war by supporting their governments, although three broad positions on the war may be identified even at this early date. If in the SPD Karl Kautsky voted funds with reluctance, his colleague to the right, Philipp Scheidemann, had few doubts about the necessity of the war effort. Vaillant, who was to join Guesde in a French coalition government, voted credits "for the country, for the Republic, for the International," and as early as 1912 Hervé had become a committed patriot.   Those who had "planted the flag in the dung-heap," it would appear, were those who most wanted to carry it to Berlin.   In Belgium, Vandervelde was more adamant still. This right-wing was to reject any compromise peace, refuse to participate in international socialist gatherings held on neutral ground—in short, have nothing to do with the enemy whether socialist or not. It later condemned the Bolshevik revolution and the methods it employed, and members were subsequently charged by communists with having never accepted Marxist revolutionary theory. As the fighting wore on, however, it was this right-wing group that steadily lost its strength.

The Center was convinced that socialist objectives could be reached by democratic routes. As casualty rates rose, however, and as they came to appreciate the difficulties in settling the question of war guilt, Centrists began to ask for pacific resistance and for a revival of international working-class solidarity. They became outspoken critics of the war and tried to find ways in which a revived International could bring it to an end. They suggested a "peace without guilt or annexations." They also urged a hands-off policy toward the Bolsheviks and willingness to suspend judgment on their revolution.   Buffeted by foreign and domestic strife, torn by more resolute forces operating on their right and left, this center was doomed. Increasingly, the more militant Left, led by men like Lenin and Liebknecht, hoped to transform the conflict between nations into revolutionary civil war between classes. It actively supported the Bolsheviks (who rejected war credits from the start) and demanded that their example of revolution be followed. In essence, the story of socialism during World War I was that of the growth of the Left with additions from the Center.

It must be said at the outset that it was the *war-socialists* on the Right who most closely reflected the position taken by labor. Lenin and Luxemburg accused the leaders of the Second International of "betrayal." Lenin denounced at length their "petty bourgeois opportunism." In substituting bourgeois reformism for socialist revolution and in insisting on bourgeois chauvinism under the guise of patriotism, he charged that they ignored the internationalism of the Communist Manifesto. He maintained that "illegal forms of organization and agitation were imperative during epochs of crisis."[1] But a majority of European workers, from antimilitarist *cégétistes* to oppressed Russians, supported these war-socialist leaders and so opposed the stand taken by the Bolshevik leader.

The patriotism displayed by the labor rank and file appeared to have reaffirmed the legitimacy of the vanguard theory. In his book, *The War and the International* (written at the end of the first year of fighting), Trotsky recognized that only after prolonged hostilities would revolutionary action be possible. This same national solidarity accounted for the failure of international socialist action. Neutrals feared that the war might spread to their own countries and made attempts to hold a congress of the Second International. But the patriotism of the Right and Center prevailed. French and Belgian delegates refused to sit with Germans until the invasion of Belgium was disavowed. Consequently, at a gathering that opened in Copenhagen in January, 1915, only the Scandinavian and Dutch parties and the Jewish Bund were represented.

An opposition nevertheless began to appear. Bolsheviks and Mensheviks in the Duma opposed credits. In Britain, the ILP denounced the war. Socialists there were convinced it was a matter of imperial rivalries, while others like George Lansbury objected on more traditionally pacifist grounds. Having put their party at the disposal of the recruitment campaign, Labour now made concern with foreign affairs paramount. The party executive deplored the British promise of support to France made without public knowledge. Still, it did not openly oppose the government and seemed receptive to its efforts to woo the workingman. Henderson joined the cabinet, serving as a liaison between government and labor. In France, the war was condemned only by a handful of intellectuals like Romain Rolland and some trade union people like Alfred Merrheim and Pierre Monatte. Centers of opposition were found in the Metals Workers Federation in the CGT and the SFIO's Federation of the Haute Vienne (one of the regional organizations of which the party was composed), led by Jean Longuet. In Germany, Karl Liebknecht was voting against further credits by December, 1914. A small group of delegates rejecting annexations, including Kautsky and Bernstein, abstained in budgetary votes. They would soon join the dissidents, Rosa Luxemburg, Franz Mehring, and Clara Zetkin.

At the invitation of the neutral Italian and Swiss socialists, a conference was held in the Swiss village of Zimmerwald in September, 1915. Thirty-eight delegates from the Center and Left of their respective parties attended. Although they unanimously condemned the policy

SOCIALISM AND COMMUNISM   113

of national coalitions, two tendencies nevertheless emerged. What came to be known as the *Zimmerwald Right* estimated that it was necessary to reconstruct the International and offer it as an agency of mediation between the belligerents. The Left adopted the *revolutionary defeatism* formulated by Lenin in *Theses on [the] War*—that is, to change the war into a civil class conflict. However, he was unable to persuade even the more revolutionary socialists despairing of their governments' war policies; not until the Bolshevik victory would the Left subscribe to his views. The minority was larger but still unable to prevail at a conference held at Kienthal the following April.

These meetings were dismissed by most socialist newspapers, which tended to be under the control of the patriotic-socialists. Still, war weariness helped to generate disenchantment, and a socialist propaganda campaign, particularly the distribution of the illegal manifestos of the *Zimmerwald Left,* helped create pressure for a negotiated settlement.[2] In the Reichstag, 20 socialists voted against credits, including such party leaders as Bernstein, Hugo Haase, and Georg Ledebour. An opposition group called the *Sparticist* emerged from the far left, and on May Day, 1916, organized the first revolutionary strike of the war. The minority rejecting credits was expelled from the SPD's Reichstag delegation and formed a dissident group. In Austria, Friedrich Adler, son of the party leader, assailed his party's war policy. His assassination of the prime minister and his speech to the court that condemned him jolted Austrian socialism.[3] But the party disassociated itself from the act. Similarly, the ILP, if sympathetic with the Zimmerwald movement, remained affiliated with the Labour party.

Like the rank and file, most trade union leaders approved of their respective governments' war policy. In Britain, an industrial truce was signed for the war's duration. In return for a promise of no strikes, the government was to seek limits on profits made by firms producing war materiel. It was easier for labor than for the government to keep its word. The Labour party soon considered itself a prisoner of other parties represented in the cabinet, with little influence on decision making. It had been forced to accept conscription early in 1916 as well as the incursion of unskilled workers into jobs long held by craftsmen. On becoming head of the government, Lloyd George provided somewhat better conditions from labor's point of view in state control of mines and shipping and food rationing. Even so, there was discontent, and in France syndicalist and pacifist groups organized a committee to resume international relations. Dissatisfaction with the coalition policy of war-socialists was growing, but this opposition was scattered and diverse, and, until 1917, more pacifist than revolutionary.

THE RUSSIAN REVOLUTION AND INTERNATIONAL SOCIALISM

The tsarist regime collapsed in March, 1917. Although the Petrograd Soviet wanted a negotiated peace without annexations, allied pressure kept the Provisional Government in the war. In Germany, war fatigue in the spring of 1917 and the effectiveness of the British blockade helped bring on a wave of strikes. Because of Spartacist intervention, they assumed a revolutionary character. The government's violent repression of the movement in Leipzig provided a taste of what was to come. In effect, a revolutionary party was being formed, consisting of a few independent socialists (USPD) and forces further to the left. This antiwar movement called for democratization of the Reich and for universal suffrage in Prussia.

Pressure for a settlement mounted in France after the failure of the much-touted Nivelle offensive. Mutinies broke out in the army, and strikes of increasing intensity at home. The government made concessions in both places—providing better leave-policies (under the new commander Pétain), a reluctance to sacrifice lives in needless offensives before the coming of the Americans, and a minimum salary and compulsory arbitration practices to workers. Both Britain and France had welcomed the overthrow of the tsar, as these Entente powers now viewed the war ideologically as one of democracy against empire. Socialists took these claims seriously and would not fight for territorial gain. In Britain, opponents of the war voted against the government on three occasions in 1917. The ILP and British Socialist party (Marxist) joined forces in the United Socialist Council, which in June called for a convention in Leeds. Attended by 1100 delegates, including such moderates as Mac-Donald and Philip Snowden, the congress endorsed the Russian peace program of "no annexations and indemnities." It asked for the establishment of workers and soldiers councils, or *soviets,* to initiate and coordinate working-class activities, but all this sounded decidedly revolutionary and was disavowed by the bulk of the Labour party.

Demands for another international socialist agreement could not be disposed of as easily. Again, the initiative was neutralist, and Stockholm was the site chosen. Russian socialists hoped the conference, scheduled for early June, could arrange a compromise peace and so permit the country to leave the war. The socialist Right in Britain and France was suspicious, but the Labour and SFIO majorities accepted, convinced the proposed meeting was the only way to keep Russia fighting. Virtually all Social Democrats in Germany and Austria approved, revealing the position that was to be given formal expression in the Reichstag's "July resolution" of 1917. The SPD, together with the Center and Liberals, called for a peace without annexations and indemnities. The conference took on symbolic significance and loomed as a great hope of peace. It was never held. The Entente governments refused to issue the necessary passports. This episode marked the effective end of the Second International and any hopes placed in it as an agent of mediation. Nothing was left but the victory of one side over the other as the means to peace. More immediately, it meant the end of socialist support for coalition governments in France and England. The SFIO opposed the new Ribot ministry. Although Labour ministers continued to sit in the cabinet presided over by Lloyd George, the real head of the party, Henderson, vowed never to return until his party controlled the government. Efforts were undertaken to revamp Labour, to change it from an interest group to a national opposition.

THE NOVEMBER REVOLUTION

The Bolshevik success in November, 1917 and Lenin's stated objective of seeking a peace appeared to the war-weary Left as a dawning in the east. The victory enhanced the prestige of the Zimmerwald Left and shed new luster on revolutionary solutions. Even so, in a last attempt to join the democratic and revolutionary traditions, Luxemburg rejected Lenin's elitism and denounced his substitution of a party for a class. Other socialists voiced their dismay after the Russian withdrawal from the war. The Peace of Brest-Litovsk permitted the Germans to rush troops from the east to the western front. Patriotic socialists in the Entente countries saw it as a betrayal. But the dictatorial nature of the Clemenceau government prevented those in France from moving too far to the right. The SFIO was equally removed from national coalition and revolutionary defeatism. Trade union leaders, on their part, found it easier to turn to more practical bread-and-butter issues.

The chief impact on the Left of the Bolshevik success was the precedent for successful revolution. Lenin had not managed to persuade radicals at Zimmerwald and Kienthal what the November Revolution affirmed in actuality. Radicals were to rally to the Third International, and in France, a month before the armistice, this minority finally became a majority. Marcel Cachin replaced the moderate Pierre Renaudel as editor of *L'Humanité* and Ludovic-Oscar Frossard became secretary of the party. For the socialist Right and for nonsocialists, the main impression was the establishment of a dictatorship. They were less concerned with the dynamics of revolution than with the support given by the Russian non-Bolshevik Left to counterrevolution.

Even less enthusiasm was shown for the Bolsheviks by British socialists. Support of even the March Revolution overthrowing the tsar was limited to industrial areas like the Clydeside, and subsequent news of terrorism in Russia reduced the number of these supporters. Alexander Kerensky visited England in June, 1918 and was warmly received by workers in London, but only a handful—chiefly the British Socialist party—identified with the Soviets.

Still, to prepare for its new opposition role, a new structure was deemed necessary for the Labour party. It took advantage of franchise reforms early in 1918 to broaden its base from a federation to a mass party open to individual membership. The organization became more centralized, with the entire conference slated to vote for the party executive. This meant greater representation for local sections and for individuals, and less from the unions. Even so, the union bloc remained dominant. In June, the party accepted the Webbs' policy statement, "Labour and the New Social Order." For the first time the party was provided with a distinct socialist orientation, demanding "common ownership of the means of production." The fact that it was still financed and controlled by the trade unions, however, proved an effective bar to extremism. These renovations nonetheless ensured that the yet unborn Communist party would make no headway in Britain.

The November Revolution made more of an impact in Italy. Socialists in that country had been neutral, not patriotic, ever since hostilities opened. (The reformists, it will be recalled, had been expelled in 1912.) In seeking a negotiated peace, the majority had taken a position similar to that of the Zimmerwald Right. After the Bolshevik success a *maximalist* majority led by Giacinto Serrati won control of the party's Rome Congress in September, 1918. As we shall see, it called for the proletariat to take power and establish a socialist republic.

THE REVOLUTIONS IN CENTRAL EUROPE

THE GERMAN REVOLUTION

Bolshevik expansion, it became clear, would depend on its reception in Central Europe. The revolution experienced by Germany was the result of war, defeat, and the Soviet example. It was foreshadowed by a political strike in January, 1918, which aimed at peace without annexations and universal suffrage in Prussia. Also foreshadowed was the aftermath. The SPD majority cooperated in breaking the strike. The alignment of socialist forces was revealed during the Reichstag vote on the peace concluded with Russia. While the USPD delegation disapproved, Scheidemann and 52 deputies abstained on this vote for a blatantly annexationist peace. This may have been due less to hostility toward the treaty than to the desire to retain the alliance with the Center party and the Liberals. Still, until the end of the war, the editors of *Vorwärts* refused to consider the likelihood of yielding Alsace-Lorraine. There was no time since 1914 at which the SPD was further to the left than the winter of 1917–1918. Even so, the party's innate conservatism, apparent before the war, was strengthened by the fear of Bolshevik "barbarism." It was not so much the November Revolution, for only fragmentary information came from Russia, but the dissolution of the Constituent Assembly in January, 1918, that turned most Social Democrats definitively against bolshevism. They remained fervent democrats and refused to weigh arguments that democracy had at best slim chances in a Russia preparing for civil war. Their fears spurred an integrationist ideology and further weakened defenses against conservatism. There was no guarantee of party life under a revolutionary government, but there was every indication that the gains won by the trade unions would be lost. The wish to avoid civil war at all costs, as well as that for domestic reform and an acceptable armistice, prompted the SPD to join a coalition cabinet.

Late in September, General Ludendorff said there was no chance of victory and advised the government to make peace. On October 4, Prince Max of Baden formed a ministry representing all parties. In entering it, majority socialists took the first step in becoming a government party. Some politicians, as well as the high command, recognized President Wilson's preference to deal with democratic governments and wanted the Kaiser to abdicate. The SPD—or at least elements of its leadership—did not join this movement. It certainly never tried to overthrow the monarchy, and, at most, asked for some sort of regency. Its chief concern was to avoid social revolution and to establish a popular government by legal means. The party was to reverse itself only after revolution forced the Kaiser's abdication on November 9. Even then, the pressure of the Berlin crowds may have influenced its support of republican demands. To preserve internal stability and forestall Liebknecht from proclaiming a German soviet republic, Schneidemann proclaimed the republic from the Reichstag balcony. Socialists further to the left were divided: Independents like Kautsky opposed bolshevism; Ledebour defended it. Many Spartacists like Rosa Luxemburg were in prison, and it was while there that her study, *On the Russian Revolution,* was published. She condemned the Bolshevik repudiation of democracy and urged the reestablishment of the *soviets.*

Revolution in Germany was made by the sailors at Kiel. They mutinied before the prospect of a futile showdown and set up workers' and sailors' councils. Their revolt spread to nearby forts and to the interior. Revolution also broke out in Munich. There it was the work of Kurt Eisner, whose anti-Prussianism was as much a propelling force as his Marxism. On October 23 he called for a republic and for peace. On November 7 the Bavarian government was overthrown and soviets established. Next came the turn of Berlin. Crowds of workers appeared on the streets demanding a change of regime, and it was under the pressure of one such crowd that Scheidemann divulged his own conversion. A provisional government was created, headed by Friedrich Ebert and including both majority and independent socialists. Prince Max had few hesitations about handing the reins of power to Social Democrats. In yielding to Ebert he observed: "The man was determined to fight the revolution tooth and nail."⁴

Unlike the program of the soviets, which demanded the socialization of the privately owned means of production as well as an immediate armistice, that of the provisional government was wholly political and moderate. It called for an election held by universal suffrage, and for social legislation as opposed to socialization. It behaved very much like a government party. The explanation given by Mehring for the SPD's vote on war credits was still appropriate. "They are now," he said, "perfectly respectable middle-class persons, who would no more think of losing their positions in life than they would of going into the streets naked."⁵ To justify his moderation, Ebert could have pointed to the hostility of the peasants and landowners. They were in a position to withhold food from the cities and so bring down a socialist regime not to their liking. It may also be said that Social Democrats never received a solid mandate for further change, and that between 1919 and 1923 the SPD was to use every means in its power to defend the new republic—from the *Freikorps* (composed of volunteers recruited to repress the rebels) to the general strike—and to do so successfully.⁶ On the other hand, revolutionaries would hardly wait for a popular mandate.

The struggle, then, was not a revolutionary one. The government had lost its support and the paralysis of the ruling class was complete. Precisely because it was a peaceful upheaval, it could not be radicalized. Moreover, few were aware of the divisions between majority and independent socialists. Both groups wanted a constituent assembly, but while independents agreed that an assembly would be considered by the allies as representative, they wanted to postpone its election until the government had time to socialize industry. When the SPD, in accord with the its promise to the army to preserve the social fabric in return for the maintenance of order, rejected proposals to democratize the army, the USPD withdrew its support. Still, both varieties of democratic socialists remained distinct from the Spartacists. The latter said that an assembly would only produce the same result as in 1848: It would rob the workers of their power. They preferred a dictatorship, and Rosa Luxemburg, for one, hoped that it would be temporary.

The Spartacists decided to attack the government. Gustave Noske, serving as defense minister, called on the Freikorps to repress them. The troops did so ruthlessly, removing any last doubts held by independents as to the usefulness of further collaboration. In January, 1919 the Spartacist revolt was crushed, and with the murders of

Luxemburg and Liebknecht, its leadership destroyed. Throughout the spring Noske continued to use the Freikorps to put down new uprisings. In as much as most Spartacists became communists, we have, in effect, the first overt clash between socialism and communism in Germany.

In the elections for a national assembly, majority socialists returned about 40 percent of the delegates; independents less than 8 percent. Ebert was elected president, and the new constitution was promulgated in August. It provided Germany with a progressive Western-style democracy. One socialist clause was included: the legislature received the authority to socialize national resources, manufacturing, and distribution.

Clearly, Ebert and Scheidemann were more concerned with national than with socialist interests. They were shocked by the chaos they saw in Russia. The natural moderation of the SPD, long reconciled to the nation, had persuaded it to call on the army and so preserve order. But, again, there was no evidence that the party lagged behind the rest of the country. Germany was not revolutionary, although a revolution had occurred. The old regime had tottered of its own weight, and an impulse had been enough to dislodge it. Workers' and soldiers' soviets were not so much engines of revolution as consequences of the disappearance of the Reich. Even the Congress of Soviets elected in December, 1918 had contained 284 SPD delegates, or 60 percent of the total. Given majority socialist strength here and the superior organizational abilities of both trade union and Social Democratic branches, in contrast to that of the radicals, it was perhaps but a question of time until the soviets fell under SPD control. The party chiefs expected that with the long-sought conquest of political power a reality, economic and social change could be introduced gradually. Their error lay in leaving untouched the structure of the previous regime: the upper administration, the military, the judiciary, and the landowning classes were not democratized. The party was to pay for its shortsightedness.

THE AUSTRIAN REVOLUTION

Similarly, Austrian socialists were not responsible for the fall of the Hapsburg Monarchy. In demanding cultural autonomy, Renner and the party leaders remained loyal to the government. Spurred by Otto Bauer, a minority came out for dissolution of the Empire. Even so, nearly all Austrian socialists shared the hope of joining a greater Germany after the war. Hostility toward Russia, also widely shared, was fragmented by the 1917 Revolutions. The Bolshevik decision to make peace set off a major strike in Vienna in January, 1918. The initiative, however, for dissolving the Empire and establishing ethnic states belonged not to the socialists but to the national minorities. Even among socialists, national sentiment remained primary. Those in the Sudeten and Moravian areas wanted to join their German colinguists and rejected integration into the proposed Czechoslovakian state. Concomitantly, they subordinated social concerns and the prospect of social revolution to nationality problems.

THE GROWTH OF COMMUNISM

THE TWO INTERNATIONALS

The Communist or Third International was founded in March, 1919. It asked workers to reapply Marxist teachings, to renounce false bourgeois democracy, and to seize power. The following year it set forth *21 Conditions* for membership, which included authority of the International over its member parties, repudiation of the reformism that had typified socialist behavior, and specific insistence that the old leadership be jettisoned. This referred to the party leaders occupying the middle ground as well as those on the Right: MacDonald and Henderson in England, Kautsky and Rudolf Hilferding in Germany, Jean Longuet in France, and Morris Hillquit in the United States. The debate and vote that followed within the world's socialist parties was to split them permanently.

Most socialists who had supported their wartime governments wanted to reestablish the Second International; revolutionaries wanted to follow the Russian example and so urged adherence to the Third. With the failure of insurrection in Central Europe, revolutionaries understandably pinned their hopes on Russia. They directed their heaviest blows against democratic socialists and called them guilty of "applying the brake to progress." Socialists, in turn, became preoccupied with justifying their existence vis-à-vis communism. The beneficiary of their inability to come to terms was to be fascism.

Socialists anxious to reconstruct the Second International scheduled a conference at Berne for February, 1919. They also wanted to influence the peace treaties, then being negotiated, along the lines indicated by Wilson. Aside from the Russians and the Belgians who refused to meet with the Germans, 102 delegates from 26 countries attended. They committed themselves to parliamentary democracy and the defense of individual rights as the sole methods by which socialist objectives could be attained. A minority led by Friedrich Adler and Jean Longuet opposed on the grounds that this formula could be used against the Bolshevik revolution, and so revealed their concern with refashioning socialist unity. But the majority, led by British Labour and the bulk of the SPD, repudiated any kind of dictatorship, including that set up by Lenin. The congress delegated the responsibility of reestablishing the International to an action committee and then turned to the question of war guilt. Here it worked out a skillful compromise. Ascribing guilt to the Germans satisfied the Entente socialists; condemnation of the Treaty of Versailles pleased the SPD.

Two currents, then, could be detected. Democratic Socialists favored reconstructing the Second International in opposition to the Communist International (Comintern). Others had opposed wartime coalition policies, but had also rejected Lenin's revolutionary defeatism. This group remained aloof both from the Third and a refurbished Second International. It included Frenchmen like Longuet, some ILP people, German independents, and Austrians loyal to Adler. At Vienna in February, 1920 they founded yet another international socialist organization. They allowed that they did not want to limit themselves to parliamentary methods alone nor to insist on the techniques used by the Bolsheviks. Not surprisingly, their association was derisively dubbed the "Two and a half International" by its critics. It proved unable to reconcile the Second and Third Internationals, and one more unity congress representing all three was called by Adler to meet in Berlin in April, 1922. It deteriorated into a forum denouncing the Communist International, and proved to be the last such meeting. The success of fascism in Italy, however, and the growth of reaction in Germany revived attempts to present a united socialist organization. The last obstacle was removed when majority and independent socialists in Germany reestablished a unified party. At Hamburg, in May, 1923 delegates from the Berne and Vienna Internationals came together to create the *Labor and Socialist International*. It was to endure as the voice of international democratic socialism until the Nazi invasions of Western Europe in 1940.

The Communist International, or, in the jargon favored by communists, *Comintern,* was the Bolshevik response to Berne. A Moscow Conference of March, 1919 founded the Third International, attended by representatives of numerous revolutionary groupings but dominated by the Bolshevik party. Luxemburg had anticipated its appearance before her death and had already made known her opposition. As much a revolutionary as Lenin, she maintained that insurrection must be based on mass support. She once more rejected his theory of the conquest of power by an elite of professional revolutionaries, and asked that the creation of a communist international be postponed until the establishment of mass communist parties.

THE EMERGENCE OF THE COMMUNIST PARTIES

Europe was at a revolutionary peak during the two- or three-year period after the war came to an end. Great political strikes indicated the extent of labor's anxiety about social reconstruction. Several hundred delegates representing 37 countries attended the Comintern's second congress in 1920. They included former socialist patriots like the Frenchmen Frossard and Cachin, as well as early pacifists and defeatists. Others who sought association with the Comintern, however, were recent converts to socialism. Those who voted to join the Third International at the SFIO's Tours Congress in December, 1920 had for the most part belonged to the party for only a few years. The sections that rallied were largely new and located in the countryside. Those in industrial areas and party veterans remained faithful to what Léon Blum was to call "the old house." The communists attracted the young; they failed to win over the trade unions. The same pattern prevailed in the successor states of the Austro-Hungarian empire. Communism made impressive gains in Montenegro and Macedonia; it experienced most difficulty in economically advanced Slovenia (northern Yugoslavia).[7] This tendency persisted in communism's subsequent successes in developing countries of the Third World.

The 21 Conditions set forth by the Comintern for membership divided every socialist party. Even the handful of existing communist parties learned they would have to expel some of their leaders. Communists had come to view socialism (which claimed working-class support) as a greater threat than capitalism. Similarly, they aimed at destroying the socialist center, seen as much of a danger as the socialist Right. Hence the ILP, USPD, Longuet's *minoritaires,* and the followers of Adler and Otto Bauer were all indicted as obstacles to working-class emancipation. Communists managed to destroy this center—either by forcing it to the Right, as in France and Germany, or by so disrupting socialism that the entire movement was imperiled, as in Italy. The insistence on wholesale acceptance of Bolshevik tactics in 1920 was much greater, but not entirely dissimilar to the acceptance of SPD tactics in 1904 insisted on by the Second International's Amsterdam Congress. Even when accepted, the conditions were in some cases done so grudgingly. Numerous intellectuals in seeking social reconstruction never felt entirely comfortable in the embrace of these tactics.

THE SFIO AND THE COMINTERN

The most prestigious victory for the Comintern took place in the French party. Léon Blum spoke for those who opposed the centralization demanded by Moscow; he wanted a pact among equals. Rejecting the suppression of minority rights and the right of initiative by local and parliamentary groups, Blum reaffirmed revolution but considered the conquest of power as a means to an end and not as an end in itself. He insisted, moreover, that the dictatorship of the proletariat was to be based on popular sovereignty. A majority within the SFIO, nevertheless, accepted the communist terms. The new militancy had become deeply rooted at home; bred by wartime discontent, French socialism seemed unable to live up to its promise, and a revolutionary epoch opened. The war had swelled the ranks of the SFIO (it boasted of 133,000 members at the end of 1919), and many of the newcomers came from nonindustrialized areas. They included revolutionary syndicalists hostile to the war and indulgent toward bolshevism. The most important revolutionary elements from labor were those led by the syndicalists Pierre Monatte and Fernand Loriot. Also won over to revolution, and subsequently to communism, were a number of sympathetic intellectuals, like Paul Vaillant-Couturier.

The ability of these "militants" to turn the party toward the Russian example was made possible by the defeat of the Left in the 1919 election. Although the socialist vote rose to 1.7 million (from 1.4 million in 1914), the number of its delegates in the Chamber fell from 103 to 68. The election was swept by a nationalist bloc in a fashion similar to Lloyd George's victory of the year before. The bloc had seized on the issues of wartime unity and fear of bolshevism. Its candidates recalled the pacifism practiced by socialists before the war. Moreover, the hybrid proportional representation system introduced gave a bonus to parties able to unite. The Right was able to do so, but Radicals and socialists could not, and ran separate lists. At the SFIO's Strasbourg Congress in February, 1920 a large majority came out for abandoning the Second International and, if not for joining the Third, for at least negotiating with that objective in mind.

Another explanation for the party's militancy was syndical, not political—the failure of the strike movement of 1920. A conservative government crushed the general railroad strike earlier in the year. Eight thousand railroad workers were dismissed and the CGT was legally dissolved (although the government did not enforce the decision). Soviet communists, in turn, were aware that the revolutionary tide was ebbing in Germany and Hungary and that it would be wise to build up the western parties, however unorthodox. Comintern officials invited a French delegation to Moscow for their 1920 congress. Duly impressed, leftist Deputies Cachin and Frossard urged and won acceptance in France, though with reservations, of the 21 Conditions. The Right, led by Pierre Renaudel and Albert Thomas, opposed. While not hostile to the Bolshevik revolution as such, Blum denied that insurrection was necessarily the solution for France. Longuet and the Center wanted to join on their own terms, which meant accepting some conditions and rejecting others. The majority dismissed this centrist position, and then voted to accept. It marked the greatest Bolshevik success in the West and opened a schism in the French Left that has yet to heal. Within labor, however, the reverse proved true. The communist CGTU found itself in a minority, although communists ultimately won control of the CGT.

The Right and Center, under the leadership of Blum and Paul Faure, set out to rebuild the party. Blum was a graduate of the renowned École Normale. Jewish, esthete, he was converted to socialism in 1893 by Lucien Herr. He was a disciple of Jaurès and hence very much a humanist, but unable to generate the fervor demonstrated by the latter. He did not start empty-handed. If the regular party lost control of its newspaper and treasury, it retained the loyalty of socialist deputies, mayors, and local officials. Moreover, the purges and crises within the Communist party (PCF) and a growing awareness of conditions in Russia led many to return to the "old house." Still, a remarkable job was done. In the 1924 election, successfully allied with the Radical party in a left-wing cartel, the SFIO won 101 seats, the PCF only 16. By 1932 socialist membership reached the 2-million mark. However, it possessed a new clientele. Socialism had made gains in rural areas and among white-collar workers and civil servants, where it displaced Radicalism. But it remained on the defensive in industrial sectors and lost members to the Communist party in Paris. Not until the time of the Popular Front was the SFIO to win back the allegiance of intellectuals. If disturbed by the subservience necessarily paid to a foreign country, many continued to find greater satisfaction in communism.

Socialism, however, was unable to respond to growing industrialization and provided little that was new in the way of theory or in tactics. While it continued to group its members according to residence, the rival PCF was organizing cells within the factories and workshops. Like its sister parties elsewhere, the SFIO relied on the same formulas and pushed by communism on its left, seemed able to do little more than defend the established order. Much of the reformism initially formulated by Jaurès prevailed. Even so, the reaffirmation of Marxism early in the century, as well as the fear of appearing as bourgeois as communist critics said, allowed neo-Guesdist leadership to endure. Both Faure and Blum may be figured in this category. Those within the SFIO who to accommodate to a changing capitalist system sought tactical and doctrinal changes received little encouragement. For Georges Lefranc, an historian of the movement, the continued repression of moderate elements within socialist ranks helped keep the party from power for over 30 years, prevented effective action when finally exercised, contributed to having Radicals seek support from their right at the expense of social legislation, alienated and thus weakened the forces of labor, and, as we shall see, in repeated purges drove from the party some of its most talented members.[8]

The SFIO could not react to new events like fascism and the New Deal. It was not unique; other western socialist parties suffered from the same deficiencies. For Blum, unity and the preservation of the party were most important. He tried to keep equally distant from bourgeois and communist parties. He remained a revolutionary, but rejected the notion that revolution had to be achieved by violence. French socialism between the two world wars may best be understood in terms of its responses to rival mass movements: communism and then fascism.

The party was also hurt by the relative aloofness of labor. Unlike Britain, where the Labour party remained composed largely of trade unions, and Germany, where important union chiefs also held major party posts, labor retained much of its syndicalist tradition of hostility toward politics. This tradition was reinforced after the defeats of 1920. Only by remaining apolitical, it was felt, could the CGT keep its coherence in the face of repeated socialist schisms. Its chief, Léon Jouhaux, kept the proper distance—close enough to the SFIO to enjoy parliamentary support, not so close as to injure communist and syndicalist susceptibilities.

BRITISH LABOUR IN THE TWENTIES

Although the Labour party held power twice between the two world wars, it produced no social transformation. Indeed, it did not try for one, or even for very much social reform. Explanations are varied—poor leadership obsessed with proving its responsibility to the nation, the absence of any economic policy, and an estrangement between the Trades Union Congress (TUC) and the parliamentary Labour party. If Labour remained within the wartime coalition until the armistice, its presence was scarcely representative. Henderson's departure more appropriately reflected the adoption by the party of its new role of a national opposition. To perform it, structural reforms were found necessary; a larger base was needed for recruitment. Sections were established as in the continental parties; individuals, as we have seen, were allowed to join; annual conferences were scheduled with an executive council providing direction in the interim.

The new program, *Labour and the New Social Order*, may have been a "Fabian blueprint for a more advanced capitalism."[9] It was also the first socialist program adopted by the Labour party. The provision for a *national minimum* committed it to work for full employment, a minimum wage, and maximum working standards. Social services were to be subsidized by heavy taxation of large incomes and by a capital levy. National surpluses would be used to expand opportunities in public education and culture. It was a program designed to appeal to all the voters, not only workingmen. In becoming a national party,

Labour set a precedent later followed by continental parties. The election of 1918, however, hastily called by the government to take advantage of prevailing wartime unity, was swamped by the Conservative-Liberal coalition. Though Labour increased its representation to 60 MPs, its leaders were defeated. But after the Liberal fall from power, the Labour party became the official opposition. A progressively worsening postwar economic depression contributed to its success. National industrial output lagged. The now antiquated plant and the loss of overseas markets made unemployment a permanent addition to British life.

On the question of relations with the Third International, the response of the party, though clear, was not unanimous. The trade unions opposed the government's interventionist policy, and dockers refused to load supplies destined for the Polish and White Russian armies. The government retreated, and Winston Churchill held working-class resistance as responsible for the difficulty of giving armed support.[10] However, a group favoring assistance to Russia, led by Lansbury, never won the interest of more than a small minority. The TUC and Labour party delegation to Moscow in April, 1920, rejected affiliation with the Comintern, and pointed to Bolshevik reliance on terror. The party agreed. Only a handful joined the British Communist party, subsequently formed, and those in it came from such left-wing organizations as the British Socialist party. The Labour party refused even to admit the Communists as an affiliated group.

The ILP kept a centrist position. It had sent its own delegation to Russia, but rejected the 21 Conditions in 1921. The commitment to Christian socialism and to utopians like Robert Owen, along with the repudiation of Marx and the class-struggle idea that had long kept the party free of ideology, both prevailed. The absence of a modern revolutionary tradition made this decision a certainty.

The Labour party added to its parliamentary representation in 1922 and 1923. It was most successful in the north of Great Britain and in the London area. In December, 1923, after the Liberal schism, Labour campaigned on a free-trade platform. In opposing the protectionism offered by Stanley Baldwin, the party won 172 seats to the Tories' 250. Because the Liberals won only 155, the King asked MacDonald to form the first Labour government. Five years of conservative rule had not solved unemployment, but neither would Labour. MacDonald was determined to demonstrate his party's political maturity. He lay stress on foreign affairs, and scored some notable successes. Trade with Russia (or the Soviet Union as it was now called) increased, and diplomatic recognition was granted. Aided by the presence of the left-wing cartel in France, MacDonald successfully began the negotiations that led to the *Dawes Plan* and opened the discussions that culminated in the *Locarno agreements*. At home, however, aside from providing some low-cost housing, the party executive could offer no remedies for unemployment. It continued to rely on such long accepted deflationary policies as cutting expenses and wages. This, rather than the party's need to rely on Liberal tolerance to govern, explained its inadequacies. A communist newspaper editor called on the military to disobey orders. In reviving fears of Labour's ties with communism, the act generated demand for a new election. These same fears brought about Labour's defeat. Conservatives took advantage of a letter allegedly written by the Comintern chief, Zinoviev, to British Communist party officials. Only 151 Labour MPs were elected, while the Liberal party disappeared as a major force affecting British political life.

The enormity of the defeat induced a left-wing response within the party. Radicals argued that it was better to reject participation in office until a majority could be won. The ILP broke with MacDonald and called for "socialism in our time." This was the message of its influential journal, *The New Leader*. Like the Austro-Marxists, they continued to condemn violence, but at the same time held that compromise was still possible with the communists. By the end of 1924 and in large part the result of initiatives taken by the miners' federation, an Anglo-Russian trade union committee was set up to promote a unified trade union movement in Europe.

The miners went out on strike in 1926. They got belated support from other major unions and provided the country with its greatest and last general strike. The defeat revealed once and for all that industrial action alone was no substitute for political involvement. Parliament voted antiunion legislation and held general and secondary strikes as illegal. It required the Labour party to have workers "contract in"—that is, to place individual responsibility on them to authorize deduction of party dues from their salaries. The new program drafted in 1928, "Labour and the Nation," was the work of the economic historian R. H. Tawney. He came out strongly for arbitration and disarmament in foreign affairs. The approach was Fabian and hence gradualist. In the 1929 election the party revealed the extent of its recovery from the defeats of 1924 and 1926. It won 288 seats, the greatest number in its history thus far, but still required Liberal support to govern. The communists, it was noted, lost their only seat. The second MacDonald cabinet anticipated major accomplishments, but it took office coincident with the onset of worldwide economic depression.

THE RIVAL INTERNATIONALS

By the time of the Fourth Comintern Congress in November, 1922, the tide of world revolution was clearly receding. Polish forces defeated a Red army at the gates of Warsaw in August, 1920. Italian workers who had occupied factories in September of that year resumed work within a month. In Russia, the Kronstadt sailors rose up unsuccessfully against the regime in March, 1921. These defeats, together with the Rapallo Treaty signed between the Weimar Republic and Russia, presaged the transformation of the Third International. Priority was formally given to Soviet interests, and henceforth the Comintern became a tool of Russian foreign policy. The same was true of the *Labor Union International,* the communist counterpart of the *International Federation of Trade Unions* established at Amsterdam in 1919.

Zinoviev rejected the possibility of reunification with socialists on anything like equal terms. Soviet hostility forced the centrists to reexamine their position. As we have seen, they called for the meeting at Hamburg of all the socialist parties not adhering to the Third International and formed the federation known as the *Labor and Socialist International* (LSI). Member parties were granted autonomy to formulate domestic policies, but decisions taken on international affairs by the LSI were to be binding. Its founders intended it to serve as the democratic counterpart to the centralized and Soviet-dominated Comintern. It was Marxist, but only in theory. The Socialist International opposed allied intervention in Russia, fearing it would bring an end to the revolution itself. It ultimately accepted the League of Nations, and came out for disarmament, arbitration, and finally, collective security.

The executive committee of the Comintern denounced the "Hamburg International" as bourgeois and predicted it would go the way of its predecessor. The Third International would work to accelerate the process, but on the basis of the struggle for the "united front of the proletariat on a national and international scale." This *united front* tactic was devised when Lenin realized that the period of revolution had passed and that the major task of communism was that of winning a majority of workers to its side. With Germany as an ally, moreover, and with the possibility of other alliances, workers might be called on to support their governments in a pro-Soviet capacity. He did not necessarily limit the formation of the front to the outcome of negotiations with the socialist leadership. It could come about as a consequence of the effort to have noncommunist workers force their leaders to acquiesce. However, the winning of workers away from their trade union and political leaders, that is "from below," became the only means envisaged for its formation. Defined in this narrowest possible sense, the united front was to remain Comintern strategy until 1934.[11]

Reconciliation between socialists and communists, at least in Germany, might have been carried out during the Ruhr Crisis. The French occupation in 1923 was opposed by all the elements of the left. But differences between political objectives were simply too great to permit the unification of the two leading groups of which it was composed. Social Democrats wanted to end passive resistance and get negotiations underway with the allied governments. Communists, together with the Soviet Union, wanted a final break between Germany and the allies, and would have preferred that passive resistance escalate into war between Germany and France. Once more, socialists sought parliamentary solutions; communists, the overthrow of parliaments. The one movement wanted to avoid civil war; the other, to promote it. The SPD opposed a nationalist, soon fascist, counter-revolution. The German Communist party (KPD) was willing to cooperate with it and so demonstrated that the proposed united front with socialists was a manoeuvre designed to destroy them.[12] Communists assured the election of Paul von Hindenburg as President in 1925 when they refused to drop the name of their chief, Ernst Thälmann, from the second ballot and support a single left-wing candidate. Hindenburg received only 904,000 votes more than the democratic runner-up. In gathering 1,931,000 votes, Thälmann's candidacy made his election possible. The ascent to the highest office in the land of this symbol of monarchism and militarism may be said to have marked the beginning of the end of the German democratic republic. Its demise was assured when communists in the early thirties preferred to cooperate with the Nazis against the SPD.

In pursuing a united front policy to win workers over to communism, it was natural for the Comintern to turn its attention to the trade unions. In aiming at trade union unity in 1924, British union leaders provided communists with their opportunity. The International Federation of Trade Unions (IFTU) met in Vienna in June of that year. Under British pressure, and after considerable opposition, its management committee agreed to open negotiations with Soviet trade unions. The Russians also wanted a single trade union international; not, however, by means of affiliation with the IFTU. The latter was willing to admit Soviet unions only on the same conditions as other member organizations. Although discussions never got off the ground, the TUC kept the question alive. The general strike of 1926 then took place. Stalin condemned British trade union leaders like Ernest Bevin as responsible for its failure, and consequently as traitors to the working class. The TUC then gave up all attempts to bring about an understanding with the Russian trade unions.[13] The gulf between socialists and communists was now impossible to bridge on either the professional or political fronts.

The peace policies pursued by the LSI were criticized by the Comintern. At their Marseilles Congress of 1925, the first held since the founding of the Socialist International two years before, socialists reaffirmed the theory that capitalism by its very nature bred war. However, they viewed the preservation of peace as one of the LSI's most urgent tasks. At Brussels, in 1928, they resolved that socialist parties should exert pressure on their respective governments to pass laws prohibiting mobilization until international conflicts were submitted to the League of Nations "or [to] other means of peaceful settlement." The "strongest possible measures" were to be taken against a government refusing to submit a dispute to arbitration.

The Sixth Comintern Congress denounced this proposal. It also denounced the Geneva disarmament talks, the Kellog Proposals to "outlaw" war as a means of pursuing national policy, and the League itself. It was but a trick, said the relevant declaration, to deceive workers about the nature of the war threat and to deter them from their real duty in the event of war, that is, from turning it into a revolution.[14] This Sixth Congress in 1928 was coincident with Stalin's Five Year Plan to industrialize the Soviet Union and collectivize its agriculture. The congress inaugurated the Comintern's *class against class policy,* which aimed at "radicalizing the masses" and convincing them that "socialist reformism" was the chief enemy of revolutionary communism. It appeared that there was no common ground on which socialists and communists could meet in order to apply themselves jointly to the solutions of the world's problems. Their animosity was to endure until communists and the Soviet leadership changed their minds under the threat of fascism.

The diverse communist parties suffered from this new and harder line. The French party lost 80 percent of its membership (131,000 in 1921; 28,000 by 1932). From a significant political force, it became virtually an isolated sect. The German party was engaging in a policy that helped the Nazis to destroy the Weimar Republic. The Yugoslav party was driven to sporadic but ineffectual terrorism and insurrection in 1929. Its membership fell to a few hundred. The British party, under the new leadership of Harry Pollitt, made massive efforts to convert trade union members to communism. Yet it admitted that in 1932 the number of cells in the nation's thousands of factories numbered only 82 and contained only 550 party members. The Czech party lost nine-tenths of its membership in a decade.[15]

Unable to carry out a single successful communist revolution, communist parties continued to preach Marxist revolutionary theory while breaking with traditional Marxist organizational and political practice. Veterans like Jules Guesde had found themselves bewildered even before 1928. "Communism," he said, "is at once what I have fought for all my life and what I have fought against all my life." Marxist theory as presented by Lenin and Stalin, an historian of the movement has written, served to maintain party order and to provide a sense of opposition between the communist and noncommunist worlds. From its first introduction into Russia, it operated less as a blueprint for action than as a justification for actions dictated by Russian conditions.[16]

COMMUNISM VERSUS SOCIALISM: CONCLUSION

In view of its hostility to communist practice, it was but natural for socialism to appear as heir to the reformist tradition and to the revisionism of Eduard Bernstein. In fact, it made use of the flexible and gradualist elements in Marxist thought. Communism appeared as the culmination of the antirevisionist tradition and stressed the revolutionary components in Marxism. However, it is fruitless to pursue this any further. Well before the Bolshevik revolution, socialism was becoming less of a doctrine and more of an attitude. After World War I it had to withstand the threats of both the far left and the far right, and so was prodded to defend the order it theoretically repudiated. It became all the more integrated into the state when in power, as in Austria, Germany, and Great Britain. In defending what communism had neglected, namely democratic procedures and a concern for the quality of individual life, socialism was forced to set aside plans for what communism had, at least in Russia, achieved wholesale collectivization.

The labor and social historian G. D. H. Cole has argued that it is necessary to regard communism as very much within the socialist tradition because it shared similar objectives. Only the means differed, and it was as much nonsense to urge that Russian socialism should proceed by parliamentary methods as it was to insist that English or Scandinavian socialism should set up a dictatorship of the proletariat. One cannot argue, he went on, that democracy is a necessary prerequisite of socialism if democracy means the exclusive use of parliamentary methods in countries where no tradition of parliamentary government exists and no parliamentary institutions are available to bring socialism about.[17] The chief difficulty with this outlook, however, was that it was limited to the ways in which socialism might be realized. It said nothing about what it did once it had won power and managed to establish itself. In focusing on revolutionary tradition to justify its actions, communism rejected the idealistic elements in Marxist thought. In relying on parliamentary machinery and in expending its energies to preserve it, socialism came to reject the revolutionary elements in that thought.

Lenin's success ran counter to Marx's insistence that revolution came when the forces of society (described as economically industrialized and politically liberal) were ready for it. The latter had accepted democracy as a necessary pacemaker. Clearly, Lenin's revolution had occurred in a country that was far from democratic. If ultimately justified, even in Marxist terms, it marked a departure from the guidelines suggested by Marx. Stalin's economic planning marked an even greater divergence, from socialist concern with distribution to concern with production and was to become something of a model to an economically underdeveloped Third World. One constant emerges: as Marxist theory became ever less directive of action, its value as a "holy writ" of communism became ever larger.[18]

As socialists came to define themselves in terms of their differences from communists, they lost their Marxist roots. On the other hand, they fought with all their strength against what they saw as a new danger emerging from the right, fascism. Their hatred encouraged them to cooperate with communists when the latter were to feel similarly threatened.

NOTES

[1] Lenin, "Theses on the War," cited in Olga Hess Gankin and H. H. Fisher, eds., *The Bolsheviks and the World War* (Stanford: Stanford University Press, 1960), p. 141. F. Borkenau, *World Communism: A History of the Communist International* (Ann Arbor: University of Michigan Press, 1962), p. 58.

[2] Merle Fainsod, *International Socialism and the World War* (Cambridge, Mass.: Harvard University Press, 1935), p. 75.

[3] Jacques Droz, *Le Socialisme démocratique, 1864–1960* (Paris: A. Colin, 1966), p. 154.

[4] Prince Max of Baden, *Memoirs* (London: Constable, 1928), Vol. II, p. 329. P. Scheidemann, *The Making of the New Germany* (New York: Appleton, 1929), Vol. II, p. 240. The phrase "tooth and nail" is not authentic. Both Max and Scheidemann wrote: "resist the revolution with all the force of his unquestioned authority."

[5] Cited in Franz Bohn, "The Reds of Germany," *International Socialist Review* XVI, 2 (1915), p. 80.

[6] Richard N. Hunt, *German Social Democracy, 1918–1933* (New Haven: Yale University Press, 1964), p. 254.

[7] M. M. Drachkovitch, B. Lazitch, "The Communist International," in M. M. Drachkovitch, ed., *The Revolutionary Internationals* (Stanford: Stanford University Press, 1966), p. 163.

[8] Georges Lefranc, *Histoire du socialisme sous la troisiéme république, 1875–1940* (Paris: Payot, 1963), pp. 161, 266.

[9] Ralph Miliband, *Parliamentary Socialism* (London: Allen & Unwin, 1961), p. 62.

[10] *Ibid.,* p. 81.

[11] Jane Degras, ed., *The Communist International, 1919–1943. Docu-*

ments, Vol. II, *1923-1928* (London: Oxford University Press, 1960), pp. 30–31. See also her "United Front Tactics in the Comintern," Saint Antony's Papers, No. IX: *International Communism*, ed. by David Footman (Carbondale: Southern Illinois University Press, 1960), pp. 10–13.

[12] J. Braunthal, *History of the International, 1914-1943*, Vol. 2, (New York: Praeger, 1957), p. 284.

[13] Lewis L. Lorwin, *The International Labor Movement. History, Policies, Outlook* (New York: Harper & Row, 1953), pp. 97–98. John Price, *The International Labor Movement*, (London and New York: Oxford University Press, 1945), p. 20. Braunthal, *op. cit.*, p. 307.

[14] Degras, *The Communist International*, II, pp. 49, 459. Braunthal, *op. cit.*, p. 340. G. D. H. Cole, *A History of Socialist Thought*, IV: *Communism and Social Democracy, 1914-1931* (London: Macmillan, 1958), Pt. 2, p. 687.

[15] Braunthal, *op. cit.*, p. 308.

[16] Guesde cited in Drachkovitch, *Revoluntionary Internationals*, p. 201. Robert V. Daniels, "The Evolution of the Communist Mind," preface to his *Documentary History of Communism* (New York: Random House-Vintage, 1962).

[17] Cole, *op. cit.*, pp. 847–850.

[18] Daniels, *op. cit.*

SUGGESTED READING

Angelica Balabanoff. *My Life as a Rebel*. Westport, Conn.: Greenwood, 1968.

E. H. Carr. *The Bolshevik Revolution, 1917-1923*. III. London: Penguin, 1966.

David Caute. *Communism and the French Intellectuals 1914-1960*. New York: Macmillan, 1964.

William H. Chamberlin. *The Russian Revolution, 1917-1921*, 2 vols. New York: Grosset & Dunlap, 1963.

Joel Colton. *Léon Blum. Humanist in Politics*. New York: Knopf, 1966.

S. R. Graubard. *British Labour and Russian Revolution*. Cambridge, Mass.: Harvard University Press, 1956.

Annie Kriegel. *Aux origines du communisme français 1914-1920*. 2 vols. Paris: Mouton, 1964.

Val Lorwin. *The French Labor Movement*. Cambridge, Mass.: Harvard University Press, 1954.

L. J. Macfarlane. *The British Communist Party. Its Origins and Development until 1929*. London: MacGibbon & Kee, 1966.

William Maehl. "The Role of Russia in German Socialist Policy, 1914–1918," *International Review of Social History*, IV, p. 19.

H. Meynell. "The Stockholm Conference of 1917," *International Review of Social History*, V, 1961.

Allen Mitchell. *Revolution in Bavaria, 1918–1919*. Princeton: Princeton University Press, 1965.

David J. Saposs. *The Labor Movement in Post-War France*. New York: Columbia University Press, 1931.

Eric Waldmann. *The Spartakist Uprising of 1919*. Milwaukee: Marquette University Press, 1958.

Robert Wohl. *French Communism in the Making, 1914–1924*. Stanford: Stanford University Press, 1966.

SIX

Socialism

and Fascism

Communism be-
came the major
threat on the
socialist Left and permanently divided the movement by winning
away numerous socialists to its cause.
Fascism, seen by socialists as right-wing reaction, was to result in socialist destruction in Central Europe and further enfeeblement in the
Western democracies. Neither the Socialist International nor its member
parties could cope with fascism in Germany, Italy, and Austria. Its
chances for success in these countries were kindled by a variety of causes,
particularly economic depression and (in Italy) the maladjustments of
the first post-war period. They were considerably heightened by the
division between the two working-class parties, particularly after the
Soviet Union—and hence the Comintern—turned sharply to the left
in 1928. Communists viewed fascism as a danger too late to prevent
its victory in Germany, and both socialists and communists appreciated
its destructive potential only at the last moment in France.

Although unable to prevail in the West, fascism exerted a powerful
attraction on some socialists. The dynamism and mass appeal that it
displayed induced them to seek a shift in strategy. Hence, there emerged
new revisionists like the Belgian Hendrick de Man, neosocialists like
Marcel Déat in France, and the New Party of Oswald Moseley in
England. They attempted to correct evident deficiencies within their
respective parties. They also demonstrated a readiness to jettison basic
principles not only of socialism but of democracy as well. The one bright
spot in an otherwise bleak picture was to be found in Scandinavia where
democratic socialists managed to escape the worst ravages of worldwide
depression and to build modern welfare states. The uniqueness of their
situation, however, in small and homogeneous populations with relatively high living standards to begin with, cast doubts on their usefulness
as models for less fortunately endowed countries.

Much of the blame for the destruction of socialist as well as democratic organizations lay with the socialists themselves. Offering no alternate economic policies, they were unable to combat the depression and so were discredited. Destroyed by fascism in Central Europe, socialism seemed a poor alternative in the opinion of most people. Socialists could offer little more than reliance on the orthodox (deflationary) financial policies of their conservative oppositions. They insisted that "the crisis must run its course" and were prepared to write off the depression as payment for capitalist errors. But if unable or unwilling to implement their socialist theories, they retained enough doctrinal purity to regard nationalization as a panacea, yet they prohibited themselves from seizing public power by any means other than parliamentary.

Socialist parties appeared more as pressure groups representing the interests of labor than as agents in the transformation of society. They seemed committed to administering capitalism and making the private enterprise system work within the framework of national controls. There was little class tension when national production increased (before 1921 or after 1936). But when it contracted (between 1921 and 1924, or between 1929 and 1934), socialists defended labor's economic concerns all the more arduously. From the standpoint of implementing theoretical goals, their close ties to the trade unions proved a source of weakness. Trade unions were naturally interested in improving the immediate economic position of their members. In becoming spokesmen for labor, socialist parties were under a certain amount of pressure to join coalition governments in the economic and political crises of the thirties, as they had in earlier crises. Individual socialists did so in Britain in 1931. Socialist parties joined in other coalitions on the Left in Spain and France in 1936. Not until after World War II, however, would most socialists in government break with orthodox economic thinking.

In 1931 the reconstructed Socialist International contained parties with over 6 million dues-paying members and could boast of a total parliamentary vote for socialist candidates reaching almost 26 million, over 300 socialist deputies and 360 newspapers defending labor's interests. This large force was helpless in the crisis-ridden 1930s.[1]

For the labor historian Adolf Sturmthal, the explanation for the "tragedy of European labor" lay in the fact that comprehensive political action and not pressure-group tactics was required. Communists stressed the former, but identified it with revolution and so made it difficult to equate politics with reformism. Socialism remained a distant objective for most socialists, one that exerted little influence on daily activity.[2] During the depression, they were concerned more with defending the level of wages and unemployment benefits than with foreign affairs or with seeking alternate economic approaches. Their inability to

satisfy a widespread desire for social peace and strong government furthered the growth of fascism. The chief dilemma for socialism, in the
thirties as before, lay in the difference between its daily behavior and
its ultimate goal. No longer prepared for revolution, it lacked any policy
for a gradual transition to socialism.

THE EMERGENCE OF FASCISM IN ITALY

After World War I, revolution seemed imminent in Italy. In the elections of 1919 socialists won 2 million of 5.5 million votes. Yet the
Italian Socialist party (PSI) never lived up to its promise, and by the
mid-twenties was crushed by Mussolini. In part it was the victim of the
long series of schisms that began with the expulsion of the syndicalists
in 1908 and continued through the formation of the Communist party
in 1921. The failure of Italian socialism may also be attributed to the
inability of the PSI to gauge the realities of post-World War I Italian
society and accept responsibility commensurate with its power.

The decision to join the allies in March, 1915 had once more
threatened to divide the party. Moderates stated their readiness to
support the government in a national crisis. For the present, they agreed
on a policy of "neither collaboration nor sabotage." The compromise
proved fragile as the war progressed, and after the Austrian successes
in the spring of 1916, many PSI deputies were expressing their patriotism. They were admonished, although not expelled, at the party's Rome
Congress in September.

When the war ended the party was still very much in the hands
of the Left. *Maximalists,* led by Giacinto Serrati, wanted to follow the
Bolshevik example and set up a socialist republic and proletarian dictatorship under the auspices of the Third International. The PSI's Bologna
Congress, meeting in October, 1919, voted by acclamation to join the
Comintern. The atmosphere of millenarianism was all-pervasive. Militant socialists in Turin, particularly Antonio Gramsci and Palmiro Togliatti, were more realistic about the difficulties that lay ahead. The party
seemed unaware of the need to win the active support of workers and
peasants, necessary for any successful transformation. The pacifism and
antimilitarism displayed during the war had already alienated the
middle classes, especially returning veterans.

Still, the desire for change matched the cry of discontent that
arose from the people. Inflation intensified long-standing demands for
land reform. Workers sought control of factories and public regulation
of profits and distribution. Both farmers and workers wanted fiscal and
constitutional reform, as well as the punishment of war profiteers. And

they believed that a better world was about to be born.[3] As the most highly organized force in the country, socialism appeared ready to profit therefrom. In general elections held in November, 1919 socialists received 32 percent of the vote and seated 156 deputies (out of 535). However, they were unable to join with the Christian Democratic Popular party founded in January and so form a left-wing majority. The divisive issue here was that of church–state relations.

In the spring of 1920, the first in a series of strikes broke out in Milan. The General Labor Federation had grown from less than a quarter million members in late 1918 to almost 2 million in the autumn of 1920. Industrial strikes during the period 1901–1913 averaged 1006 (201,000 strikers) annually and reached 1881 (1,268,000 workers away from their jobs).[4] In September, workers occupied their factories, while peasants in the south and in Sicily seized the uncultivated lands of absentee owners. The sit-ins were spontaneous and not the result of any socialist initiative. Other workers asked their leaders to order the occupation of additional factories. The uncertain trade union and socialist chiefs hesitated, wholly unprepared for and clearly overwhelmed by the events unfolding before them. Trade union chiefs narrowly rejected a radical suggestion to use the occupation as the beginnings of revolution, and the PSI accepted the unions' decision to negotiate with employers. With Giolitti's prompting, the government agreed in principle to union demands for working-class control of production. He used the same tactics (and reached the same results) as in the strike of 1904. Mixed committees, set up to study the workers' demands, talked themselves to exhaustion. In the absence of any effective outcome, labor became discouraged, and the frightened bourgeoisie was determined to suppress any recurrence. A revolutionary moment had in fact passed.

L'Avanti published the 21 Conditions in its issue of September 21, 1920. They shattered the majority reached at Bologna. The 7th demand identified Turati as a "notorious opportunist" and not to be "tolerated" by the Communist International. At the PSI's Leghorn Congress, reformists flatly rejected the Russian proposals as unsuitable for the Italian situation. Communists, like Gramsci, voted for unconditional adherence to the Third International. Finally, *unitary communists,* like Serrati, who wanted to join the Comintern, refused to accept all the conditions set forth. When this last group won a majority, the communists broke away and founded the Italian Communist party (PCI). Hence it was a divided Left that had to face the fascist threat.

The economic as well as the political situation deteriorated. In November, 1919 unemployment reached 2 million. At the same time inflation was rampant. Prices rose almost 150% between 1914 and 1918, 50% more the next year, and another 100% in 1920. The value of the lire fell proportionately. Responsible were war expenditures that had reached 148 billion lire—twice all the government expenditures from 1861 to 1913.[5]

On September 12, 1919, the poet and nationalist Gabriele D'Annunzio marched on the city of Fiume and claimed it for Italy. Disappointment over the peace treaty (which failed to grant the nation the territory promised in 1915 for entering the war), the economic crisis, and fears of socialism aroused national pride and a yearning for order. In March, 1919, at Milan, Mussolini founded his first fascist group, a ragtag and bobtail collection of disgruntled army veterans. In the November election his local slate of candidates attracted ony 4600 votes compared to the PSI's 160,000. But the mock funeral held by Milanese socialists for their former colleague proved premature.

In keeping with its Bologna program of 1919, the PSI refused to participate in the cabinet formed by Francisco Nitti, or in that of his successor, Giolitti. The latter called for new elections in May, 1921. He hoped for fascist as well as socialist support, and hence for the former to be brought into the web of *transformismo*. The elections were marked by fascist intimidation and violence. The socialists lost some 30 seats, but with 123 deputies they remained the single largest party in the chamber. The communists won 15 seats, and the fascists entered national political life with over 30 deputies.

No longer able to press for a revolutionary solution, socialists lacked plans for alternate ones either. When Bonomi replaced Giolitti in June, 1921, the PSI's Milan Congress could only reaffirm its condemnation of either participating in or giving support to the government. Nor did the growth of fascism change its mind. The new movement was viewed by the maximalists as the last phase of bourgeois domination; no change in course was therefore required. Gaetano Salvemini, a renegade socialist more in the line of Mazzini than Marx, pointed out that it was not fascist reaction that was bringing an end to socialism, but the socialist decline that was making fascist reaction possible. In refusing "any participation and any vote" to the government, democratic socialism was, in fact, signing its death warrant.[6]

The auto-defense groups organized by workers appeared too late. Their call for a labor alliance, an early version of the united front, was rejected by the communists over Gramsci's objections. Socialist deputies finally agreed to support the Facta government in June, 1922. They were disavowed by *Avanti* and the party leaders. When Turati and his friends were expelled by the party's Rome Congress, reformists, including most of the parliamentary socialists, bolted and formed the Unitary Italian Socialist party (PSU). Giacomo Matteotti was named secretary. The Serrati group, meanwhile, again indicated its readiness to join the Comintern. These opposed factions were nearly equal in size, and their mutual opposition, in addition to the hostility between them and the communists, paralyzed the Left. The *March on Rome* took place a few weeks later. Asked by the King to form a government, Mussolini ruled by parliamentary means for two years. Even so, his ascent to power marked the end of Italian socialism. Not even the destruction of the movement brought an end to the divisions within it. Serrati proposed that the PSI and the communists come to terms and plan for joint action. Thanks in large part to the opposition of the radical Pietro Nenni, he failed to win Moscow's support. The fraudulent election of 1924 gave the fascists a majority. The socialist Matteotti was murdered for denouncing the fascist victory, and the decision by antifascist deputies to withdraw as a moral protest meant an end to open opposition to the regime.

In spite of the marked desire for social change, then, and regardless of the success of radicalism within the PSI, socialism could make no headway in postwar Italy and was ultimately suppressed by a dictatorship. The party lacked any strategic policy. It established no ties with peasants seizing land in the south or workers occupying factories in the north. From the standpoint of tactics, socialists were too radical to collaborate with the Popular party after the 1919 elections, or to form a socialist-liberal coalition government in the fall of 1921. They were too closely affiliated with labor to regard the sit-ins as the onset of revolution or to accept a communist proposal to form a counterparliament (a possible resistance organization) after the Aventine secession (the withdrawal of the antifascist deputies from parliament). They were stymied by the legacy of their divided past. From the standpoint of theory, socialists saw in fascism a sign of imminent capitalist collapse. Consequently, there was nothing to balance their fears of communist domination of any mass nonparliamentary opposition movement.

THE END OF GERMAN SOCIALISM

The SPD was the strongest of the European socialist parties after World War I. It enjoyed the support of the great majority of German workers. If it was never in sole control (aside from a few months following the 1919 revolution), it was often in a position to influence policy. More so than in the case of Italian socialism, the party's ties with organized labor constituted an important reason for its ultimate demise. For this party had also become a pressure group, unable to define national policy and committed to preserving its institutions and the republic that sheltered them. It was also rivaled by a strong communist party on its left, which had already absorbed many independent socialists. The SPD could provide no solution to the depression of the early thirties, and, as in Italy, the appeal of a dynamic nationalist movement swept all before it. In both nations, it was the failure of the Left that helped make the fascist seizure of power successful.

With socialist support, the Weimar Republic weathered the first nationalist attempt to overthrow it. In March, 1920 the *Kapp Putsch* was broken by a general strike. However, workers continued to stay off their jobs, many of them waiting for a sign that the government was carrying out its promise to stem reaction. They received communist support and then leadership. The newly formed Weimar coalition of majority socialists, the Catholic Center, and conservative democrats sent in the army to overwhelm the strikers, and it was the army that proved the real victor.

In June, in the first Reichstag election, the nationalist parties gained at the expense of the coalition. Supporters of the Right were critical of the socialists for the terms agreed to in the peace treaty and won middle-class approval. On the left, independent socialists increased their representation from 22 to 81, while communists saw their vote grow from 112,000 to half a million. A new cabinet of the Center and the right-wing German People's party then took office with socialist support. At its Halle Congress in October, 1920, the infuriated USPD voted to accept the Comintern's 21 Conditions. Negotiations began with the communists, and most independents joined the KPD in December. The minority that did not went to the Social Democrats in 1922.

The communists were also experiencing internal difficulties. Paul Levi, a realistic party leader, was aware that most German workers were not inclined to make a revolution. Consequently, he opposed those whom he called romantic adventurers. Ultimately expelled from his party, he joined the SPD where he reestablished a left wing. But his departure from the KPD was to mean greater Soviet control.

After the occupation of the Ruhr and the events accompanying it (inflation, threats of separatism, and the attempted Nazi *putsch*), the SPD decided to enter the Stresseman cabinet. As a result, it was linked with the repression of a socialist-communist government in Saxony. The latter had formed a proletarian guard in order to fight the *Freikorps*, and pressure by the army to yield in favor of a more docile government forced it from office. Socialist ministers resigned in protest. The dissatisfaction of socialist voters was revealed in the elections of May, 1924. The SPD retained only 100 seats (from the 171 it held together with independents), while the communists increased their representation from 17 to 62. In a subsequent election held in December, however, the socialists regained some of their losses.

The mid- and late twenties were years of economic prosperity and Stresseman's policies generated a semblance of normality. Socialists were not represented in national government until 1928, yet they shared power in Prussia and on local and municipal levels elsewhere, notably

Berlin. The party's Heidelberg Congress of 1925 reaffirmed the concessions made to reformists in 1921, but devised no strategy for subsequent economic or political crises. Its chief concern lay with assuring the immediate welfare of labor.

It was during this period of economic expansion that party theoreticians developed the concept of *organized capitalism*. Rudolf Hilferding, the former Austro-Marxist and now the SPD's leading economic expert, told the Kiel Congress of 1927 that the age of blindly free capitalism was over, that business objectives were scientifically planned, and that a democratic state would necessarily influence the economy in a democratic way. His assessment that an economy directed by a democratic government amounted to socialism further dissuaded socialists from revolutionary action.

These ideas only reinforced the conviction of German communists that social democracy was indeed the left wing of fascist reaction. As early as 1923 the KPD had fallen into the hands of the ultra-left leadership of Ruth Fischer and A. Maslow. Under the stewardship of Ernst Thälmann the party became wholly subservient to Moscow. We have already seen how Thälmann's refusal to withdraw in favor of a stronger democratic candidate assured Hindenburg's victory in the presidential election of 1925. Unable to act on behalf of the workers or to take power, the party lost three-quarters of its membership by 1928. Socialists, meanwhile, took advantage of widespread dissatisfaction with the government's decision to build a naval cruiser, benefited from restored independent support, and in the elections of May, 1928 won 30 percent of the vote and 152 seats in the Reichstag. The Weimar coalition once more governed with the SPD's Hermann Müller as chancellor.

The Republic seemed safe at last. It was solidly supported by the socialists. The SPD boasted of 3 million members, an immense trade union base, consumer cooperatives, sports and youth movements, and even its own paramilitary organization. Few noted that in the process of rebuilding the party was again moving toward its right. Mounting prosperity, revealed by a rise in per capita income, conceivably smothered any outcries that might have been made. More likely, the party lacked any significant analysis of the economy and the society. It had certainly failed to mark the plight of the middle classes, squeezed between powerful industrialists on the one hand and the trade unions on the other. The inflationary period of 1918–1923 had drained the resources of the small businessman, while the factory owner had benefited from cheap money to further his investment in plant. He had also received additional help from the foreign loans distributed by governments anxious to revitalize the economy. The few criticisms made were stilled by the insistence that large industries were also large employers and consequently had to be preserved. Eager to gain more protection for workers against the ill effects of concentration and to win for them a larger

share in monopolistic organizations, the SPD did little to further bourgeois interests. Fearful of becoming proletarianized, neither capitalism,
socialism, nor even democracy offered any ideological balm for this
group. Not until the advent of the Nazis was solace to be provided for
the German middle classes.[7]

Social Democrats, then, returned to office in 1928; however, the
depression ruined any of their chances to preserve democracy or the
Republic. The crisis struck quickly, given the country's financial ties to
the United States, and harshly, in view of the millions of unemployed.
Few socialists urged devaluation or abandonment of the gold standard.
Like his counterpart in the Labour government, Philip Snowden, Hilferding in the Ministry of Finance was convinced of the "natural
causes" of the depression and resolved not to interfere. In seeking to
balance the budget and not to tap any idle capital funds or go into
debt, the government pursued an orthodox deflationary policy. Its lack
of any coherent economic plan was most strikingly revealed by socialist
unwillingness to prevent the fall of the Müller cabinet. The SPD refused to vote unpopular measures like the increased workers' contributions to unemployment insurance called for by the Reichsbank. The
trade unions had opposed and the party agreed.

In the face of growing Nazi success at the polls, two courses
seemed open to the socialists. One was to create a united front with
the communist party and stage a revolution, even though (in view of
the latter's greater discipline) it might well mean subordination to the
KPD. The alternative appeared to be cooperation with the existing government in an attempt to ward off the Nazis. This policy of the *lesser
evil* was adopted, and the party supported or tolerated the centrist
government of Heinrich Brüning. In abandoning all initiative, however,
the nation's second largest party had placed itself in a pitiable position.
Admittedly, even after the election of September, 1930, which sent 107
Nazis to the Reichstag, most socialists saw no major threat in fascism.
The Italian example was still regarded as unique.

The *class against class* policy decided on by the Sixth Comintern
Congress proved disastrous for German democracy. Communists considered Social Democrats as "Social Fascists" and their worst enemies.
Not unlike socialists, they evaluated fascism as a right-wing phenomenon,
one best explained as the last stage of monopolistic capitalism. Consequently, they rejected all cooperation with the democratic Left. In point
of fact, they joined forces with its opponents. As late as November, 1932,
the KPD was cooperating with the Nazis in a Berlin transit strike directed against the socialist-controlled municipal government. The
previous December the communists repudiated the republican *iron
front,* established to unite trade unions, the SPD, and the *Reichsbanner.*
Their strategy proved suicidal.

It was in pursuit of the lesser evil that socialists supported the reelection of Hindenburg in 1932. They were poorly rewarded. He dismissed Brüning, because he resented his proposed land reforms in Prussia, and replaced him with Colonel Franz von Papen. Two months later the socialists in the Prussian government were forced from office. Fearful that the Prussian police would be crushed by the army if ordered to resist, and convinced that a call for a general strike would lead to fighting between the employed and the jobless, the SPD decided to ignore spontaneous mass mobilization and yield. Trained to fight parliamentary battles, socialists continued to place their faith in the voters. In fact, they registered no substantial loss in the July and November elections of 1932, retaining almost a fifth of the vote. In the longer period, between the 1928 election and that held in November, 1932 (the last free election), the SPD lost only about one-tenth of its share. Measured in percentage of the vote cast, the loss in terms of socialist voters was very much smaller. That the communists also increased their vote revealed that the Nazi victories were due not to any transfer of working-class allegiance, but to the support of the middle classes. When Hitler became chancellor on January 30, 1933, workers appeared once more ready to take to the streets. Once more party leadership drew back before the threat of civil war. It found the coalition carrying the new government to power full of contradictions and estimated that its term in office could not be long. Socialists fought the Enabling Act, and so were the only party (the communists having been outlawed on March 21) to oppose granting full powers to Hitler. On June 21, the SPD was declared illegal; its goods were seized and many of its leaders, together with trade union chiefs, interred in concentration camps.

The inadequacies of the Left were not responsible for the Nazis, but they help to explain their coming to power. Communists persisted in viewing socialism as a greater danger than fascism. Socialists lacked programs for economic and political crises and preoccupied themselves with defending working-class interests and safeguarding their party apparatus. At the same time, they rejected all nonparliamentary solutions. Although conditions had changed, SPD tactics remained constant, and the party was unable even to call for a general strike in face of the Nazi onslaught. Socialists continued to yearn for the discredited Weimar system. On the other hand, it may be said they never expected the Nazi regime to endure and (eyes fixed on Bismarck's antisocialist laws) never anticipated such harshness. Consequently, no preparation for underground resistance was made. Whatever opposition there was after 1933 came from socialists acting individually, from communists, and from elements within the army.

In the final analysis, German social democracy was destroyed because of the reasonableness of its practitioners, their faith in the reason of others, and hence their trust in democracy. Socialists were incapable of dealing with a demagogue who used the democratic process only to subvert it and were unable to appreciate the fact that most Germans had washed their hands of the Republic. Because they hoped their protest and the spectacle of being prevented from carrying out their duties would arouse a response, they did not fight their ejection from the Prussian government. Because the Nazis were voted into power, they took no action against them. The party leaders could not believe that people would continue to support Hitler. Conceivably, a general strike would have unleashed widespread resistance, but effective leadership was required. They at first refused to act. Then they were unable to. The greatest labor force in history was wholly paralyzed.

THE DESTRUCTION OF AUSTRIAN SOCIALISM

Third largest in Europe, the Austrian socialist party was the next to be destroyed by fascism. Its dissolution in 1934 shocked the socialist world. Situated physically and ideologically between Hungarian communism and German social democracy, the party was viewed as a model for socialism after World War I, and the city of Vienna, as a consummate socialist administration. Although fascism was present from the outset, it lacked widespread support for almost a decade. Fearful of the short-lived Hungarian Soviet republic (March through July, 1921), the Austrian middle classes acquiesced in socialist demands—until reaction triumphed in Italy and Hungary. Even then, without the threat of a strong communist party, fascism in Austria proved less severe than the German variety.

As in Germany, socialists in Austria constituted the nation's largest party at the end of the war and were called on to administer peacetime reconstruction. They wanted to have Austria become part of Germany, invoking the right of national self-determination and maintaining that the truncated new republic lacked economic viability. Socialists won a plurality in the election to a constituent assembly in February, 1919, defeated their chief rivals, the Christian Socials, by six votes. Karl Renner became chancellor of a coalition cabinet. Extremist efforts to promote revolution, particularly those of the communist-Hungarian leader Bela Kun who wanted Vienna to go the "way of Budapest," did not succeed. Most socialists estimated it would mean war with their neighbors, civil war at home, and the end of allied supplies. The Austrian communist party never became much more than a sect. But the fear of *red peril,* together with the appearance of reactionary regimes in neighboring countries, turned the peasants and elements of the bourgeoisie further to the right. The allied prohibition of an *Anschluss* prompted the resignation of Otto Bauer as minister of foreign affairs. Others soon followed. Christian Socialists, with the support of the small petit-bourgeois parties, took control of the government and maintained their majority throughout the life of the Republic. They drew their strength from the Catholic and conservative countryside. Socialists controlled Vienna and made striking contributions in the areas of housing, education, and recreation.

During the First Republic, Austrian socialism was dominated by the *Austro-Marxists* in the party. We have noted their additions to socialist theory before 1914, particularly those relating to subject nationalities and imperialism. Although few in number, their opposition to the revisionism of Eduard Bernstein had checked its progress in the party. Austro-Marxists persisted in their attempts to reconcile Marx and neo-Kantian thought, and preferred to stress the sociological aspects in the writings of the former. Representative of the group was Otto Bauer. Like Victor Adler before him, he placed a premium on party unity and was willing to cooperate with the communists as part of a larger effort to maintain the scientific character of Marxism. In acknowledging that power was to be won by democratic means, Bauer feared the corruption of revolutionary faith caused by participation in government. At the party's Linz Congress in 1926, he rejected a dictatorship of the proletariat, but reaffirmed the use of force in the event that the middle classes repudiated working-class victories won at the polls. Violence as a means of defense was held entirely legitimate. This position, reminiscent of Kautsky's *centrism,* sought a Marxist middle ground between revolutionary communism and the embourgeoisement of Western socialism.

To the right of the Austro-Marxists were the so-called *empiricists,* responsible for much of the social legislation enacted. Renner and his colleagues would cooperate with bourgeois parties and so improve labor's position in existing society. For the Left, however, political democracy was purely formal; social democracy alone real and capable of establishing a classless state.[8] In proportion to total population, Austrian socialism was the strongest in the world, both in dues-paying members and voters. They won 42 percent of the vote in 1927 and enjoyed a two-thirds majority in Vienna, viewed as the most progressive city in Europe. The Christian Social chancellor, Monsignor Ignaz Seipel, however, successfully kept them from national power.

Fascism became a significant political force in the late twenties. The *Heimwehren,* a paramilitary force composed largely of the sons of wealthier peasants and led by imperial army officers, held the support of the government, business elements, and the church. The socialists countered with the *Schutzbund,* labor's armed militia. Their proposal that both forces be disbanded was rejected by Seipel. Nazi successes encouraged fascists in Austria, already winning greater representation in provincial elections and, to a lesser degree, in the capital. Their victories, however, came at the expense of the Christian Socials, not the socialists. Chancellor Engelbert Dollfuss, possessing a majority of one vote over his opposition, the socialist and pan-German parties, staged a coup after the Nazi triumph in Germany and prohibited parliament from meeting. He ruled by decree in an attempt to refashion Austria as a Christian corporate state. Although he had been expected to ally with one against the other, Dollfuss repudiated both socialists and Nazis. The *Schutzbund* was dissolved and Vienna deprived of considerable state revenues. The Nazi party, too, was officially abolished, but Nazi atrocities continued. Socialists preferred Dollfuss to the Nazis, and estimated that a struggle against the former would ensure the success of the latter. Consequently they offered no armed resistance. Bauer later admitted that Austrian social democracy's greatest error lay in its rejection of even a general strike at the time of the Dollfuss coup. He rightly concluded that the party's refusal to respond severely undermined working-class morale.

The riot of February 6, 1934, in Paris set off civil war in Austria. To secure French loans, Dollfuss had pledged the preservation of democratic institutions. The fall of the government that had demanded this promise, together with his conviction that the last great democracy on the continent was about to collapse, persuaded the chancellor to accept *Heimwehren* demands for the dissolution of Austrian social democracy. Workers in Linz resisted the police search for arms. Strikes, and then shooting in Vienna ushered in a short, but bitterly fought civil war.

Socialists were poorly prepared for street fighting. Secret arms stores proved inaccessible; only party leaders knew of their location, and they were the first to be arrested. The party could scarcely publicize its call for a general strike because it had neglected to make arrangements with striking electrical workers to keep the socialist presses operating. Railroad workers, moreover, demoralized by unemployment, refused to support the strike. Although heroically defended by the *Schutzbund* in house-to-house fighting, Vienna succumbed, and democracy as well as socialism legally came to an end.

A number of socialist leaders had managed to flee to Czechoslovakia and helped to set up an underground resistance. During the next four years small groups within Austria coalesced into larger opposition formations. When Hitler issued his ultimatum to Chancellor Kurt von Schuschnigg in February, 1938, socialism was once more a national force. Aware that the country could no longer count on Italian support, and in return for socialist aid, Schuschnigg promised freedom of expression and trade union autonomy. Negotiations began, but Nazi troops invaded Austria before they were completed. The conquest marked the disappearance of the socialist movement that had tried to steer a middle course between social democracy and communism. It meant the expiration, too, of one of the most constructive of all the socialist parties of post-World War I Europe—the one on the noncommunist left most anxious to maintain a Marxist identity and reunify the Left, and consequently the one most harshly denounced by the Communist International.

INTERNATIONAL SOCIALISM AND FASCISM

What was the response of international socialism to the growth and successes of fascism? Socialists preferring to revive the Second International (the Berne International of 1920) and adherents of the "Second and a Half" International (Vienna, 1921) had joined forces in 1923 in part because of concern over the fascist victory in Italy and early signs of nazism in Germany. But Italian fascism was viewed as a peculiarly Italian phenomenon. In his report on the world political situation to the LSI Congress of 1928, Otto Bauer touched on a variety of topics but hardly mentioned the word fascism. Like most socialists, he failed to see much international significance in the movement and took literally Mussolini's own assurances that "fascism [was] not for export." Its development was held as related to technologically retarded areas, not to industrialized democracies. Hence, at the outset, socialists were unable to appreciate the anticapitalist dimensions of fascism and its ability to gain popular support during periods of economic distress.

Both nazism and the depression were extensively discussed at the Socialist International's Vienna Congress. The interpretation of fascism as the resort to gangsterism by a dying capitalism resembled that offered by the communists. But the congress sought a remedy when it proposed that capitalist countries be asked to restore the German economy and bring an unconditional end to that country's reparations payments. The delegates were divided on the attitude the SPD should take toward the Brüning government. Some, like Blum and Bauer, favored "toleration"; others, like James Maxton of the ILP, called instead for an open struggle.

After Hitler's accession to power, leaders of the Socialist International met in Paris in August, 1933. They were unable to agree on the formation of a common left-wing front against fascism, although some, like the Italian emigré Pietro Nenni, urged adoption of the revolutionary tactics demanded by the Comintern and the immediate seizure of power. Most Scandinavian socialists called for a total rupture with communism. They preferred to reinforce the democratic states by having socialism make overtures to the middle classes. Midway between these outlooks was the position defended by Otto Bauer and Léon Blum: to have socialism retain its own identity yet work for rapprochement with communism. In point of fact, few perceived that fascism constituted an international force to be met with by united action from the Left. It was regarded rather as a "Boulangism that succeeded" and hence an internal affair.[9] In fact, it was an unprecedented mass movement, a new historical phenomenon, and not a form of decadent capitalism best put in the framework of the struggle between bourgeoisie and proletariat. The error was similar to the underestimation of nationalism made before 1914, but of even greater magnitude. Not until the initiative taken by the socialist and communist rank and file in popular front coalitions (over the reluctance of their respective leaderships) would the Left successfully unite in an attempt to preserve democratic forms.

THE NEW REVISIONISM

Socialism was crushed in central and southern Europe. What impact did fascism and the support it apparently enjoyed have on socialism in the Western democracies? The effort to revitalize socialism and supply it with a new dynamism was characteristic of the 1930s. It took the shape of the neosocialism of Marcel Déat in France, the New Party of Oswald Mosley in England, and the Labor Plan Movement of the Belgian Hendrik de Man. A comparative study of these men and their ideas would doubtless be of importance to the historian of socialism. They all called for firmer direction by the government, an appeal for mass support, and reliance on economic planning. In nearly every case they were defeated by majority socialist opposition, broke with their parties, and evolved in a quasi-fascist manner. The process further divided and demoralized European labor.

NEOSOCIALISM

One of the first socialist movements determined to profit from the lessons learned from fascist successes was neosocialism within the SFIO. Its leaders were Adrien Marquet, mayor and deputy from Bordeaux, and Marcel Déat, a former Normalian, seen as Blum's successor, and "crown prince" of the party. In 1930, in his book, *Socialist Perspectives,* Déat asked his party to try to reach the middle classes and to participate in power. The SFIO's secretary-general and long-time disciple of Guesde, Paul Faure, promptly accused him of revisionism. At the meeting of the Socialist International in 1933, called to hold a post-mortem on the death of German social democracy, Marquet described socialism as stagnating and as having lost its mass appeal. He said that at the present moment of crisis and confusion order took on revolutionary meaning. "If we, as socialists," he went on, "do not speak of the matters indicated by concepts like will, action, and order . . . we may suffer the fate of the countries where Socialists have been exiled."[10]

At an earlier French socialist congress, Déat and Marquet held the lesson of the failure of German socialism as the need for "order, authority, and nation." They considered internationalism as a romantic and utopian ideal. Neosocialists, then, correctly interpreted fascism as a mass movement and not mere reactionary extremism. They insisted that new conditions called for new tactics of socialist combat. They wanted to match some of the appeals of fascism, particularly satisfaction of the longing for strong government. The abuses of capitalism would be countered not by revolution but by "planning." In promising a strongly "national" socialism, neosocialists acknowledged they would borrow from fascism even as the latter had taken its social program from socialism.

Léon Blum said that he was appalled by these ideas and reiterated his belief that fascism might be a necessary form of transition from capitalism to socialism. A majority of the party agreed. The SFIO's national council rejected neosocialism in its entirety and expelled Déat, Marquet, Pierre Renaudel, and four other converts. Some sympathetic deputies and intellectuals like Compére-Morel and Paul Ramadier followed them out of the party. They founded a new Socialist party of France, but it never reached a membership of more than 20,000. Whom did neosocialist ideas appeal to? Largely to activist youth elements and dissatisfied right-wing reformists who had condemned Blum's refusal to enter a coalition cabinet in 1932. The differences between these allies were too great to afford the new party any real chance of success. And if they both opposed socialist condemnation of middle-class governments, their economic and financial solutions were found too progressive by Radicals. Neosocialists were overtaken by the events of the Popular Front, and after Renaudel's death many of his supporters returned to the SFIO. Déat himself was defeated by a Popular Front candidate in 1936. Rejected by the Left, he became a leading exponent of appeasement toward the Nazis, and in 1939 was to coin the phrase "Why die for Danzig?" If obsessed by authoritarian and national appeals, the movement nevertheless revealed the contradiction within a party that for all practical purposes repudiated revolution yet refused to participate in power. And the *planisme* it denounced was to reemerge in socialist thought after World War II.

DE MAN AND THE LABOR PLAN

Some neosocialist ideas corresponded to those of the Labor Plan Movement in Belgium. Designed to transform the economy, the Plan called for the nationalization of key industries and finance as well as the expropriation of large land holdings. However, it would leave nonmonopolistic activity, at least in the foreseeable future, in the hand of private ownership. The objective was to halt the growth of fascism, and that required winning over to socialism large elements of the middle classes. Its author, the brilliant but unstable Hendrik de Man had served in the Belgian army. He traveled widely in the United States and was long a professor in Germany, which he regarded as his spiritual home.

De Man correctly interpreted the depression as an era of shrinking income. Consequently, pressure-group tactics aimed at procuring for labor a larger share of the economic pie were seen as self-defeating in as much as it was the size of the pie itself that was diminishing. The object was rather one of increasing national income (and that could be achieved only by changes in the structure of society). By dividing the economy into a public and private sector, by placing both sectors within a planned arrangement operating within a national framework, and by offering free development in the latter, it was hoped the middle classes would respond and hence be prevented from becoming the instruments of fascist domination. Enlisting the support of at least the lower-middle classes in alliance with the workers—both of whom shared a common enemy in finance capitalism—and providing for national economic planning under the control of a strong government, the Plan corresponded in many ways to the neosocialists' "order, authority, and nation." It impressed numerous socialists in Europe and was adopted by the Belgian Workers party at the end of 1933.

That it was never fully implemented was the result of accidental causes. One was the breakdown of the Belgian Workers Bank, which, because it held the funds of working-class organizations, ruined the movement financially. In March, 1935 a national union cabinet was formed in Belgium. The Labor party at first refused to join because the new ministry had refused to adopt the Plan. King Leopold III finally induced it to do so, and to win the support of the party's left wing, its chief, Paul-Henri Spaak, was named postmaster-general. Thus the party took responsibility before the major political objective of the Plan was achieved—the splitting of the Catholic party. Though pursuing an antideflationary policy, the government did not put the Plan into force. Finally, its energies were expended in combatting the Catholic fascist movement (the Rexist party) led by Léon Dégrelle, which it managed to defeat in the election of 1937. The emergence of Popular Front governments in France and Spain and the preponderance of foreign affairs in European labor and socialist strategy councils further pushed the Plan to the background. When the Germans invaded Belgium in 1940, De Man, now head of the party, chose not to follow Spaak and others to Britain. He urged a collaborationist policy, but was discredited with the Nazis and forced into exile in 1942. After the war, he was tried and condemned *in absentia*. His Plan, nevertheless, was of major importance in turning socialism from a pressure group into a political party and was to become a major plank in socialist platforms in post-World War II Europe.

One explanation for these strategical divisions within international socialism was the absence of any coherent ideological position. There was no theoretician during the period 1919–1939 comparable to Kautsky and the position he held in the Second International. The LSI contained a centrist group: notably Austro-Marxists, elements of the Independent Labor party, and assorted personalities. In condemning violence, it recognized the achievements of the USSR. However, events prodded this center to association with the anticommunist Right. It was this Right that found De Man's ideas most attractive, particularly his repudiation of the materialistic and deterministic components of Marxist thought and his replacement of them by a psychological basis for socialism. As national planning was to be adopted by the European Left, so was his insistence on providing socialism with an ethical content. His sociopsychological explanation for the working-class mentality contained elements of the *socialist humanism* that later emerged.

THE FORMATION OF THE POPULAR FRONT IN FRANCE

The first successful electoral coalition of socialists and communists designed to combat fascism was forged in France. An inquiry into its origins throws light on the difficulties involved in its formation and particularly on the reluctance of respective party chiefs to abandon their mutual hostility. It would appear that pressure for a working-class alliance was generated by the socialist and communist rank and file, initially over the objections of their respective leaders. Moscow's role lay not so much in instituting the agreement as in ratifying it.

The Nazi victory in January, 1933, caused more concern on the French left than in Soviet Russia. It did not at once suggest to Stalin the need for some revision of the pro-German policy set forth at Rapallo. Marxist interpreters, we have seen, saw in fascism the desperate resort to violence by a frightened bourgeoisie; once in power, however, it would open an era of revolutions. Viewing Hitler as a precursor of communism, Moscow ordered its Berlin embassy to break all contact with the Social Democratic leadership after he came to power. In point of fact, the Comintern only intensified its class-against-class policy adopted in 1928, and in France continued to denounce the SFIO as the "party of treason."

French workers, including communists, scarcely welcomed this analysis. In his report to the Comintern's executive committee, Maurice Thorez, the leading figure in French communism, gave a picture of "confusion, doubt, and indiscipline" in party ranks. He described how some communist municipal councillors had supported a resolution calling for the "defense of bourgeois democracy." Communist trade union leaders had negotiated, and in a number of strikes had formed joint committees with their socialist and Christian Democrat counterparts. Following its own investigation, the Comintern agreed that many PCF members wanted a change in the communist attitude to the socialist party.[11] While calling for antifascist action, however, it insisted on continuing the struggle against social democracy and proving to workers that its bankruptcy and that of the Socialist International were "historically inevitable." In regard to tactics, the chief objective lay in winning over socialist workers to communist leadership. One way was the creation of a united front, but only by means of joint committees of communist and socialist workers—that is, "from below"—and given the tighter discipline in communist ranks, doubtless at the expense of the socialist leadership. Hitler's nonaggression pact with Josef Pilsudski (enlarging the threat of a German invasion of the Soviet Union through Poland) caused no change in Russian policy, at least none that would suggest joint action with socialists against fascism. In early March, 1934 the Comintern attributed the destruction of Austrian socialism to the "inept social democratic leadership" and contrasted the defeat to Bolshevik success in 1917.[12]

By the summer of 1934, however, it was evident that additional elements within French communism had rejected the Comintern's interpretation of fascism as a necessary stage and showed interest in meeting the threat by means of common action with socialists. We have seen how the party underwent a *bolshevization* phase in the late twenties. Its exclusion from political life and refusal to support any national defense, foreign, or colonial policy caused the party to lose force as a national movement. With its existence threatened, its younger members demanding a change, and older *militants* and intellectuals suffering from long isolation from their country and eager to discover lines of continuity between "Capetians and communists," internal pressure was generated for a reversal of course. The rank and file remained animated by the desire to defend democratic institutions, if necessary together with socialists.[13]

The animosity between socialists and communists since 1920 had been a distinguishing feature in French political life. By 1932 relations had deteriorated to the point where in the elections of that year the communist leadership (although not always followed by the communist voters) refused to withdraw its candidates in favor of socialists and thus ensured several conservative victories. On the local level the rival parties competed intensely for the recruitment of membership. The communist executive, it was clear, would cooperate neither with the established order nor with the democratic opposition to it. Thorez insisted that "nothing was more false and dangerous for the masses than to distinguish bourgeois democracy from fascism." Anyone failing to understand the necessity of striking the first blow against those who apply the brake to mass pressure, he went on, "does not understand the 'A.B.C.' of communism" and was "afflicted by parliamentary cretinism."[14] Communist tactics therefore consisted in unmasking socialists and Radicals as having become integrated into the apparatus of the bourgeois state and as now serving as instruments of capitalism. The party executive, following the Comintern lead, did not reverse itself after the Nazi arrival in power despite mounting discontent. For ever-larger numbers of the rank and file it was obvious that German socialists and communists, whatever the division of responsibility, represented the defeated force.

As Thorez had noted, events were leaving the party leadership (and the Comintern) behind. Budgetary problems giving rise to austerity programs, and then the depression with increasing unemployment contributed to greater ministerial instability. From June, 1932, to February, 1934, a 20-month interval, there were 6 governments; in the six and a half years between 1930 and 1936, there were 18. As on past occasions in modern French history the apparent impossibility of effective government aroused an antiparliamentary response, now in the form of extraparliamentary leagues. Disenchanted by the inadequacies of democratic procedures, they began to seek other models. A financial scandal involving left-wing politicians led to the organization of street fighting on February 6, 1934. The results included 15 dead and scores of wounded, the installation of a conservative national union government, and the conviction on the part of labor that the riot represented the greatest domestic threat to French democracy since the Dreyfus affair.

After February 6, fascism no longer denoted a vague and foreign ideology; the attention of the French Left focused on France. Socialist and communist workers experienced the revival of a mystique of unity, perhaps the chief element in French socialist history before 1905 and after 1920. Events now brought the Left together. The next day, at the invitation of the CGT (then the socialist trade union federation), delegates from the CGTU (its communist equivalent) as well as from the two parties met to discuss a joint program of counteraction and reached general agreement on the need for mass demonstrations and strikes. Several were held in the days that followed, the first united action between socialists and communists in any country since 1928. Regardless of a reluctance to negotiate by leaders, French workers and intellectuals began to set up common agencies to combat fascism: leagues, watch committees, and cartels.[15]

After another visit by Thorez to Moscow, *Pravda* published an important article reproduced in the PCF's *L'Humanité* on May 31. It repeated the necessity of seeking a united antifascist front under certain conditions, but added that these conditions had been realized in France, "where the social democrats had not yet gotten power" and where it was "necessary for the masses to experience struggle directly." There can be little doubt that this article prompted the PCF leadership to make renewed and energetic attempts at unity. In the same edition that carried the *Pravda* report, *L'Humanité* printed an appeal to SFIO members and leaders (it marked the first time that the socialist executive had been addressed) to undertake joint action on behalf of the imprisoned German communist chief, Thälmann. A second letter, printed June 5, repeated the offer. Conversations between Thorez and Blum were held on June 11 and four days later, on the condition that mutual criticisms come to an end, the SFIO accepted the principle of joint demonstrations. At his party's Ivry Congress in late June, a reluctant Thorez called for union with socialist workers against fascism "at any price." The implication was clear: Negotiations could be held with the socialist party chiefs.

In view of the abruptness of the change, one can readily understand why the SFIO saw the proposal as a new manoeuvre and further proof that the communists wanted unity only on their own terms. That agreement was nevertheless reached was due to the pressure put on Blum and Faure by the growing number of unity pacts at the federation level. Not only the communist, but the socialist rank and file desired it. By July 16 a draft unit of action pact was proposed. Paul Faure, Jean-Baptiste Lebas, and others opposed to unity still hesitated, fearing a Moscow-directed movement but having little choice other than to yield. The ultimate SFIO decision to participate had been predicted by Blum in *Le Populaire* the previous February 25. He then intimated that the masses would not understand a socialist refusal. The SFIO leadership never overcame its conviction that the sudden amenability of the communists was due to the changed demands of Soviet foreign policy and especially growing Franco-Russian rapprochement. To the impatient membership the hesitancy and insistence on guarantees strengthened the impression that the PCF had seized the initiative in establishing working-class unity and was in fact the "champion of the Left." A unity of action pact was signed July 27. The accord was defensive, not yet an electoral alliance, but aware of some mutual withdrawals made in favor of the stronger candidate in local elections that fall, few doubted that such an alliance was forthcoming.

On the international level, the LSI rejected the SFIO's request that similar action be undertaken by other socialist sections. A majority, from its president, Vandervelde, to its largest delegation, British Labour, was further to the right than French socialism. Unwilling, however, to condemn the important French section, the International recognized the SFIO's right to join with the communists in view of the fascist threat to French democracy.

The Seventh Comintern congress, on the other hand, meeting in the summer of 1935—and after the transformation of the united front into an electoral popular front—congratulated the French "proletariat" and applauded its "delegation." The new secretary, Dimitrov, stated that French workers had provided the international proletariat with an example of the means necessary to fight fascism. In contrast to the LSI, the Comintern recommended that under certain conditions communist parties enter united front governments provided they were antifascist and were supported by powerful mass movements. International communism, according to Dimitrov, had entered a "new tactical orientation." It had, in fact, entered its "fourth period"; class collaboration replaced class antagonism.

Suffice it to say that the enlargement of the front to an electoral alliance was due to a combination of communist initiative and socialist practice. First the pact was extended to include the middle classes. On June 30, writing in *L'Humanité,* Thorez recognized the Radicals as the "largest of parties" and acknowledged its influence on French political life. A wing of the party, led by Edouard Daladier, ignored the objections of more conservative elements under the direction of Edouard Herriot and responded to the communist appeal. A number of fringe groupings then joined the coalition. A number of difficulties were ironed out in time for the 1936 elections: for example, socialist demands for increased nationalization were restricted by communists and Radicals, while communist demands for extraparliamentary action were curbed by Radicals and socialists.

The cooperation among the three parties made possible the victory of the Popular Front. Socialists replaced Radicals as the leading group in the new Chamber of Deputies. The communists returned 70 deputies and doubled the size of their vote from 6.8 percent to 12.5 percent. The parties on the right, however, had lost only 1.5 percent of the votes gathered in 1932, slipping from 37.4 to 35.9 percent of the total number cast. Nothing demonstrated so well the general usefulness of electoral coalitions in French politics and their particular indispensability to the Left.

This account of the establishment of socialist–communist unity of action suggests that although Soviet policies were furthered by it and that Soviet approval was ultimately necessary, *de facto* unity was being achieved independently of Comintern mandate and only after-ward received Comintern compliance. The Soviet role can best be described as that of exercising a veto. The Third International could either have broken the tendency toward unification of the Left or reinforced it, and chose the latter.

With 146 deputies to give it a plurality in the legislature, Léon Blum accepted the post of premier, to which he was entitled as head of the party. Since the early 1920s he had distinguished between the exercise of power, undertaken by socialists within a capitalist frame-work (without transforming society), and the conquest of power by revolution. Communists, taking the position long held by socialists, re-fused to participate in his cabinet and preserved their freedom of action.

At the time the government was constituted, the greatest strike movement yet experienced by the nation broke out, one involving 2 million workers. For the first time in France, workers occupied fac-tories, in part to prevent employers from resorting to lockouts and the use of scabs, in part as an attempt to reaffirm their identity. Unlike the Italian strikes of 1920, however, where the object was to reject capital-ist rights of ownership, most French strikers saw themselves, in Blum's words, as "guardians and co-proprietors." The sit-ins were undertaken in a spirit of cheerfulness and with a buoyancy probably matched only by the students-workers uprising in May, 1968.

Employers indicated their willingness to come to terms, and asked the government to intercede. The subsequent Matignon accords granted French labor a *new deal* in guaranteeing collective bargaining, and by implication the right of the trade union to exist, industrywide shop stewards, and salary increases ranging from 7 to 15 percent. Subse-quent legislation established the principle of paid vacations and the 40-hour week. Still, only by exerting all his authority was Thorez able to persuade workers to leave the factories, which prompted some observers to label the movement as revolutionary. In the summer of 1936 the Blum government undertook a public works program to combat unemployment and realized an old socialist demand in founding a national wheat office empowered to fix prices. It also nationalized the armaments industries and began to institute state control over the Bank of France.

However, both international and domestic problems plagued the ministry. Blum's refusal to intervene in the Spanish Civil War alienated communists and the socialist Left; what help he did provide infuriated conservatives. At home, schemes to increase public purchasing power foundered on persistently low production levels, and the 40-hour week was blamed. The employing classes returned to the offensive, to the extent of exporting capital and artificially inflating prices. Unable or unwilling to undertake structural reforms, buffeted by a deteriorating political climate, deserted by the withdrawal of support from many within his party, Blum called for a *pause* in March, 1937. When refused emergency financial powers by the senate three months later, the cabinet resigned.

SCANDINAVIAN SOCIALISM

A different and brighter image of socialism in the 1930s was presented by Scandinavia, and particularly Sweden. Social Democrats came to power for considerable lengths of time in Denmark in 1929, Sweden in 1932, and Norway in 1935. They introduced a series of significant reforms, establishing modern welfare states if not socialist societies, and by virtue of enlightened fiscal policies staved off the worst effects of worldwide economic depression. Their achievements, however, must be placed in the perspective of small civilized countries with relatively homogeneous populations and few class tensions. There was no question of the overthrow of democracy or a threat from abroad. Even so, their work was remarkable and their governments hailed as models of economic democracy.

Scandinavia was comparatively late in industrializing. Hence socialist parties came on the scene at about the turn of the century and were spared much of the conflict between the economic and political branches of working-class movements that had plagued their predecessors. Their belated appearance also meant that they had to contend with well-established liberal and conservative parties. The renowned flexibility and realism of Scandinavian socialists may best be explained as political imperatives and not as manifestations of Nordic national character. In any case, their socialism was less a matter of doctrine than a desire for greater social justice. What nationalization and redistribution of income there was took place for the sake of efficiency and not theory.

The three parties were not identical. The socialist party in Denmark was more reformist than that in Norway, which for a time worked closely with the Communist International and was regarded as one of the most radical. Unlike their equivalents in Central and Western Europe, however, they were armed with definite programs to combat the depression and introduce the welfare state and a determination to carry them out. On taking office in 1935, the Norwegian party launched an extensive public-works program and reduced unemployment sharply. It also established a national retirement benefits plan, expanded unemployment insurance and factory legislation, and before war broke out was making arrangements for a planned economy. Danish socialists won a majority on a program calling for nationalization of the country's central bank, of insurance, and of some industries enjoying monopoly status, as well as greater social legislation. But the party that was to appear as a model to others and capable of providing a "middle way" to nonsocialists was Swedish social democracy.

From its establishment in 1889, the Social Democratic party aimed at securing a broad electoral base. As early as 1911 it defined socialism as a humanist ethic and promised to defend small peasant proprietorship. It supported the movement for universal suffrage and became its chief beneficiary. By 1920, Swedish socialists formed the world's first regularly elected labor government. (A left wing, hostile to the party's decision to join a coalition cabinet in 1917, had broken away and constituted the antecedent of the Swedish communist party. Like its Norwegian counterpart, a large dissenting group within it came to resent the impositions laid down by the Comintern and was expelled.) The subsequent history of the Social Democratic party is one of unparalleled political success. It had formed three all-socialist governments by 1925, was returned in 1932 and, aside from a brief interval in 1936, has been in power ever since. The feat was all the more remarkable inasmuch as the socialists rarely held a majority in the *Riksdag* (parliament). Theirs became the oldest, largest, and best-organized party in the country. In the developmental process, it lost its Marxist origins and dropped such ideological demands as separation of church and state, the replacement of the monarchy by a republic, and demilitarization. It had evolved into a national party well before mid-century and was following the precepts of its present program long before it was adopted:

In every case the Social Democratic party will choose those forms of enterprise and ownership which best serve material progress and human welfare. It stands for public ownership and public control of natural resources, banks, and industrial and other undertakings in so far as it is necessary to safeguard the important interests of the community.[16]

What accounted for this evolution? Certainly leaders like Hjalmar Branting, who were willing and able to compromise and subordinate doctrine to pressing issues. The neutrality observed by the nation for a century and a half permitted funds otherwise spent on war to be administered for welfare needs. The homogeneity of race and religion reduced tensions and allowed major political parties to draw closer on basic issues like national defense, taxes, and social welfare. Politics had become more a question of tactics and personalties than of goals and issues. Finally, there were the traditions of local government and *folkrörelser* (a non-translatable term referring to noneconomic popular movements). These organizations appeared at the turn of the century and promoted causes like suffrage extension, education, temperance, and trade unionism. In granting Swedes opportunities to participate in small-scale democratic bodies, they served as schools for democratic politics and accounted for high participation in political affairs with an accompanying readiness to modify objectives and engage in compromise. A strong cooperative movement lessened the desire to increase nationalization and reinforced tendencies toward welfare legislation rather than socialization. The Social Democrats drew much of their strength from a close alliance with organized labor. Unlike the British Labour party, however, it rose above the immediate demands of its clients and successfully fought the depression.

The party's conservative predecessors in office had clearly failed to do so. Unemployment in 1932 reached a level of 25 percent. Socialists elsewhere accepted deflation but opposed its application to wages and unemployment benefits. The Socialist International, continuing to think in terms of the workers-employers struggle and not of government policy, asked that the costs of increasing consumer purchasing power be borne entirely by management. Swedish socialist leaders urged that public investment be expanded to compensate for the reduction of private spending in times of depression.

The cabinet that implemented this program constituted a brilliant team. Its leading lights were the popular prime minister, Per Albin Hansson, the foreign minister, Rickard Sandler (who had translated Marx), and the minister of finance, Ernst Wigfors. It was supported by the Swedish School of Economic Science, closely affiliated with the government and directed by Gunnar Myrdal and Erik Lindal.

Public spending was increased to stimulate consumption and production. The money was used not for relief purposes alone, but for works projects. It came not from taxation, which would only have shifted—not have created—purchasing power, but from borrowing. This constituted the first great experiment in deliberate deficit financing. Myrdal in particular rejected the concept of the balanced budget as sound fiscal policy; he wanted the state to influence the business climate and not merely reflect it. Consequently, budgetary cuts were not only avoided, but expenditures increased. The debts incurred were to be repaid in more prosperous times when tax revenues would be higher. The party was aided by the fact that Sweden had withdrawn from the gold standard in 1931. A free currency, not tied to gold, created a favorable condition for economic recovery.

The government was determined to enforce its program. Following the socialist victory, the country's leading banks demonstrated their hostility to the new economics by raising interest rates. Plans for large-scale borrowing were at once jeopardized. However, the government exerted pressure and forced the banks to yield.

Recovery began in the second half of 1933. In March of that year unemployment reached 187,000 (average unemployment for the year numbered 164,000). In 1934 the figure fell to 115,000; in 1937 only 18,000 people were out of work, and by 1938 unemployment in Sweden virtually ceased to exist. Moreover, debts were being repaid, and a vast program of social services had been put into effect. It ranged from maternity and child benefits, paid vacations, and the right of collective bargaining for state employees to a national health insurance scheme and old-age pension reform. Returned to power in 1936 (with 112 of 230 seats), socialists chose to ally with the peasant and not the Communist party to ensure its legislative majority. It did so in order to retain its freedom in foreign affairs and pursue an independent policy. Scandinavian socialists in general, and those in Sweden in particular, established a new concept of the state's role in times of economic crisis and served as a pioneer in the area of welfare legislation. Accordingly, they were held in widespread repute as having found a "middle way" between laissez-faire capitalism and Marxist–Leninist collectivism.

SOCIALISM VERSUS FASCISM

THE SOCIALIST INTERNATIONAL AND FOREIGN POLICY

In view of overt and repeated German violations of the Treaty of Versailles after the Nazi accession to power, fascism could no longer be considered the domestic concern of any one country. International socialism felt obliged to make a response. Although the constitution of the LSI stated that decisions on all international questions were binding on its membership, no one had imagined that measures of enforcement should be created. Member parties were voluntarily to impose limits on their autonomy. The Socialist International consequently became an agency for exchanging information and devising mutually acceptable, nonoffensive policies.

The prevailing outlook on international affairs may be found in the remark made by the German Otto Wels: "Never again shall there be war." Socialists supported the League of Nations as an instrument for furthering disarmament and international arbitration. At the same time they pointed out its inadequacies and demanded enlargement of its authority. The LSI considered capitalism as the chief cause of war. It was committed to a gradualist approach in foreign as well as in domestic affairs and to the maintenance of peace. Consequently, while criticizing the League as an instrument of capitalist governments, it tried to cooperate with it. The weakness of the socialist response to foreign issues, then, lay in the structural deficiencies of the International, in policy differences among its member parties, in the tendency of the latter to support the foreign policies of their respective governments, in a fundamental misunderstanding of the nature of fascism, and in a persistent pacifist and antimilitary tradition reenforced by the experience of World War I. It was this last, perhaps, that proved the greatest obstacle to the formulation of an active and coherent socialist stand.

Before Hitler came to power there was no question but that the LSI wanted to preserve peace through international disarmament and arbitration. At its Brussels Congress in 1928, delegates like Paul Löbe, President of the German Reichstag, and Paul Faure asked for an early allied evacuation of the Rhineland in the interests of binding Germans to disarmament and so contributing to the preservation of peace. We have already observed the divided response accorded the SPD's *toleration* policy, and the International's request that the nations of the world grant credits to Germany in an effort to stave off threats to its democratic republic.

In the special session of the Socialist International held in Paris, in August, 1933, left-wingers led by Spaak attributed the destruction of German social democracy to the inadequacies of reformism. Attempts to establish "proletarian unity" and the "dictatorship of the revolutionary classes," they said, must take precedence over collaboration with nonsocialist groups. But the resolution embodying these ideas and calling for negotiations with the Communist International was defeated. Anti-Bolshevik sentiment was too strong. Traditional demands for disarmament and arbitration prevailed. The congress recognized the German claim for equal treatment, but opposed German rearmament to attain it. In so doing, they implicitly called for British and French disarmament.

Socialism's unswerving devotion to peace was less ambiguous. Léon Blum argued that every chance offered by the fascists to ensure its permanence should be seized.[17] Hence socialism was put in the difficult position of preserving peace from a position of unconditional pacifism. As Hitler consolidated his regime, conflict intensified within the Socialist International over the means to deal with the Nazi threat. With the demise of the SPD, British Labour and the SFIO became the two most powerful parties. They were notoriously pacifist. Many of the other delegates who attended LSI congresses were internationalist minded and often opposed to their own party's policies. Together with delegates from some neutral lands and aware that their home countries would not be called on to act, they voted for strong anti-Nazi measures. Thus it was that the International often appeared more critical of Germany than the British and French socialist parties. The LSI opposed further concessions to Germany. They would, it was held, lead only to new demands. At the same time, most British and French socialists fought attempts to strengthen the military establishments of their respective governments and so limited their ability to refuse German demands for concessions.

After Hitler took power, the British and French parties resisted their governments' rare attempts to contain him. Fiercely seconded by Paul Faure, Blum opposed any increase in arms expenditures and any extension of his country's two-year draft. Lessons learned from the origins of the first world conflict and legitimate hostility to the Treaty of Versailles continued to guide their behavior. Admittedly, the socialist decision was not an easy one. Stories of Nazi inhumanity circulated, and many socialists were torn by uncertainty and by the contradictions in their position.[18] Still, in 1935 Blum drafted and the LSI's bureau adopted a resolution demanding general disarmament (with or without German participation). It was hoped that the Nazis would be forced by world opinion to sign. French socialists had feared British "warmongers" during the Ethiopian crisis and were not about to let France or the League of Nations be used as instruments to further British colonial ambitions. Hence they supported economic, but repudiated military sanctions against Italy. The Labour party seconded the British government's reluctance to take action and reiterated its wish to see the Versailles treaty amended. The response of the Socialist International was a renewed call for disarmament by international agreement. The following year, the SFIO rejected any military response to the German reoccupation of the Rhineland.

LABOUR AND FOREIGN POLICY: THE EVOLUTION OF A POSITION

Regardless of their reluctance to take preventive action, the Nazi triumph in Germany and Japanese aggression in the Far East required the British Labour party to place new urgency on foreign affairs in 1933. Conflicts over which paths to follow quickly surfaced. Wholly pacifist, George Lansbury, then party leader, rejected rearmament for self-defense and also denounced the League of Nations as a society of the rich against the underdeveloped nations. Other elements within the party, while not going as far, retained the illusion that disarmament was somehow synonymous with security. However, trade union leaders, particularly the national council of the Trades Union Congress, influenced and directed by Ernest Bevin, came out for collective security and for armed resistance to aggression. Nonetheless, they rejected proposals for a united front with communists. Labour party leaders may have been feeling their way toward a new policy. They stated their readiness to support a defensive war, according to a resolution adopted at their Southport conference, but it was vaguely worded. Certainly, the bulk of the party was pacifist, as much opposed to the French as to the Nazis, and seeing considerable justification behind German demands for greater self-determination and equality of treatment in matters of disarmament.

The so-called Peace Ballot of 1935 asked whether an aggressor should be stoppped by war. Nearly 7 of every 9 Englishmen and women who replied said yes. The Labour party's annual conference, held shortly after Italian armies invaded Ethiopia, resolved that "all the necessary measures provided by the [League] Covenant" should be taken against the aggressor. Even so, the formidable voices of Stafford Cripps, who said that "every war entered upon by a capitalist government is and must be an imperialist war," and the pacifist George Lansbury were raised in opposition. The latter thereupon resigned and was replaced as head of the party by Clement Attlee. In the election campaign of that year, in which Labour increased its representation by over 100 seats, both parties urged all sanctions short of war.[19]

The party remained divided, however, and continued to oppose arms expenditures. It was through the efforts of the chairman of its national executive Hugh Dalton, and leading Labour advocate of large-scale rearmament Ernest Bevin that prodded the party to take a position in support of collective security. The Spanish Civil War completed its evolution. By 1936 Labour defended rearmament in principle, but did not feel obliged to vote for armaments credits under a government whose foreign policy it distrusted. Earlier fears of imperialism had proven justified. Pressure for a united front with the communists and ILP was exerted by the Left Book Club founded by Victor Gollancz, a leading exponent of an antifascist alliance, and managed by John Strachey and Harold Laski. The war in Spain posed the issue clearly. In allowing all opponents of fascism to fight it overtly, it understandably encouraged them to think of joining together.

Neither organized labor not the Labour party, however, would have much to do with the drive for unity on the left. The latter expelled Cripps' Socialist League in January, 1937 and threatened similar action for individuals supporting it. Association with the Communist party, no matter how small and isolated, evoked memories of the twenties and was viewed as an electoral liability. Although it refused to enter any antifascist alliance with France and the USSR abroad, or with communists and the ILP at home, Labour finally voted for rearmament in 1937. Its mind once made up, the Labour party, unlike the SFIO, was unanimous in its support for the defense of Czechoslovakia. It rejected the concessions made at Munich by Neville Chamberlain. After war broke out, only a very weak minority within the ILP rejected socialist support for a war effort in a capitalist regime.

In supporting the Russo-German pact of 1939, the communists lost whatever ground they had previously gained in attracting left-wing sympathy.

SOCIALISM AND THE COMING OF WORLD WAR II

After the failure of the League in Ethiopia and the remilitarization of the Rhineland, many of the smaller European socialist parties no longer relied on collective security, although they continued to pay lip service to it. Dutch socialists wanted full unilateral disarmament. Danish socialists were even more pacifist and dissolved their nation's armed forces almost in their entirety. Many in the Belgian Workers party doubted the value of the French alliance. But socialists in Czechoslovakia and Poland called for stronger measures of national defense and collective security. Still, it was the attitude of the British and French parties that counted most. The former supported collective security after 1936; the French remained very much divided.

The Spanish Civil War also persuaded the Socialist International to change its outlook. The British and French governments had decided on a policy of nonintervention. Yet Germany and Italy provided aid to the insurgents and so created a very real dilemma for socialists who hesitated to risk war and yet wanted to aid the loyalists. In the first great sign that it was about to revise its policy, the LSI and IFTU condemned these violations of the noninterventionist program agreed to, and called on all labor organizations to work for the lifting of the embargo against the Spanish government. By July, 1937, the Labour party asked for an end to nonintervention. Most French socialists continued to support their government's policy.

German forces occupied Austria in March, 1938. Meeting shortly afterwards, the Socialist International and the Trade Union Federation agreed that the event destroyed any remaining illusions about Hitler's real intentions. They again demanded an end to the Spanish embargo and as well as effective guarantees for Czech independence. When during the crisis of 1938, the British government told Germany it would support France in the event that Czechoslovakia were attacked, the LSI's executive bureau applauded the act. But the situation worsened in the summer and fall of 1938 and the risk of war was heightened; pangs of anxiety shot through European socialism. The Labour party momentarily wavered in its support of collective security. Still, it denounced the Munich Pact as a shameful betrayal. The faction headed by Paul Faure within the SFIO, however, its gaze riveted on the summer of 1914, called it a preferable alternative to war. The left wing of the SFIO, represented by Jean Zyromski, unequivocally denounced appeasement. Blum stood between both, convinced since the 1938 *Anchluss* that only willingness to use force could preserve peace, but desperate to retain party unity and apparently upset not so much about the decision taken at Munich as over the absence of Czech representatives there. Most socialist deputies, like most Frenchmen, supported Daladier. The communists, a lone socialist, and a single conservative were the only ones to vote against the pact in the Chamber of Deputies.

The LSI's executive committee condemned the Munich agreement. Its protest, however, had to be acceptable to the anti-Munich British, the pro-Munich French, and inoffensive to the neutralist Belgian, Swiss, and Scandinavian sections. Consequently, it objected to the form and not to the substance of appeasement. Czech Social Democrats thereupon resigned from the International; Hungarian and Polish socialists welcomed the Czech territory acquired. For all practical purposes the Socialist International was brought to an end. Its unswerving commitment to peace had proved its undoing. Still, it had reflected the views of the leading democracies and peoples of Western Europe. Appeasement in France collapsed only when it became clear that Italy was not to become an ally. Zyromski and Blum defeated Faure, but too late to aid the loyalists in Spain. Even so, a heartsick Blum watched a majority of his party's deputies vote full powers to Marshal Pétain in June, 1940. Labour's opposition in the House of Commons led to Chamberlain's departure, but it was Churchill who profited most from the victory.

The Left was to do much to redeem itself during the resistance. Although only a comparative history permits identification of the similarities and divergencies of the various resistance movements, particularly from the standpoint of their political compositions, resemblances emerged. They stirred a mass response and the ideology developed gave a large place to socialist ideas. They formulated plans for national renewal which were to give left-wing coloration to politics in the immediate postwar period. Finally, because they shed luster on the Left (and because the Right was tainted by its support and/or affiliation with fascism), socialists were given an opportunity to hold power after 1945.

NOTES

[1] Daniel Bell, "Socialism," *International Encyclopedia of the Social Sciences* (New York: Macmillan, 1968), Vol. 15, p. 519.

[2] Adolf Sturmthal, *The Tragedy of European Labor* (New York: Columbia University Press, 1943), pp. vii, 5.

[3] Christopher Seton-Watson, *Italy from Liberation to Fascism* (London: Methuen; New York: Barnes and Noble, 1967), p. 511.

⁴ *Ibid.,* pp. 520–521.

⁵ Dennis Mack Smith, *Italy. A Modern History* (Ann Arbor: University of Michigan Press, 1959), p. 313. Pietro Nenni, *Storia di quattro anni, 1919–1922* (Rome: G. Einaudi, 1946), pp. 36, 65. S. W. Halperin, *Mussolini and Italian Fascism* (Princeton: Van Nostrand, 1964), p. 28.

⁶ Jacques Droz, *Le Socialisme démocratique, 1864–1960* (Paris: A. Colin, 1966), p. 197.

⁷ Franz Neumann, *Behemoth. The Structure and Practice of National Socialism, 1933–1944* (New York: Octagon Books, 1963), pp. 17–18, 260–261, 284.

⁸ Charles A. Gulick, *Austria from Habsburg to Hitler,* 2 vols. (Berkeley: University of California Press, 1948), II, pp. 1371–1380, 1389.

⁹ Sturmthal, *op. cit.,* p. 183.

¹⁰ *Ibid.,* p. 221.

¹¹ Jane Degras, ed., *The Communist International, 1919–1943. Documents* (London and New York: Oxford University Press, 1956), pp. iii, 313. See L. Derfler, "Unity and the French Left: Some Views of the Popular Front," *Science and Society* (Spring 1971), pp. 34–47 for a survey of some of the current literature. I have excerpted freely from this article.

¹² Degras, *op. cit.,* pp. 308–309.

¹³ Louis Bodin, "Le PCF dans le front populaire," *Esprit* (October 1966), p. 440.

¹⁴ Georges Dupeux, *Le Front populaire et les Elections de 1936* (Paris: A. Colin, 1959), pp. 11–12.

¹⁵ John Marcus, *French Socialism in the Crisis Years, 1933–1936* (New York: Praeger, 1958), pp. 59–60, 69–81.

¹⁶ Joseph B. Doard, Jr., *The Government and Politics of Sweden* (New York: Houghton Mifflin, 1970), p. 93.

¹⁷ Carl Landauer, *European Socialism. A History of Ideas and Movements,* 2 vols. (Berkeley: University of California Press, 1959), II, p. 1535.

¹⁸ Sturmthal, *op. cit.,* pp. 237–238.

¹⁹ A. J. P. Taylor, *English History, 1914–1945* (Oxford: Clarendon Press, 1965), pp. 379, 381–383.

SUGGESTED READING

J. M. Cammett. *Antonio Gramsci and the Origins of Italian Communism.* Stanford: Stanford University Press, 1967.

Julius Braunthal. *History of the International, 1914–1943.* New York: Praeger, 1967.

Julius Braunthal. *The Tragedy of Austria.* London: Gollancz, 1947.

Daniel Brower. *The New Jacobins. The French Communist Party and the Popular Front.* Ithaca: Cornell University Press, 1968.

Joseph Buttinger. *In the Twilight of Socialism. A History of the Revolutionary Socialists of Austria.* New York: Praeger, 1953.

Joel Colton. *Léon Blum: Humanist in Politics.* New York: Knopf, 1966.

Hugh Dalton. *The Fateful Years. Memoirs, 1931–1945.* London, 1957.

Peter Dodge. *Beyond Marxism: The Faith and Works of Hendrick de Man.* The Hague: Nijoff, 1966.

Michael Gordon. *Conflict and Consensus in Labour's Foreign Policy, 1914–1965.* Stanford: Stanford University Press, 1969.

Richard Hunt. *German Social Democracy, 1918–1933.* Chicago: Quadrangle, 1970.

Journal of Contemporary History. Vol. I. "International Fascism, 1920–1945."

J. A. Lauwerys. *Scandinavian Democracy.* Copenhagen: Danish Institute, 1958.

George Lichtheim. *Marxism in Modern France.* New York: Columbia University Press, 1966.

Richard W. Lyman. "The British Labour Party: The Conflict between Socialist Ideals and Practical Politics Between the Wars." *The Journal of British Studies.* V (1965).

Erich Matthias and Rudolf Morsey, eds. *Das Ende der Parteinen 1933.* Düsseldorf: Droste Verlag, 1960.

Ralph Miliband. *Parliamentary Socialism.* London: Allen and Unwin, 1961.

C. L. Mowat. *Britain Between the Wars, 1918–1940.* Boston: Beacon Press, 1971.

Henry Pelling. *The British Communist Party. A Historical Profile.* London: A. and C. Black, 1958.

Henry Pelling. *A Short History of the Labour Party.* London: Macmillan, 1965.

Hugh Thomas. *The Spanish Civil War.* New York: Harper and Row; London: Eyre & Spottiswoode, 1961.

Alexander Werth. *The Twilight of France, 1933–1940.* New York: Harper & Row, 1942. Reprinted New York: H. Fertig, 1966.

SEVEN

Contemporary

Socialism

European social-
ists before World
W a r   I I   s a w
themselves and not the communists
as the true heirs to the Marxist tradition. By 1970 they had diluted the
deterministic aspects of their programs, and had placed emphasis on
the moral and humanistic rather than the materialist values inherent
in Marxist thought. They searched for and found socialist roots in
ethical, philosophical, and religious sources. Although opposed to
both capitalism and communism, many viewed the greater danger to
democracy as coming from the Soviet Union; to forestall it they elected
to cooperate with the democratic middle-class parties. However, the
new revisionism displayed by socialists gave rise (as had the old) to
a new and more militant Left.

The story of socialism in the post-World War II period properly
begins with the resistance movements that emerged during the war. The
planning that took place provided for national liberation. It also envisaged a new departure for postwar society, and many of the ideas
formulated matched socialist objectives. Once again, however, only a
comparison of the resistance movements and of their ideological pre-
occupations can reveal the degree to which any one of them was so
committed. Because there was official collaboration in France, the
resistance there necessarily took on the dimensions of a civil war, with
the Left ranged against the Vichy regime. In Germany, with socialism
long defunct, what there was of a resistance was necessarily conservative. But conservatism failed to halt a revolutionary Nazi movement.

After the German invasion of the Soviet Union in the summer of
1941, communists joined in the resistance movements. By virtue of
their greater discipline and experience in working underground, they
were able to assume a major role. Still, socialist objectives were not
communist-imposed but widely shared. Technical and tactical questions remained paramount. The old communist-socialist schism and

even the revolution–reformist controversy had little meaning for underground organizations operating in fascist-controlled countries. Divergent views, to be sure, were expressed. Walter Ulbricht, head of the German Communist party since 1935, opposed the proallied policy of the Social Democrats from Moscow. In urging a German-Soviet pact, he hinted of postwar difficulties to come. Most socialists and communists, however, worked for the establishment of democratic and humanitarian values in institutional forms.

SOCIALISM IN POWER

Until at least 1950, socialism appeared as postwar Europe's destiny. The Labour party was swept into office in 1945. Together with communists and Christian democrats, socialists governed in tripartite regimes in France and Italy, continuing to govern without the communists after 1947. Socialists constituted the chief opposition in West Germany, and socialist parties were predominant in Scandinavian legislatures. Western Europe seemed to have committed itself to socialism. In Eastern Europe, socialists and communists had come to power in coalitions known as *people's democracies*. They repudiated the quasi-fascist or reactionary regimes of the interwar period.

What accounted for the success of socialism at the end of the war? In large part the answer rests on the prestige of the Left, which had long fought fascism and had participated extensively in the resistance. The Right was discredited. In most Nazi-occupied countries, collaborationists came from the ranks of conservative business elements. This seemed to confirm the view that fascism was essentially a middle- and upper-class reaction to socialism. The men and women of the liberation were determined to limit the pressures of organized business on democratically elected governments. The nationalization measures undertaken in Britain and France (the former, with noteworthy exceptions, enjoyed Conservative or Tory support; the latter, the approval of General de Gaulle) reaffirmed their new socialist character and testified to widespread recognition of the need for social change. It was anticipated that as World War I had brought capitalism to an end in Russia, so World War II would result in the victory of socialism.

THE LABOUR GOVERNMENT, 1945–1951

The "revolution" carried out during Labour's term of office began in 1940. Labour ministers in Churchill's wartime cabinet were given control over domestic affairs, and men like Clement Attlee, Arthur Greenwood, Ernest Bevin, Herbert Morrison, and Stafford Cripps out of necessity and choice began considerable state intervention in daily British life. Party designs for postwar Britain called for extensive socialization. The Beveridge Plan for "full employment in a free society," asked for universal social security and aimed at abolishing mass poverty and unemployment. That the Liberal Beveridge drafted such a plan revealed the degree to which nearly all British leaders agreed on the need for major societal change (although not collectivization). Labour wanted to extend social insurance schemes, establish minimum working and living standards, free health, food for school children, and greater educational opportunity. Specific party programs added nationalization of the Bank of England, the coal and gas industries, electricity, railways and trucking, and the metals industries. They did not aim at nationalizing all industries, but only those "ripe" for it. Others would only be regulated and small business left alone.

The voters returned 393 Labour candidates against 213 Conservatives and their allies, and Attlee replaced Winston Churchill as prime minister. What accounted for the size of the victory? Certainly the memory of Conservative errors and unemployment before the war coupled with Labour's own effective wartime role. Despite shortages, government controls were so efficient that more people were better fed and clothed during World War II than ever before. Moreover, Labour offered a carefully detailed program and won considerable middle-class support. Nor were those elected to office entirely of the working class; trade union-sponsored members of the new parliament amounted to less than one-third of the total. Many younger and professional men represented all classes and occupations.

The TUC's Ernest Bevin was named minister of foreign affairs. As chancellor of the exchequer, Hugh Dalton was responsible for much of the domestic legislation, as was Aneurin Bevan, the minister of health. There was little opposition to the nationalization of the Bank of England and to the declining coal industry, and only a little more to the slightly more profitable railways. Tories resisted the taking of the trucking and metals industries, deliberately left until the last. They especially condemned the National Health Service. Bevan had to accept demands that Englishmen be given the right to choose between private doctors and public hospitals. Compensation was paid to former owners of the nationalized industries. The Left said this made vast sums available for profitable investment in the private sector and also saddled the government with enormous debts, later ascribed to the character of public ownership. The new state-owned industries were administered by boards, or public corporations, and seated on their governing councils were men still associated with private industry. From a functional point of view little substantive change had taken place.[1]

In foreign affairs, Labour pursued the policy inherited from its predecessors in office. Bevin found the Russians intransigent and Western Europe weak and exposed. He decided on full cooperation with the United States. The Left repudiated the party's support of Western European defensive alignments. It preferred a neutralist position to bridge the widening gulf between East and West in the Cold War. It urged the party to "keep left." There was less to complain of with regard to the Empire. India, Burma, and Ceylon were granted independence. Only Burma refused to maintain its ties with Britain in the Commonwealth. The parliamentary term expired in 1950. In the election held in February, only 315 Labour candidates (and 298 Conservatives) were elected. The Labour program had called for additional reform, particularly in education. Loyal trade union support made the victory possible. With the Cold War well underway and with the establishment of the *Cominform* in 1947 (Stalin had abolished the Comintern in 1943 as a goodwill gesture to his Western allies), union leaders feared communist infiltration. They reacted by expelling communists and supporting Bevin's policies all the more arduously.

Divisions nevertheless intensified. Economies forced on the Ministry of Health by Hugh Gaitskell (who had replaced Cripps at the Board of Trade when the latter died) led to the resignations of Bevan and then Harold Wilson at the Ministry of Commerce. Attlee estimated that a stronger majority was necessary and called for another election. Thanks to renovated electoral machinery and to a redistribution of seats that benefited the less highly concentrated Tory vote, the Conservative party won a small 26-seat plurality. It was to remain in office almost 13 years. Still, it would not dismantle the welfare state that had been established in Britain.

FRENCH SOCIALISM: TRIPARTISM TO THIRD FORCE

Basking in the glory of the resistance, French socialism did not attempt structural transformations, in either its own organization or for society as a whole. The SFIO expelled those who had voted for Marshal Pétain. Party regulars, however, particularly in the countryside, were suspicious of the new "resistance men," and the latter were not integrated into party ranks. Also rejected was any ideological facelifting. Léon Blum defended a more humanistic version of socialism, one that would subordinate the class-struggle concept and materialistic determinism to individual emancipation and fulfillment. Chief spokesman for this position was Daniel Mayer, but it foundered on the opposition of Marcel Pivert and the young deputy from Arras, a former English teacher, Guy Mollet. They were determined to have the

SFIO remain a class party committed to anticlericalism. A party congress in 1946 approved this stand and named Mollet secretary. More a neo-Guesdist than a Marxist, Mollet led this congress to accept a *Declaration of Principles* embodying demands for collectivization and reaffirming the "class" and "revolutionary" nature of the party. When General de Gaulle resigned suddenly as chief of the provisional government in January, 1946, socialist leader Felix Gouin replaced him. In the next few months the Assembly nationalized the gas and electricity industries, insurance, mines, the Bank of France and the chief deposit banks, and transportation.

The SFIO agreed with Blum not to fuse with the communists, and the two parties ran separate lists in every election. However, the party joined with communists and Christian democrats in a tripartite electoral and parliamentary coalition. Situated between their two partners, they received most cabinet posts, and one of their chiefs, Vincent Auriol, was voted the first president of the new Fourth Republic. The government of the socialist Paul Ramadier began to implement the *Monnet Plan* for remodernization and retooling.

However, the tripartite regime came to an end as the Cold War worsened. Like their counterparts in the Labour party, French socialists found themselves settled in the Western camp. One country after another in the East fell to communist control, and Communist party support of a wave of strikes in France in the summer of 1947 was seen as a prelude to the same process at home. Ramadier dismissed the communist ministers in his cabinet. The PCF, consequently, entered the opposition and was to remain there. French socialists experienced few misgivings. They had seen their colleagues in the East imprisoned, and remained convinced that communist leaders placed the interests of the USSR over those of France. The anticommunist reflex that developed eased the country's entry into the Atlantic alliance.

Consequently, there was a change in socialist strategy. The SFIO was required to cooperate with centrist parties to form a *third force,* equally opposed to communism on the Left and De Gaulle's Rally of the French People movement (seen by some socialists as possessing fascist overtones) on the Right. But cooperation with the Center meant the abandonment of much of the socialist program. The 1951 elections favored the *third force* parties (socialists returned 106 deputies, a loss of 40). By refusing to support state financing of private (religious) schools, the SFIO, however, could no longer collaborate with Christian Democrats. As on so many other occasions in French political history, the Right was able to take advantage of these divisions. It formed a cabinet under Antoine Pinay in March, 1952. Aside from the Radical government of Pierre Mendès-France in 1954–1955 and that put together by Mollet a year later, socialists and the French Left have remained in the opposition ever since.

SOCIALISM IN BELGIUM, AUSTRIA, AND ITALY

A somewhat similar pattern emerged in Belgium. Socialists and social Christians formed a left-wing coalition government immediately after the war. Then Paul-Henri Spaak presided over a socialist ministry until 1949. In that year, the opposition won the elections, and aside from coalition cabinets in 1954–1958 and again in 1961–1966, repeatedly formed governments. The situation in Austria approximated that in France and Belgium. Karl Renner was named president of the republic and socialists participated in coalition governments between 1947 and 1966. It then went into the opposition.

Although represented in Christian democratic governments in 1945 and 1946, Italian socialism departed from this pattern of postwar participation in or control of government followed by opposition to it. The party was torn by schisms. Because a section of the PSI insisted on close cooperation with the communists, moderates broke away and reconstituted themselves as the Social Democratic party. It was led by Giuseppe Saragat, returned from the United States, and the antifascist writer, Ignazio Silone. Pietro Nenni spoke for those seeking to maintain a communist alliance. The PCI was headed by Togliatti. All in keeping a revolutionary outlook, he displayed a greater flexibility than did his equivalents in France and wanted once more to have his party participate in government. Under Nenni, the PSI kept its electoral coalition with the communists for over a decade, but it was the Saragat faction that joined in Christian Democratic-led coalition governments. The main socialist party was not to become part of any center-left coalition until 1963.

SOCIALISM IN THE OPPOSITION

Within a few years after the war, European socialists found themselves in the opposition. In West Germany they had never come to power. In Eastern Europe they were engulfed by communism in the late forties; in the West, by Cold War realities and by the appeal of a liberal capitalism. In the 1950s socialist parties everywhere were on the defensive. Their successive defeats were to have profound strategic and ideological effects.

THE PEOPLE'S DEMOCRACIES

A curious form of postwar government emerged in lands marked either by the reactionary rule of large landholders between the two world wars, or by open support of Germany during World War II, or both. Aside from Bohemia, great landed estates predominated; in the scattered industrial sectors, foreign investment prevailed, giving them a semicolonial status. The effects of war were devastating. Germany had exterminated 20 percent of the Polish population, particularly intellectuals, and 17 percent of that in Yugoslavia. Famine and economic ruin were characteristic of the postwar social and economic scene.

Resistance movements were strong in Eastern Europe, but unlike in France, they were represented in postwar coalition governments. Composed of such diverse forces, they could agree on short-term programs focusing on economic recovery and reprisals against Nazi collaborators. Long-range objectives differed, but all contained fundamental agrarian reforms and at least the beginnings of nationalization plans. Socialism attracted support in advocating an end to the authority of the landed estates and in limiting that of the aristocracy and church. Would these coalition governments (or, as they were known, people's democracies) return to a modified capitalism or would they press on to socialism once their reforms were carried oue? If the latter had occurred, there would most certainly have been a major political struggle, for champions of both causes were amply represented. Property holders, the church (particularly influential in Poland and Hungary), and parts of the liberal middle classes would have confronted peasants demanding greater agricultural reform and workers profiting from social legislation.[2]

The issue was never joined. The democracies fell subject to communist rule. With the subjugation of Czechoslovakia in 1948, the process was complete. These states became Soviet satellites, and, as the examples of Hungary and Czechoslovakia proved in 1956 and 1968, remained very much under Soviet control. Independent and social democratic regimes, it became clear, were not to be tolerated behind the Iron Curtain. What brought about the demise of the postwar democracies in Eastern Europe?

For Western historiography the answer is clear. The presence of the Red army and the support given by the Soviet Union to local communist leaders put socialists and other democrats under an impossible handicap. Anticommunist leaders of socialist parties were either not permitted to return from Nazi-imposed exile, or once returned forced to flee. Within the provisional governments, communists got hold of key cabinet posts: particularly police and communications. Socialists were induced to accept united-front agreements with communists, who proposed common lists of candidates. If the Socialists refused and (as in Czechoslovakia) had majority support, police were called on to oust their leaders from power. After elections were held, communists proposed a merger of the two parties, and with the support of deputies elected on the combined lists, were able to enforce their demands. Then "unconvinced" socialists and other opponents were expelled. A mass party emerged, with socialist followers, but led by reliable pro-Soviet leaders.[3]

There is considerable truth in this scenario, but it is incomplete. The presence of the Russian armies that did so much to eject the popular democracies cannot be used to explain their establishment.[4] The very legitimate influence and support of communists in Eastern Europe immediately after the war and the extent to which anticommunist forces were agents of their own isolation is passed over—their discountenance of wholesale agricultural reform, for example. There appears to be some evidence, moreover, that noncommunist parties in Rumania and Hungary were forced out of the government by popular (as opposed to Soviet-inspired) hostility. Their distintegration permitted communists to *satellize* the left wing of these parties and created national—but communist controlled—fronts, and socialists committed to democratic processes were repressed.

THE SPD IN THE OPPOSITION

A glance at Europe's leading socialist parties reveals the extent of their difficulties while in an opposition role in the 1950s and early 1960s. It will also permit us to appreciate the major doctrinal and strategic changes generated by their lack of success.

The Social Democratic party (SPD) in Germany differed from its French and British equivalents in that it did not fall from power. Socialists in West Germany long played a secondary role to the Christian Democratic Union (CDU) of Konrad Adenauer and his successors. This party, together with its Bavarian allies, dominated German political life between 1949 (when the Federal Republic was established) and 1969. This in itself requires explanation. Of all the parties, the socialist party emerged from the Nazi holocaust with an unblemished record. It had been outlawed and decimated under Hitler. Certainly, the inability of the SPD to take the power it anticipated receiving was not due to the presence of a strong and competitive communist party. Although initially authorized by the allies in 1945 as antifascist, the KPD (Communist party) never received more than a fraction of the vote and in 1956 was outlawed as incompatible with the "fundamental liberal and democratic order."

In part, the explanation rested with the new tragedy that socialism —and Germany—experienced after 1945. The division of the country into eastern and western zones deprived the party in the West of its Protestant and working-class majority. Women voters tended to support the Christian Democrats. It also rested on the personality of the SPD chief, Kurt Schumacher. Intensely patriotic but equally anti-fascist, he had been interred in a concentration camp. Schumacher met with Erich Ollenhauer, a member of the party's executive committee in exile in London, and Otto Grotewohl, who had returned from the USSR. The SPD chief rejected any fusion between the socialist and communist parties. Like his predecessors in the Weimar Republic, he was convinced that communism would return to its Moscow orbit. Subsequently, a unified socialist party under communist control emerged in the east.

The election of September, 1949 gave the CDU one vote more than the number required for a parliamentary majority, made Adenauer chancellor, and forced the SPD into an opposition role. Schumacher insisted on comprehensive nationalization at home and an independent foreign policy abroad. The Hanover Congress of May, 1946, the party's first since the war, recalled the aid received by Hitler from the business classes and stated that capitalism always constituted a threat to democracy. Schumacher adamantly opposed Adenauer on the Saar and Ruhr issues, rearmament, and the integration of Germany into the Atlantic camp. He saw in all these things obstacles to German reunification. He was determined to respect what he regarded as national feeling and not repeat the mistake made by the party in 1919—hence his categorical denial of the collective responsibility of the German people for the war and the atrocities committed. As Cold War intensified, Berlin became its leading battlefield. It was Adenauer, rather than Schumacher and his socialists, who was favored by allied officials unwilling to distinguish clearly between democratic socialism and communism.

Party affairs, as before 1933, remained in the hands of a bureaucracy. It was fully parliamentary, yet used revolutionary terminology and so discouraged potential voters. Strong personalities in local or municipal governments, concerned more with efficiency and results than with ideology, could not dent party machinery. The SPD adopted no new program; it continued to use that ratified by its Heidelberg Congress of 1925. Identification of his party with a class, not with the population in its entirety, deprived Schumacher of wider support. Moreover, the growing prosperity of postwar Germany, carried out along liberal lines, shed luster on nonsocialist approaches (ignoring the absence of wasteful arms expenditures as well as the examples of similar increases in places like Sweden, where socialists governed; in Austria, Denmark, Holland, and Switzerland, where they participated in government.)[5] There would be no ideological weakening, however, until after Schumacher's death in 1952 and replacement by Ollenhauer. The party never managed to win an election. Cold-war events seemed to conspire against it. The Berlin blockade preceded the election of 1949; the uprising in East Germany, the election of 1953; the Soviet invasion of Hungary, that of 1957; and the Berlin Wall went up shortly before the election of 1961. All of these events suggested the exercise of prudence to German voters.

BRITISH LABOUR OUT OF POWER

Socialist parties elsewhere in Europe also held minority status. The fortunes of each were subject to local conditions, but some uniformities emerged. Because socialist or socialist-inspired regimes governed immediately after the war, they administered the wage cuts, rationing, restrictions of trade union freedom, and other austerity measures dictated by scarcity. They suffered a loss of popularity and saw new stringency legislation become confused with socialism in the minds of voters. These measures were carried out most easily in England, where a strong civic sense prevailed. On the continent, however, there was widespread evasion and a considerable black market. Disobedience, after all, had been an expression of patriotism under Nazi-imposed regimes. Controls were viewed as intolerable and associated with socialist governments, doctrinally identified with restrictions on the free operation of the marketplace. The longing for economic liberalism was translated into conservative victories. Only subsequent research, moreover, can determine the extent to which American influence furthered this evolution. The United States enjoyed great authority, and, whether intentional or not, its example and presence in such agencies as those administering aid under the Marshall Plan worked against socialist parties and favored laissez-faire liberals.[6] For its part, socialism seemed unable to respond. It retained its class identity, and middle-class growth therefore worked to perpetuate its minority status. No longer revolutionary, but bristling with revolutionary symbolism, socialists turned many voters aside.

The division within the party brought about by the hostility of Bevan and other left-wingers explained Labour's weakened position in 1951. It also helped to explain why, once defeated, it remained out of office for so long. The Left wanted to reduce military spending and move away from the Atlantic alliance. It also sought more explicitly socialist measures, like a tax on capital. It profited from disappointment that the nationalized industries were proving no panacea. Economic growth slackened. Sick industries like coal and railways provided a partial explanation. And Labour's policies, while helping to keep employment figures stable, did not expand productivity.

The party's left wing had long promoted efforts to win approval of more radical programs. It worked under the slogan "socialism in our time" after the failure of the first MacDonald government in 1924. Elements of the Left organized the Socialist League after the collapse of the second MacDonald government in 1931. The militant journal established by the League, *The Tribune,* either helped to initiate or stood behind every successive left-wing campaign. In the 1950s, supported by the influential *New Statesman,* the Left rallied under the leadership provided by Bevan.

To be sure, the divisions within Labour did not by themselves explain the party's inability to return to power. Its electoral machinery had been allowed to run down. Wisely, Conservatives did not reverse Labour's achievements and profited therefrom. The welfare state was not dismantled, and aside from trucking and steel, nationalized industries were left alone. Labour's subsequent losses in 1955 and 1959, however, made its defeat look conclusive.

THE NEWEST REVISIONISM

GAITSKELL AND WILSON

In Labour's prolonged absence from power, mutual recriminations and faultfinding intensified divisions. They were expressed most bitterly in the debates over the foreign policy Labour was to follow. In 1952, at the height of the Korean War, the party executive favored rearmament in principle. Fifty-five Labour MPs rejected the heavy costs this would involve. Bevanites managed to win a number of seats on the executive and expelled Morrison and Dalton from it. It 1955, 62 MPs refused construction of the hydrogen bomb and demanded firm restrictions on its use. Bevan, who opposed the rearmament of Germany, had quit the shadow cabinet the year before. But he returned after the disastrous Suez invasion by the Eden government had aroused hopes for a Labour victory, provided the party could close ranks. The able Harold MacMillan, however, replaced Eden and kept the Conservatives in power.

As the Left sought more radical policies, the executive, since 1955 in the hands of Hugh Gaitskell, wanted to revise the collectivist elements in the party's program. Repeated and larger electoral defeats had prompted this reexamination of party objectives. Was a Labour party with its class bias viable in postwar Britain? Gaitskell estimated that demands for nationalization constituted a liability at the polls and were irrelevant in a *postcapitalist* society. His wish to have the party accept a mixed economy stemmed from the *New Fabian Essays,* published in 1952, and C. A. R. Crosland's *The Future of Socialism,* in 1957. Both works attempted to analyze the party's inadequacies

in the period 1946–1951 and to provide a program when it was returned to office. The latter, especially, became something of a text for
the party chief. Crosland wanted to have the party drop its ideological baggage and focus on the modernization of industry, both private
and public. He would make efficiency and not status-of-ownership
the test. He would also lay stress on social rather than on economic
goals and work for improvements in education to eliminate class distinctions.

However, Gaitskell was unable to persuade the party to drop
Point IV, the clause in its program calling for common ownership of
the means of production and exchange. At Labour's Scarborough Conference in 1960, he was also unable to overcome left-wing opposition
to nuclear disarmament. It sought the unilateral disarmament of nuclear weapons. For the first time since 1931 a Labour leader was defeated on a major issue in party conference. Much of the explanation
lay in the fact that the trade unions, long moderate, now supported
the Left. They were spoken for by Frank Cousins, the militant chief
of the Transport and General Workers Union, who rejected all nuclear defense and wanted a return to a more socialist-sounding program. Given the huge bloc vote held by the trade unions at party
conferences, their opposition sufficed to defeat the leadership.

However, this left-wing pressure did not turn the party from its
antiideological course. The same Scarborough Conference ratified an
executive declaration which, while alluding in theory to class conflict
and socialist objectives, held that "both public and private enterprise
have a place in the economy." Evidently, the party was interested
more in winning over the middle classes than in its own Left and
demonstrated that it was more of a rival than an enemy of the Conservatives. Gaitskell stumped the country to win approval of his hostility to unilateral nulcear disarmament. Its supporters found they
were in a minority. Three trade unions reversed their earlier stand,
and at the party's Blackpool Conference the following year, the leadership's policies carried by a 3 to 1 margin. The executive shared the
Left's hostility to closer affiliation with Europe. Gaitskell opposed entry
into the Common Market as indicating "the end of a thousand years
of history" and was seconded by Cousins.

The succession to Gaitskell (who died young) by Harold Wilson
marked no change in the party's development, for Wilson was no
longer the militant who had supported Bevan. On a platform calling
for the renationalization of steel, greater government subsidies for
housing, and restored economic growth, Labour won a 24-seat majority in the election of 1964. The party could subsequently claim a
number of successes: an increase in old-age pensions, the removal of
charges on medical prescriptions, a capital gains tax, the abolition of

capital punishment, more housing starts, and the approval of wage increases (by a government board established to keep down inflation). Wilson increased his majority to 64 two years later. However, his government was beset by economic problems, particularly an adverse balance of payments. The pound was devalued at the end of 1967 in an attempt to bolster exports. The white minority in Rhodesia broke away from British rule, and the policy of sanctions, designed to bring down the regime in weeks, failed dismally.

The government's support of America's Vietnam policy aroused the most intense hostility of the Left. Wilson was determined to keep close ties with the United States, in part as an attempt to ease his country's financial woes. He lost further credibility in refusing entry to British citizens of Asian descent and unwanted by newly independent east African republics. The country was frightened of mass colored immigration. Finally, he reversed his stand on the Common Market. A long-time opponent of British entry—or more precisely an advocate on the basis of terms (like keeping Commonwealth trading advantages) that could never be accepted by the European Economic Community—Wilson was converted to the pro-Market position in 1966. Britain plus the Market, it was held, could best resist American domination. After his surprise defeat in June, 1970 and the success of the Conservative Prime Minister Edward Heath in negotiating an entry, Wilson and the Labour Left rejoined forces and unsuccessfully fought parliamentary approval.

The Labour defeat ran counter to forecasts made on the basis of public opinion polls. The country had brighter economic prospects as devaluation and import restrictions seemed to work, although at the cost of lower productivity. The party's inability to end inflation (the pound had lost nearly half its purchasing power since 1953), coupled with frozen wages and high taxes, proved decisive for the voters, and Conservatives won a majority of 31 seats. During the campaign, there was little talk of socialism.

In retrospect, the revisionism espoused by Gaitskell appears to have won out. Will Labour take on the shape of an American political party, "an election machine" lacking ideology or the support of a mass movement? Many of Labour's young technocrats prefer precisely this. They want to modernize the party, master television, advertising, and market-research techniques in order to learn of the public's wants, and make party programs compatible. Accordingly, they want Labour to drop whatever doctrinal orientation that remains and present a more dynamic image. This, they say, will appeal to an electorate which is becoming classless and nonideological. The Left, on the other hand, sees the party as still embarked on a crusade for socialism. A complicating feature has been the emergence of a new and revolutionary Left. Stimulated by the French students and workers uprising in May, 1968 and consisting largely of young people, this revolutionary Left has not joined the party, despite pleas to do so and make its voice heard. This new Left is probably right in saying that socialism will not come through Parliament. Party regulars are probably right in saying it will not come through revolution.

Gaitskell's failure to have his party drop its goal of public ownership of the means of production and distribution (not to be confused with collectivization—there are various forms of common ownership, including state, municipal, and cooperative) has been all but forgotten. The Labour party may be identified as progressive and reformist, aiming at a speedy return to office. Responsible for the revisionist surge has been the party's very success in constructing a welfare state, its long tradition of parliamentarianism, its monopoly on detailed policy thinking (Bevanites, for example, were little interested in the complexities of taxation and administering the welfare state), and Gaitskell's qualities of leadership.[7] The victory, however, has been costly, leaving a residue of bitterness and suspicion.

THE GERMAN SOCIALISTS DISCARD MARXISM

The Labour party threatened to forego the socialist aspects of its program and become a progressive liberal party in theory as well as practice. German Social Democracy has actually done so. For a growing number of members, the solution to the party's inability to win an election lay in its abandonment of Marxist principles and closer identification with the populace as a whole. At its Berlin Congress in 1954, the SPD resolved to focus on inadequacies in the government's economic policies and downplay nationalization. It laid stress on the need for a more equitable distribution of national income and for economic planning. The absence of attacks from both Right and Left (as under Weimar) no longer made defense of the movement a primary objective. Greater foreign stability, thaws in the Cold War, a more prosperous working class, and Schumacher's death all lessened the need for ideological appeals and permitted consideration of winning a broader electoral base. Moreover, a new generation of leaders, men who gained popularity after the war, moved into the SPD executive. When they consolidated their position, reformers were in control of party machinery.[8]

The electoral defeat of 1957 and the ability of the Christian Democrats to win an absolute majority in the upper house provided further ammunition to those who advocated discarding the party's Marxist base. Resolutions adopted at congresses in that and the following year indicated the change in course made official at Godesberg. At the Bad Godesberg Congress in 1959, a new program was substituted for the one held since Heidelberg in 1925. It offered a humanistic ideal—the self-fulfillment of the individual—for the economic determinism long professed. The plurality of views within the party was acknowledged; only the fundamental moral values agreed on by all were to be implemented. Socialist roots were explicitly listed as Christian ethics, classical philosophy, and humanism.

The Social Democratic party identified itself not as one of the working class, but of all the people. It called for a mixed economy, a middle way between collectivism and capitalism. It accepted the free market and rejected central planning for the entire economy. Specifically abandoned was the "eschatology of nationalization." The formula employed asked for "as much competition as possible; as much planning as necessary." Because economic power and not property was important, the party would oppose its concentration in either state or private hands, but vaguely asked only for economic decentralization. Also vague were references to the representation of labor's interest, the public interest, and consumers' interests in managerial structures. Anticlerical statements were avoided; the basic law of the Federal Republic was to be obeyed. Struggle, then, would take place only along "democratic" lines, and communists were denounced as "radically oppressing liberty . . . and violating the rights of men and the right of self-determination of men and peoples."

The program was conspicuous for what it omitted; it made no mention of Marx's name or of terms like "class" and "class struggle." No social doctrine was offered; democracy was seen as an end and no longer as merely a means. The document was characterized throughout by restraint. In its wish to appear capable of governing, the SPD also jettisoned its foreign policy. The party had opposed the Schumacher Plan in 1952 (because of the clerical and capitalist nature of its subscribers) and the European Defense Community (EDC) (as an obstacle to reunification and to closing the gap between the West and the Soviet Union). The party had preferred to cooperate with states containing strong socialist movements. It now accepted NATO as the necessary condition for reunification, with West Germany paying its fair share—that is, the party accepted the basic premises of the CDU's foreign-policy program.

The SPD registered only a slight improvement in the 1961 election, receiving 36 percent of the vote to the CDU's 45 percent. Its candidate for chancellor was the mayor of West Berlin, the attractive Willy Brandt. He replaced Ollenhauer as head of the party on the latter's death in December of 1963. Yet another disappointment was experienced in the election of 1965. The defeat further encouraged the rise of men with political experience at municipal and regional levels. Was ample opportunity for expression given to those within the SPD who rejected its adoption of an evermore pragmatic outlook? The answer must await further research. However, in 1959 the critical SDS (German Association of Socialist Students) was expelled. Four years earlier, the hostile revue, *Die andere Zeitung,* run by former *Vorwärts* editors, was denounced as a communist dupe.

The fall of the Erhard government in November, 1966 left the SPD with little choice other than to enter into a *Grand Coalition* with the CDU and the latter's Bavarian affiliate. Christian Democrats had not wanted to govern with the Free Democratic party, considered as an unsure ally, yet lacked the absolute majority required to govern alone. On the other hand, an SDP-FDP coalition enjoyed only a 6-vote plurality. (Liberal in outlook, the Free Democrats held economic views similar to those of the CDU, becoming more sympathetic to some state intervention, but insisting on maintaining a clear distinction between church and state. More significantly, a minority of FDP members wanted to grant diplomatic recognition to the German Democratic Republic [DDR] in the east.)

This decision ended one of the gravest political crises faced by the Federal Republic. Still, many members of the SDP disapproved of their party's entry into Chancellor Kurt Kiesenger's cabinet on December 1, 1966. Participation in power benefited the party, as the policy's chief instigator, Herbert Wehner, had predicted. It permitted the SDP to shed the stigma of opposition and endowed it with greater legitimacy. It showed itself capable of governing, and its leaders—Brandt was Minister of Foreign Affairs—received public exposure. The party was thereupon able to propose bolder policies, and so gave voters the opportunity to judge it with greater confidence in the 1969 and 1972 elections. Brandt opened a new relationship with the communist world to the east. He restored diplomatic ties with Yugoslavia and Rumania and paved the way for others. As minister for all German affairs, Wehner proposed expanded contacts with the German Democratic Republic. Minister of Economics Karl Schiller eased the country out of the recession that had contributed to Erhard's fall in 1966. Still, there was considerable fear that the absence of any opposition could hardly enhance the image of German democracy.

The election of September 28, 1969 made possible an SDP-FDP governing coalition. The single greatest initiative taken in the years that followed was in the realm of foreign affairs. First the Social Democrats, then the Free Democrats, and finally a good part of the population became aware that, without repudiating Adenauer's policy, greater freedom from the U. S. and France, and greater realism in the nation's relationship with East Germany and the Soviet Union had to be explored. A nonaggression pact was signed with Russia in August, 1970. This was followed by pacts with the German Democratic Republic and Poland. In recognizing the Oder-Niesse line as the boundary between the two, the "inviolability" (as contrasted to the "permanence") of Germany's boundaries was affirmed. In 1971 agreements were reached over the status of Berlin, and in that year Brandt won the Nobel Peace Prize. The victory of November 19, 1972, when the SPD topped the conservative opposition for the first time since the founding of the Federal Republic in 1949, revealed widespread voter approval of his Eastern Policy.

In reevaluating the mark, Schiller had dealt successfully with the recession of 1966–1967. He convinced Germans that the SPD could defend their living standards and dispelled suspicions that the party would resort to provoking inflation as a means of ensuring full employment. The party was penetrating Catholic groups and the middle classes. The CDU took on a more conservative image and received greater support in the rural sectors.

Although reestablished in 1969, the Communist party has not aroused any appreciable response from West German voters. It wants to win to its ranks all those to the left of the SPD. More significant as competition is the so-called New Left. The young feel ideologically frustrated by what they see as SPD compromises with capitalism. Neo-Marxists within the party defy its leadership, which prohibits collaboration with the communists. They admire the Yugoslav model of workers participation in managerial decisions as more meaningful than the "co-determination" scheme set up by Christian Democrats and accepted by socialists. They also seek structural reforms in German industrial life and are eager to organize international trade union action in order to confront the power of multinational corporations within the European Economic Community. Their strategy aims at winning control of local governments, in much the same manner as the revisionists first contested the party bureaucracy.

To what degree did the party owe its success at the polls to its new, nonideological program? The answer remains a matter of speculation. Certainly, other explanations may be offered. They include a relaxation in the cold war situation, the Catholic Church's (or Pope Paul's) greater acceptance of the SPD, the increase in the size of the urban working-class vote (presumably at the expense of the rural vote), and the inability of the CDU to find a suitable replacement for the prestigious Adenauer.

German socialists were especially gratified to see an Austrian socialist victory within a few months of their own. On March 1, 1970, the Austrian party ended 25 years of conservative or coalition rule. The party had gradually come to adopt a revisionist program, dropping its revolutionary and anticlerical tone. It narrowly lost the election of 1966, but this time went into the opposition rather than participate in a governing coalition. Four years later Bruno Kreisky formed a socialist government and became the country's first Jewish chancellor.

CONTEMPORARY FRENCH AND ITALIAN SOCIALISM AND COMMUNISM

The presence of larger and stronger communist parties on their left made the situations of the French and Italian socialist parties exceptional. Unable to expose themselves to charges of betraying working-class interests, and reluctant to leave the field to communist parties enjoying more members, voters, and trade union control, socialists in these two countries did not abandon Marxist ideology. Still, many years in the opposition or as junior partners in conservative-dominated coalitions accounted for revisionist overtures and the rejection of class militancy. In both nations the unification of the Left is a prerequisite for its return to power. France, for example, is the only Western democracy in which the Left has been out of office for a decade and a half.

It was natural for dissent to crystallize as French socialism spent long years in the opposition. Repeated and legitimate complaints were made about the lack of democracy within the party. Critics charged its executive with subordinating questions of doctrine and strategy to those of organization and apparatus. Only tried and tested members—that is, those loyal to the leadership, were installed in positions of influence, while younger people, or those with differing views were excluded. In theory, the executive was popularly elected and representative of all views. In practice, the party was dominated by its secretary-general. He relied on the support of a handful of powerful regional federations, assuring him a majority in party congresses. Dissidents could not gain much of a foothold in either the party's executive councils or its press. Consequently, criticism was sporadic and spontaneous, expressed in nonofficial meetings and publications.

The gradual bureaucratization and embourgeoisement of the SFIO after World War I became more rapid after 1945. Party members tended to come from small towns and from the ranks of white-collar employees, particularly civil servants. Perhaps as much as one-third of the nation's lower echelon civil servants voted socialist. As it "matured," the party displayed ever less dynamism. It could no longer win mass support or keep that of intellectuals. Its ideology, like its name, was that adopted in 1905—only anticommunist themes had been added. Certainly, socialists lacked any coherent or carefully formulated economic program. Those who had tried to present one, many of the party's best thinkers (including men like André Philip), were driven off and so lost to politics. The SFIO lost members gradually and, aside from the success in 1956, steadily. From over 350,000 in 1946 there were fewer than 100,000 in 1960. In the first postwar election of 1945 it had won 23 percent of the vote and returned 139 deputies. By 1962 it could claim only 12 to 15 percent of the vote and 40 deputies.

French socialists were also divided over national issues throughout the 1950s. Many opposed economic or political integration into a community composed of capitalist and Catholic governments, into what they called a *Black International*. The party split over German rearmament. If the executive forced its acceptance at an extraordinary congress in 1954, socialist opposition in the Chamber of Deputies helped bring about the defeat of the European Defense Community.

The major crisis within the party, however, stemmed from debates over the Algerian War. No group of French socialists, like the Fabians in British Labour, had ever developed a comprehensive approach for the party on imperial matters. While its record on decolonization was not particularly good, the SFIO had condemned the war in Indochina. Socialists initially opposed government repression of the Algerian rebels. After the election of 1956 and the victory of a socialist and Radical coalition (the success of many right-wing Poujadist candidates indicated this was more of a protest vote than a swing to the left), Mollet became premier. Although he had campaigned on a promise to end the war, he reversed his position during a trip to Algiers and called for the repression of the rebel National Liberation Front. Gaston Deferre, Alain Savary, and other critics charged him with having yielded to the pressure of the Europeans in Algeria and of nationalists at home, and consequently, with having debased socialist ideals. Mollet and his supporters denied sustaining a colonial elite and held that only a French presence could prevent a dictatorship and the suppression of individual liberties. They also pointed to the government's domestic accomplishments (an increase in retirement benefits, longer paid vacations, and agricultural reform) and argued that only a pro-Algerian foreign policy could retain the support of the Chamber. To his credit, Mollet resigned when it became clear that he would have to sacrifice his reform program in order to stay in office. The party executive was doubtless unnerved by the intense criticism; it had defended with equal vigor every act of the government, even the invasion of Suez, however incompatible with socialist thinking.

The advent of the Fifth Republic proved disastrous to the SFIO. It produced the first of several schisms, along with the need to rethink objectives and strategies in a presidential regime. A small number of socialists, following the lead of Mollet and regional chiefs like Gaston Deferre, supported De Gaulle's investiture in May, 1958 and ratification of his new constitution the following November. Three socialists, including Mollet, joined De Gaulle's cabinet but resigned within a year. They gave as reasons for their initial support the wish to avoid both a military dictatorship and a communist-dominated popular front.

Still, several party leaders and 5 or 6 thousand members rejected the Gaullist republic. They broke away in November to form an autonomous socialist party. Led by Edouard Depreux and former minister Alain Savary, it later combined with other left-wing groups hostile to the SFIO to create a unified socialist party (PSU). Other discontented socialists, opposed to the evolution of the Fifth Republic toward a stronger executive, preferred affiliation with independent political clubs.

Hostility to the party leadership and concern with modernizing party structure had emerged in the Fourth Republic. The development of a powerful presidential regime furthered it and was to produce for the first time in French socialist history a program of detailed objectives and procedures. (The party possessed only its 1905 *Declaration of Unity* and Blum's 1946 *Statement of Principles*.) With a minority of deputies, the SFIO had been able to form a government in 1956 that could survive for 16 months. Now the Gaullists enjoyed a massive parliamentary delegation of 231 deputies (after the 1962 election; as the second largest party, socialists held 66 seats) and considerable power was held by the president of the Republic. Clearly, the size of a party was vital to its chances for success. These new circumstances gave rise to discussions about the SFIO's role and future.

The former socialist minister of the interior, Jules Moch, had previously urged the formation of study groups, and their reports had been published in the party's *Revue socialiste* between 1959 and 1961. André Philip, expelled in 1958 for denouncing the Mollet "dictatorship," had wanted to give the party a humanist dimension and turn it toward comprehensive economic planning. Dissidents had joined with Christian Socialists and Mendès-France Radicals. At the same time, the need to unite the forces of the Left was more obvious than ever, that is, ally with the communists.

The outcome of these efforts and deliberations was a new *Fundamental Program*, ratified in 1962. It was not revisionist—the SFIO had not experienced a *Godesberg*—and was received with considerable indifference. Still, it marked a more revisionist stand than that taken in 1946. It omitted direct references to collectivism or to the class struggle. It called for transferring the means of production to the community only when warranted by economic oppression. The new program recognized the rapid growth of the tertiary sector of the economy, but offered no tactics for winning over the middle classes. The same Mollet who had criticized Blum's efforts to *deradicalize* the party in 1946 said 15 years later that the SFIO was revolutionary only in the sense that changing an economic system was revolutionary; it was not synonymous with *bloody revolt*.[9]

Why did the French and Italian socialist parties fail to embrace revisionism as had the German (explicitly) and British (tacitly) parties? The role played by revolutionary tradition cannot easily be dismissed. Much of the explanation, however, rests on the presence of powerful communist parties in both countries and on an understandable reluctance by socialists operating in multiparty regimes to risk losing their working-class support. Unlike the essentially two-party systems of Britain and Germany (Liberals and Free Democrats scarcely make these systems analogous to those found in the two Latin republics), there was no large uncommitted vote to be won. Certainly, there were few independent voters on the Left, where every position had found political expression. Hence the absence of doctrinal revision in the Fourth French Republic, its continued absence within the main Italian socialist party, but its beginnings in the Fifth French Republic. The huge Gaullist majority necessitated a new approach.[10]

Together with demands for revision came those for the establishment of an alliance with the communists, who were beginning to show signs of at least theoretical modification. The advantages of an alliance were demonstrated in the election of 1962. Mutual withdrawals in favor of the stronger candidate on the run-off vote increased the number of deputies returned by both parties. Not all socialists, however, could accept a communist alliance. Like Gaston Deferre, they preferred to create a new political force by uniting the noncommunist Left and extending it toward the center. Hence the complexities of the French and Italian political scene. Pressure for change came from both Right and Left, and at the same time.

Since the emergence of the Cold War, fear of the communist parties had become a hallmark of Western socialist life. The French party was especially subservient to Moscow, having been thoroughly *Stalinized* in the thirties and forties. The PCF denounced unequivocally the Titoist heresy. It staged trials of dissidents who had refused to toe the party line. It even rejected any active role in the Algerian War debate because of the priority placed by the Soviet Union on retaining the support of French nationalists opposed to German rearmament. Although in opposition since 1947, it retained municipal strength, control of the General Confederation of Labor, and regularly amassed about a fourth of the vote in nationwide elections.

As the Gaullist majority showed no signs of weakening, the PCF began to reassess its role as a political party. If followed the lead of the more flexible Italian Communist party and accepted the thesis of polycentrism in international communism. It acquiesced in such revisionist overtures to social democracy as the theoretical affirmation of the pluralism of parties in a socialist regime and the toleration of previously inadmissible divergencies from the executive's stated position. In May, 1968 the French Communist party played no part in the general strike that followed the students' uprising. Rather it negotiated with the Pompidou government to get the workers back on their jobs—much to the disgust of the revolutionary Left. Aware of changes in the labor force brought about by modern industrial society and of the absence of any substantial increase in the number of blue collar workers in the previous decade and a half, PCF Chief Georges Marchais, in 1971, envisaged a wholesale revaluation of party strategy.

Earlier, however, most Frenchmen—and socialists—were not at all sure that once democratically elected, the PCF, in the event of a subsequent defeat, would voluntarily relinquish power. Still, there seemed little alternative if the Left was to return to power. The presidential election of 1965 provided another opportunity for an electoral alliance. The SFIO, elements of the Radical party, and most of the political clubs came together on behalf of the candidacy of François Mitterand. The communists gave him unconditional support. He won 45 percent of the vote and forced De Gaulle to an unprecedented second vote. The alliance was renewed for the legislative elections of 1967. There was no common program other than hostility to Gaullist objectives and approaches. Even so the communists won 73 seats and the allied noncommunist Left, 116 (of which the SFIO held 76).

This alliance fell apart after the sweeping Gaullist victory in June, 1968. The Federation of the Left lost half its seats; the SFIO received only 8 percent of the vote. Under the impetus of the need to field a candidate after De Gaulle's sudden resignation the following year, major renovation was undertaken. The SFIO voted itself out of existence and, together with elements of the political clubs, reemerged simply as the Socialist party. In two founding congresses held in May and July, 1969, it named Alain Savary as first secretary (later replaced by François Mitterand) and endorsed a new *Declaration of Principles*. The party condemned the opportunism of the SFIO by repudiating any alliance with the "political representatives of capitalism." Participation in government for the sake of republican defense or social legislation was similarly rejected. Only insofar as the act helped advance the country to socialism was the party authorized to join a government. Its program aimed at minimizing "all inequalities of power, wealth, and dignity" compatible with maintaining social efficiency and placing a priority on collective social needs. On the other hand, it recognized the force and complexity of modern capitalism and promised to achieve necessary reforms without lowering living standards. No class or class conflict was cited, and like socialist establishments in Britain and Germany, the party no longer identified with any one group. The statement embodied ideals and was not a program—hence no mention of the means by which power was to be won.

Ideologically, the declaration offered little that was new. Sociologically, it provided for a party that could no longer be considered Marxist. In containing the representatives of the political clubs, the party had formally opened its membership to non-Marxists. In temporarily retaining the program of the Federation of the Left, it continued to distinguish itself from the PCF and PSU by supporting NATO and the Common Market. It made specific mention of the wish to open a dialogue with the communists. Consequently, it stressed recruitment in order to negotiate from a position of strength.[11] Thus the French Left remains very much divided. The Socialist party, as the second largest on the Left and the third in the nation, is making efforts to face the realities of industrial society. At the same time, it is trying to form a left-wing majority to prepare for a transition to socialism. In the winter of 1972–1973 the socialists finally formed an electoral coalition with the communists.

In the story of postwar Italian socialism we find similar themes, with one major variation. We note the same tripartite governments before 1947 containing socialists, communists, and Christian Democrats. We see, too, the polarization, thanks to the Cold War, of parties on the Left and non-Marxists. But while most French socialists rallied to the Atlantic alliance and European economic integration, we have seen that the Nenni's PSI kept its alliance with the communists for over a decade.

Why could most Italian socialists remain allied with the communists when their French equivalents could not? Probably because Italian communists were never as Stalinist-oriented as were the French. Twenty years of fascist domination imposed a certain necessity on socialists and communists to cooperate, and the latter party never became isolated from the democratic community. Togliatti long denied that revolution was an absolute prerequisite for the installation of a socialist regime and insisted that individual freedom was not to be sacrificed. He had early adopted, indeed, invented the term *polycentrism*. This is the position that there need not be any one center of world communism. However, the disclosure of Stalin's crimes at the Soviet Communist party's twentieth congress, the Soviet invasion of Hungary in 1956, the admittedly authoritarian structure of the PCI, weariness with being in the opposition, and sincere desire for reform legislation prompted Nenni to join a center-left coalition in 1963. Three years later, the Nenni and Saragat wings of Italian socialism were reunited. They sought to win votes from disillusioned communists and left-wing Christian Democrats and so bid for the nation's leadership. A conspicuous absence of reform, subsequent losses of votes and seats, and charges of having sold out to the Christian Democrats have thus far not led socialists to repudiate their revisionism. Nenni's declaration that the party was not to be "the slave of ideological fetishes" was rightly interpreted as meaning that the last old line Marxist party in Western European socialism was committed to reform.

INTERNATIONAL SOCIALISM SINCE 1945

The Socialist International was moribund before World War II. Socialist delegates had it call for resistance to Hitler; their own countries remained neutral or appeased him. They had tacitly agreed that it should remain silent on the great issues and act as little more than a liaison and information center. It finally came to an end when member parties on the continent were repressed during the war. In December, 1944, at a Labour party conference, contacts were resumed with a number of socialist parties and the question of reviving the International arose. In May, 1946 19 parties set up an International Socialist Committee. It was to serve as a liaison among them with headquarters in London and to organize an annual conference.

With the advent of the Cold War and the absorption of East European socialists into communism, the organization took an anticommunist line. Ultimately, it contained only NATO or NATO-affiliated members. It expelled the Nenni socialists and accepted the Saragat group. It urged the formation of a *third force* between the two superpowers to unite Western Europe and to be led by democratic socialists. Neutralist and socialist governments were markedly absent.[12]

What accounted for the International's close ties with the West? To begin with, the prewar Marxist center, containing men like Blum, Adler, and Bauer, no longer existed. The experience of first Nazi and then Stalinist totalitarianism made Western socialists skeptical of comprehensive planning and nationalization. They placed emphasis on individual choice and moral values—hence, came to view communism as the chief enemy. The large number of contacts with American labor representatives at embassies and in Marshall Plan missions had made an impact on European trade unions supporting the parties.[13] Not even the temporary working-class dictatorship was acceptable, envisaged by some centrists before the war as inevitable in the event that the bourgeoisie resorted to unconstitutional resistance to a socialist majority. There was to be unconditional allegiance to democracy and to civil liberties.

The Socialist International was formally reestablished at the eighth postwar socialist conference, held at Frankfurt in 1951. The membership reached almost 50 parties. Anticipating charges of acting as Western agents, Asian parties established their own conference. The declaration of principles adopted at Frankfurt was directed as much against communism as capitalism. It recognized that changes had taken place in capitalism, but held that under it workers still exercised no influence over production; the rights of ownership had taken precedence over the rights of man. A free market economy, moreover, was seen as incapable of satisfying the needs of the world's population. Socialism was described as having wider appeal and as more capable of raising living standards for more people. Public ownership, either through nationalization or cooperatives, was considered not as an end in itself but as a means of controlling basic industries and services required by the community. It would end exploitation and improve efficiency. However, it need not be comprehensive; how much and what kind would depend on the situation in any given area.

Communism, on the other hand, was viewed as incompatible with the critical spirit of Marxism—hence not in the socialist tradition. As the dictatorship of a single party, it had sharpened rather than eliminated class divisions, and served as an instrument of imperialism. No uniform approach to socialism was prescribed. Marxist "or other methods of analyzing society whether inspired by religious or humanitarian principles" would suffice. Only the goal remained constant: "social justice, better living, freedom, and world peace." Its achievement, however, was by no means held as inevitable; active and prolonged effort was required. But only democratic means were to be used. Indeed, socialism was defined as "democracy in its highest form." It could be attained only through democracy and vice versa. The Oslo Declaration of 1962 expanded on these principles, and described the economic and fiscal policies demanded by the modern industrial state. It also stressed the humanistic element in socialist thought, as well as the need to assist the underdeveloped world.[14]

These statements were not new. They had emerged independently in a number of socialist movements. However, very little guidance was offered for socialist success and the long-held distinction between a maximum and minimum program had been dropped. How useful was this eminently civilized and highly democratic statement for an impoverished Third World? What room did it leave for nondemocratic workers' movements that wished to remain independent of Moscow? What was to be socialism's role in wars of national liberation? (Admittedly, both the Third International and its successor, the Cominform, also largely ignored these questions.) Still, for the economically developed West, for which it seems to have been intended, the International recognized that social parties were no longer identifiable as working-class organizations. The awareness of a changing capitalism, the diminution of ideology, the emphases placed on ethics and humanism, and the dictum that socialism was becoming the affirmation of a moral principle were all present.

THE END OF IDEOLOGY?

The apparent success of revisionism matched socialism's readiness to identify itself with the larger public and not with any class. Nationalization was downplayed and stress laid on political rather than economic structures to achieve stated objectives. The unlimited marketplace had already given way to the mixed economy, and public ownership had proved no cure-all. Communism revealed that the exploitation of the invidiual could be carried out more ruthlessly by bureaucrats than by property owners, and that it was the former who held more power. There was mounting awareness that even in a welfare state individual development was endangered by industrial society and mass culture, whether socialist or communist. The organization of production was seen only as a means to an end (as originally stated by Marx), and self-fulfillment as more important. The readiness to equate democracy and socialism implicitly meant rejection of earlier estimates that the latter was but a facade for the former. The repudiation of revolution and the willingness to rely on the methods of science to solve social problems all seemed to point to a society without ideologies or permanent political factions.

Somewhat similar tendencies could be seen emerging in the communist states. Economic revisionism suggested rejection of complete centralization and at least a partial return to the market place. Efficiency, it was argued, might be increased by reestablishing profit-taking (recognizing that it was not profits themselves that counted, but the uses to which they were put). The emergence of mainland China as a rival to the Soviet Union in the matter of providing communist leadership, and the success of national liberation movements independent of both countries encouraged the acceptance of polycentrism. Peasants, rather than industrial workers, it became clear, constituted the great revolutionary force in the twentieth century.

These and similar considerations in the late 1950s and early 1960s prompted thinkers like Raymond Aron in France and Daniel Bell in the United States to conceive of an end to ideology. Radical demands for social reconstruction no longer proved appealing. In seeking solutions to concrete problems, technicians—or, to use today's word, technocrats—and not theorists were required. Social scientists described how people were becoming integrated into their respective states and concluded that political socialization was becoming characteristic of a mature and modern society. In the degree to which this integration advances, it was argued, ideology gives way to pragmatism and class-conscious parties are replaced by the heterogeneous bargaining variety found in the United States.[15]

SOCIALIST HUMANISM

Revisionist thinking was given impetus by the postwar popularization of Marx's early writings. At the age of 26 he wrote the *Economic and*

Philosophic Manuscripts of 1844, discovered only in the 1930s and not widely read until the 1950s. They revealed him as very much of a humanist, for the young Marx seemed relatively unconcerned with ultimate objectives. In speculating on postrevolutionary socialist society, he denied that the abolition of private property was in itself a goal. The raw communism that was to follow would equalize rather than abolish labor. The ultimate aim of socialism was identified with humanism—to move beyond necessity and beyond history to a world which resolves "the strife between existence and essence, objectification and self-confirmation, freedom and necessity, individual and the species. It is the riddle of history solved and knows itself as this solution."

For Léon Blum, Erich Fromm, and others in the humanist tradition, the substitution of one kind of property system for another served only as the means for the transformation of the human condition. This ethical content was very much in the tradition of pre-Marxist socialism, of Western philosophy itself. Socialist literature from Fourier to Jaurès to Bernstein had criticized industrial society under capitalism, rather than capitalism itself. In sponsoring social reform and the welfare state, socialist movements aimed at helping workers to escape the harsher effects of uncontrolled industrial growth.

Cited for special condemnation by socialist humanists from Marx onward was that aspect of capitalism that resulted in the alienation of man from his work. For Albert Camus, the "basis of the Marxist dream," and that which constituted his greatness and the very core of his theory, was the notion of work as

"profoundly dignified and unjustly despised. [Marx] rebelled against the degradation of work to the level of a commodity and of the worker to the level of an object. To him we owe the idea which is the despair of our times . . . that when work is degradation, it is not life, even though it occupies every moment of life. . . . By demanding for the worker real riches, which are not the riches of money but of leisure and creation, he has reclaimed . . . the dignity of man." [16]

Hence the continuity between the revisionism of Bernstein and that carried on today becomes clear; both see Marxism as a moral imperative and not so much as historical necessity.

Concern over whether Marx was led to condemn private property because it was a product of alienated labor or whether his hostility to the property system, in which some men were led to become the object of others and hence dehumanized, led him to see alienation as its chief evil need not detain us. In either case for Marx the beginning of a solution lay in the abolition of private property. Individual development and enrichment were held as the proper objects of society, and economics reduced to an agent in their attainment. This humanist element is associated more with socialist than communist parties. Even so, uncovering and disseminating the *Economic and Philosophical Manuscripts* was the work of East European scholars seeking a humanistic foundation for their rejection of Stalinism, and finding doctrinal support.

The socialist attack on the structure of property (regardless of how much of it is to be collectivized) has now been given an ethical basis. For humanists, property is associated with the replacement of all the physical and intellectual senses by the sense of "having." Consequently, freedom (thanks to socialism) means emancipation of human qualities from the psychological tyranny of property. That Marx applied the concept of alienation chiefly to the working classes and not to the equally susceptible middle and ruling classes, proves no obstacle for a socialism no longer anxious to identity itself with any one class.

For both socialist and communist theoreticians, alienation can exist any place in which work is regarded as only a means to a livelihood. The individual can be manipulated in a system directed by experts of the private or public sector. The enemy is considered to be the system itself, or rather the control over it exercised by bureaucrats. Theoretical ownership of the means of production makes little difference here. It was precisely those efforts aimed at depriving the bureaucracy of some of its power and rendering it to workers that brought forth Soviet repression of an enlightened Czechoslovakian communist regime in 1968.

The most realistic socialist program, in which workers are offered control of the plant in which they are employed, may be found in the Yugoslav model. In his break with Stalin in 1948, Marshal Tito refused to follow Soviet economic patterns. The demands of regional autonomy and decentralization encouraged an approach marked by self-management, perhaps the most original feature of the regime. The scheme was introduced in 1950 as an alternative both to managerial capitalism and bureaucratic socialism. Briefly, ownership is vested in Yugoslav society. Workers act as trustees and are expected to participate through councils and managerial boards in actively running the firm (taking decisions ranging from personnel to pricing and sales). With an annual growth rate of 6 percent a year, the rise in living standards in the late 1950s and 1960s proved remarkable. The gross national income figured on a per capita basis matched that reached by France in 1939. Still, only a relatively small number of decisions are really taken by workers' representatives. There are complaints that because of mergers any one firm may be controlled by experts operating at a distance. How much of the improvement in the country's economic performance was the result of workers' enthusiasm because of their involvement in self-management? How much has been due to other factors: western aid, association with the Common Market, the removal of the worst managers, and the partial reintroduction of a market economy? These questions are all legitimate. Most observers, however, would agree that self-management is far from being the economic failure described by cynics in communist lands.

THE FUTURE OF SOCIALISM

Proponents of the *end of ideology* concept point to industrial society's need of political and social technicians as more desirable to create efficient procedures than ideologically minded politicians. Critics have rejoined that this analysis is at the very least premature. To begin with, they deny that technicians are somehow devoid of ideology. On the contrary, they are influenced by their common background and education; that is, by their class position. Hence technical choices are permeated by political values. More importantly, property managers, by the very nature of their position, work to maintain the privileges of property. The fact that they must take decisions in a particular political and economic framework inclines state technicians to collaborate with the private sector.[17]

The appearance of revisionism is also explained in terms of socialism's very successes. They have been notable. During the past century of the European Left, which was either socialist or socialist-inspired, pressure was successfully exerted for the extension of universal suffrage, for significant modifications of the previously unlimited control of the free market, and, in this latter regard, for greater state activity as a mediator between the interests of property and the public at large. Indeed, one of the interpretations of revisionism rests on the fact that the state no longer represents exclusively the interests of the property-owning class.

It would be an error, however, to suppose that these successes meant the implantation of socialism. From the standpoint of the "historic aims of the labor movement," and considered essentially as "a civilizing influence," its accomplishments have indeed been splendid. From the standpoint of its expectations for capitalism, socialism has thus far failed. For, despite considerable modification, the basic characteristic of capitalist society prevails. It hinges on the status of the wage earner who, by definition, does not own the instruments of his labor—that is, the means of production. (Admittedly, the ownership, as we have seen, cannot be individual in industrial society and must be collective.) Without collective ownership, profits return to the owners of capital. The Western welfare state, while alleviating working conditions and adding to the workingman's security, is not a substitute. Nor is the bureaucratic control of industry practiced in communist states. It is in the lack of ownership and control by workers that there are created the conditions in which exploitation—and hence alienation—become possible.[18]

Consequently, for at least the socialist Left, the movement has many real tasks before it and its historic role is far from over. It can well function as a distinct political party. It need not, however, differ from other progressive parties only by degree and rest content to urge more reform, more welfare, and more guarantees that with the rise of living standards there will be no erosion of individual liberty. It has basically to turn over to the community the ownership of production and the control of the economy, finding a meaningful way of so doing. Only when this is carried out can socialism be equated with economic democracy. There are no ready solutions. If boards or corporations have failed, other means of administering nationalized industries, as, for example, in Britain, must be found and the idea of common ownership not be abandoned. The Fabian Society has already accused the Wilson government of 1964–1970 of having failed even to attempt social democracy.

Socialists see a number of subsidiary tasks as well. To ensure world security by raising living standards in underdeveloped countries is among the most important. The Third World appears committed either to violence or to nondemocratic procedures in order to industrialize. The inability of socialism to provide a formula for its economic modernization other than state repression must surely rank among its most conspicuous failures. At home, socialists seek ways to eliminate poverty; to bring the forces of labor together in the European Economic Community as part of a larger attempt to prevent Common Market members from pursuing wholly national objectives and to provide a counterweight to the huge multinational firms within it; to eliminate regressive taxation systems like the added value tax; and to work for meaningful political integration on a socialist basis. Within advanced industrial societies they can work to prevent the responsibilities of the *technocrats* from degenerating into privileges. They will do none of these things without having first acknowledged the changes that have occurred in organized labor. It is no longer the dominant force in the population. Yesterday's proletariat exerts limited political dynamism. Socialists are trying to convert to socialism those who earn wages but reject identification with other wage earners, arguing that a new socialism is required for a new capitalism.

How much likelihood is there that this program will be carried out by European socialists? The Third World, we have seen, tends to equate industrialization with repressive forms of political organization. It would appear that socialism, which we have characterized as an extrapolation of democracy, is impossible to come by except in stable regimes enjoying economic security. The most distinguished analyst of the movement is pessimistic about its chances elsewhere: George Lichtheim has pointed to the hesitation of voters, still not affluent, to make the long-term sacrifices required to bring about social equality.[19] Nor has the labor movement, whose support is necessary in view of the fact that most voters are salaried, shown much interest in forgoing short-range economic gains. If it is argued that it is entirely reasonable to expect people to seek steady improvements in their living standards, the conclusion is forced upon us that socialism will remain an ideal until the satisfaction of human economic wants, another ideal, is attained. But, then, revisionists have always maintained that socialism is more of a quest than a goal.

At the heart of the matter is the apparent inability of the wage earner to act as an agent of social change. Herbert Marcuse has argued that the proletariat, in having become integrated into society, no longer exists. Industrially advanced societies have demonstrated their ability to satisfy the worker's immediate wants and so dissuade him from contemplating alternative forms of social organization. This domination is carried out by democratic and economically satisfying means, not by terror, and hence constitutes the most insidious of all forms of suppression. The lesson drawn by Marcuse is that any chance of success held by socialism lies not in working-class action, but with social classes outside the industrial system and the benefits it bestows.

People excluded from the system include the disinherited masses of the underdeveloped Third World. For Frantz Fanon they constitute the great majority of the rural population and appear as a potentially revolutionary force which either the colonial power or the indigenous business classes ignore or try to keep divided and impotent. They do so by fostering tribal antagonisms or by pitching the hinterland against the seaboard, to cite but two examples. In industrial society their equivalents would include ethnic or racial minorities and people living in depressed areas. They may well remain a discontented force because of the present system's inability to absorb them. And job creation in the private sector, aside from services, has slowed up (apparently one of the more unspoken requisites of the new capitalism).

That the industrial working class, neither in culture nor in politics, is "a harbinger of the future or a revolutionary force" is subscribed to by the sociologist Norman Birnbaum. He points to today's avant-garde in industrial society as found among the young, particularly students "without immediate responsibilities or bondages to the existing order" and intellectuals, "those with a certain freedom from routine and a certain proclivity to employ their critical faculties."[20] In fact, the most revolutionary outburst to appear in industrial society in recent times, one that came within a hairsbreadth of toppling the Gaullist regime, was the May–June (1968) students–workers uprising in France. The revolutionary Left has made it something of a model, though seeking to avoid the Gaullist ending. Briefly, student strikes would ignite assorted industrial strikes, which could, in turn, set off a general strike and so bring down the entire governmental system.

Undisciplined student revolutionary activity, it may be noted, concentrating on demonstrations and confrontations takes place precisely where socialism has lost its vitality, in both Western and Eastern Europe. The scantiest of readings of the objectives held by those involved would suggest a concern with ideology that is very much alive. Still, there are few signs that the presence of a New Left in Europe has had much of an impact on European politics.

Must labor, then, be written off as even a potential agent of societal change? In the May uprising it was labor (to be sure, younger elements within the rank and file) that responded to the students' appeal and launched the greatest strike in French history. There is additional evidence that European labor—and its leadership—is not as moribund as generally depicted. In the oldest of industrialized countries it is making new responses to imposed presures. In the depression of the 1930s unemployment in Britain was regarded as an inevitable aspect of another order, run by other men. Some of the unemployed marched in protest. Most stayed at home and cursed their luck. The closure of a plant or shipyard meant the death of a town. No one suggested that plant or yard be worked in defiance of the closure, still less that it could be occupied and held for ransom in exchange for guarantees of full employment. That such ideas prevail among working men and women today was demonstrated by Scottish workers along the Clydeside in 1971, and points out the difference in their attitude to that of their prewar predecessors.[21]

New techniques of protest, moreover, reveal a meager relationship between a small union treasury and the readiness to undertake widespread industrial action. Striking British coal miners early in 1972 used their funds to send pickets to close down power stations and not to support their families. A few thousand workers thus managed to paralyze the economy and succeeded in doing in six weeks what the armed might of Nazi Germany failed to do in five and a half years of war. (In allowing the union to correctly anticipate that smaller strike benefits would mean higher welfare payments, industrial society displayed its vulnerability in yet another way.) None of this means, of course, that British workers are interested in reconstructing society, or even that workers integrated into society will strike. It does, however, reveal a militancy and sense of social involvement that was not present before. Socialism became a mass political force, we have noted, when this sense of involvement was generated.

NOTES

[1] Ralph Miliband, *Parliamentary Socialism* (London: Allen & Unwin, 1961), p. 288.

[2] Claude Willard, *Le Socialisme de la renaissance à nos jours* (Paris: Presses Universitaires de France, 1971), pp. 134–136.

3 Adolph Sturmthal, "Democratic Socialism in Europe," *World Politics* III, 1 (October 1950), 97.

4 Francois Fejtö, *Histoire des démocraties populaires* (Paris: Éditions du Seuil, 1952), I, p. 123.

5 George Lichtheim, *A Short History of Socialism* (New York: Praeger, 1970), p. 325.

6 Sturmthal, *op. cit.*, pp. 98–99.

7 Stephen Haseler, *The Gaitskellites. Revisionism in the British Labour Party, 1951–64* (London: Macmillan, 1969), pp. 236, 246–247, 251–252.

8 Harold K. Schellinger, Jr., *The SPD in the Bonn Republic. A Socialist Party Modernizes* (The Hague: Nijoff, 1968), pp. 191–192.

9 Harvey G. Simmons, *French Socialists in Search of a Role, 1956–1967* (Ithaca: Cornell University Press, 1970), p. 222.

10 *Ibid.*, p. 250.

11 Christiane Hurtig, ed. *De la S.F.I.O. au nouveau parti socialiste* (Paris: A. Colin, 1970), pp. 83–84.

12 Sturmthal, *op. cit.*, pp. 109–113.

13 Sturmthal, *Unity and Diversity in European Labor* (Glencoe, Ill.: Free Press, 1953), pp. 134, 137–140.

14 Socialist International, *Aims and Tasks of Democratic Socialism* (London: Socialist International Council, 1951) and *The World Today . . .* (London: Socialist International, 1962).

15 See the conclusion to Schellinger. Also Seymour Martin Lipset, "The Changing Class Structure and Contemporary European Politics," *Daedalus* (Winter 1964), pp. 271–303.

16 *The Rebel* (New York: Random House–Vintage Books, 1956), pp. 200–209.

17 Norman Birnbaum, *The Crisis of Industrial Society* (London and New York: Oxford University Press, 1969), pp. 80–83, 87.

18 See the conclusion to Lichtheim's *A Short History of Socialism*. For an opposing view, see John Mander, "The Future of Social Democracy," *Commentary* 50 (September 1970), pp. 63–64.

19 Lichtheim, *op. cit.*, pp. 325, 327.

20 Birnbaum, *op. cit.*, p. 94.

21 *(London) Sunday Times Magazine*, December 5, 1971, p. 36.

SUGGESTED READING

Daniel Bell. *The End of Ideology: On the Exhaustion of Political Ideas in the Fifties.* Glencoe, Free Press, 1960.

Donald Blackmer. *Italian Communism and the Communist World.* Cambridge, Mass.: M.I.T. Press, 1968.

Léon Blum. *For All Minkind.* New York: Viking Press, 1946.

Claude Bruclain (pseud. for Jean Moulin Club). *Le Socialisme et l'Europe.* Paris: Éditions du Seuil, 1965.

David Childs. *From Schumacher to Brandt. The Story of German Socialism, 1945–65.* Oxford: Pergamon Press, 1966.

C. A. R. Crosland. *The Future of Socialism.* New York: Schocken Books, 1963.

C. A. R. Crosland. "The Future of the Left," *Encounter,* XIV (March 1960).

R. H. S. Crossman, ed. *The God That Failed.* New York: Harper & Row, 1965.

R. H. S. Crossman, ed. *New Fabian Essays.* London: Turnstile Press, 1952; Mystic, Conn.: L. Verry, 1970.

R. H. S. Crossman. "The Spectre of Revisionism: A Reply to Crosland," *Encounter,* XIV (April 1960).

Lewis Edinger. *Kurt Schumacher: A Study in Personality and Political Behavior.* Stanford: Stanford University Press, 1965.

Frantz Fanon. *The Wretched of the Earth.* London: Penguin, 1967.

François Fejtö. *History of the People's Democracies.* New York: Praeger, 1971.

François Fejtö. *The French Communist Party and the Crisis of International Communism.* Cambridge, Mass.: M.I.T. Press, 1967.

Michael Foot. *Aneurin Bevan, A Biography.* New York: Atheneum, 1963.

Erich Fromm. *Let Man Prevail: A Socialist Manifesto and Program.* New York, 1960.

Erich Fromm, ed. *Socialist Humanism: An International Symposium.* New York: 1966.

Roger Garaudy. *The Turning Point of Socialism.* London: Fontana, 1970.

B. D. Graham. *The French Socialists and Tripartism, 1944–1947.* London: Weidenfeld and Nicolson, 1965.

Michael Harrington. *Socialism.* New York: Saturday Review Press, 1972.

Martin Harrison. *Trade Unions and the Labour Party Since 1945.* Detroit: Wayne State University Press, 1960.

Robert L. Heilbroner. "Socialism and the Future," *Commentary,* XLVIII (December 1969).

Joseph La Palombara. *The Italian Labor Movement: Problems and Prospects.* Ithaca: Cornell University Press, 1957.

Richard Lowenthal. "The Principles of Western Socialism," *Twentieth Century,* CL (August 1951).

Arthur P. Mendel. "The Rise and Fall of Scientific Socialism," *Foreign Affairs,* XLV (1966).

John Vaizey. *Social Democracy.* London: Weidenfeld and Nicolson, 1971.

Katherine S. Van Eerde. "Socialism in Western Europe at Mid-Century," *Social Research,* XXVI (Winter 1959).

Frank L. Wilson. *The French Democratic Left, 1963–1968. Toward a Modern Party System.* Stanford: Stanford University Press, 1971.

Harold Wilson. *The Labour Government, 1964–1970. A Personal Record.* New York, Boston: Little, Brown, 1971.

Glossary

SOME REPEATED INITIALS

CDU   Christian Democratic Union (West Germany). The largely conservative party of Adenauer, Erhard, and now Barzel.

CGL   General Confederation of Labor (Italy). Founded in 1906; ousted syndicalists shortly afterwards, by 1947 communist-dominated.

CGT   General Confederation of Labor (France). Founded in 1895 and committed to independence from political parties. Anti-communist between the two World Wars; communist-controlled after World War II.

CGTU   Unitary General Confederation of Labor (France). The communist counterpart of the CGT, founded after the socialist-communist split in 1920. Merged with the CGT in time for the Popular Front.

FDP   Free Democratic Party (West Germany). "Liberals" situated between the CDU and SDP. Its presence required by one or the other parties to form a governing coalition.

IFTU   International Federation of Trade Unions. The trade union equivalent of the LSI. Founded at Amsterdam in 1919. Replaced (in the West) after 1945 by the ICFTU, International Confederation of Free Trade Unions.

ILP   Independent Labour Party (Great Britain). Founded in 1893. Socialist, but not necessarily Marxist or revolutionary. Long a left-wing spur to the Labour party.

KPD   German Communist Party. Founded after the 1918 Revolution, outlawed by the Nazis, and reformed in 1945.

LRC   Labour Representation Committee (Great Britain). Direct antecedent of the British Labour Party. Founded by the Trades Union Congress in 1899 and changed name to Labour Party in 1906.

LSI   Labor and Socialist International. International Socialist organization founded at Hamburg in 1923 by means of a merger of those who favored reconstructing the Second (Berne) International and supporters of the "Second and a Half" (Vienna) International. It spoke for democratic socialism until World War II.

PCF   French Communist Party. Founded by the majority at the SFIO's Tours Congress of 1920 supporting affiliation with the

Comintern. Represented in the government in the post-liberation years, but has played an opposition role ever since.

PCI   Italian Communist Party. Formed when socialists refused to give unconditional acceptance to the Comintern's "21 Conditions." Today the most important communist party in the noncommunist world.

PSU   Unified Socialist Party (France). Founded in 1960 by SFIO and PCF dissidents, Mendès-France Radicals, and others. Like the PCF but unlike the Socialist Party it rejects the Atlantic Alliance and Common Market.

SD   Social Democratic Party (Russia). Formed in 1898 by Marxists; outlawed, and then divided into its Menshevik and Bolshevik components in 1903. In theory, a single party survived until 1918; in fact, Bolsheviks organized a separate party in 1912.

SDF   Social Democratic Federation (Great Britain). Founded in 1881 and endowed with Henry Hyndman's Marxism. Rent by subsequent schisms and transformed into the British Socialist Party in 1912.

SFIO   French Section of the Worker's International. The unified French socialist party founded in 1905. Led by Jaurès, Blum, Mollet, and now (reorganized in 1969 as the Socialist Party) by François Mitterand.

SPD   German Social Democratic Party. Founded by Marxists and Lassalleans in 1875. Became the most prestigious—and most bureaucratic—of all the socialist parties. Driven underground by the Nazis. Re-emerged to become the chief opposition to the CDU after 1945. Held a minority status in a CDU-SDP coalition government in 1966 and majority status in a coalition with the FDP since 1969.

SR   Social Revolutionary Party (Russia). Founded in 1901. Heir to the agrarian socialism of the 1880s, it sought a peasant rather than a bourgeois revolution. By 1918 even left-wing SRs opposed the Communists.

TUC   Trades Union Congress (Great Britain). National confederation of labor unions. First annual congress held in 1868. Long a lobbying agency, it's Parliamentary Committee urged formation of the LRC. The TUC assumed a greater political voice in the 1930s, but no longer exercises control over Labour Party decisions.

USPD   Independent German Social Democratic Party. Emerged from growing opposition to World War I by SPD Reichstag delegates and given organizational structure after the Russian Revolution of March, 1917. Split by the Bolshevik Revolution, the majority in 1920 joined the Communists; the minority returned to the SPD two years later.

SOME SIGNIFICANT SOCIALIST AND LABOR LEADERS

Victor Adler (Austrian: 1852–1918). A founder of the Austrian Socialist Party and dedicated to retaining party unity. Influential in the Second International. Entered the Austrian parliament in 1905.

Jean Allemane (French: 1843–1935). Former typographer and Communard. In 1890 broke with the Possibilists and organized his own party. Called for a greater role by workers and favored the general strike.

Clement Attlee (English: 1883–1967). Socialist MP in 1922. Deputy leader of party under Lansbury, 1931–1935 and his successor. Prime Minister after 1945, he presided over Labour's extensive reform and nationalization program.

Michael Bakunin (Russian: 1814–1876). The great anarchist revolutionary contested Marx's leadership of the First International and was expelled in 1872.

Otto Bauer (Austrian: 1881–1938). Spokesman for the left wing of the Austrian Social Democratic Party. Wrote on nationalities and imperialist questions and was a leading exponent of Austro-Marxism. As Foreign Secretary in 1919 he favored *Anchluss* with Germany.

August Bebel (German: 1840–1913). One of the few socialist leaders of working-class origins. With Wilhelm Liebknecht founded the Marxist party which, with the addition of the Lassalleans, became the SPD.

Eduard Bernstein (German: 1850–1932). The founder of Marxist revisionism. Rejected German war policy and helped found the USPD in 1917.

Aneurin Bevan (English: 1897–1960). Former coal miner. In Parliament from 1929 to 1960 and left-wing party leader. Minister of Health, 1945–1951.

Ernest Bevin (English: 1881–1951). Founder and General Secretary of Transport and General Workers Union. Chairman of TUC's General Council. Minister of Labor in Churchill's wartime cabinet. As Foreign Affairs Minister from 1945 to 1951 followed a Western and pro-NATO policy.

Auguste Blanqui (French: 1805–1881). Long-time revolutionary and advocate of a professional revolutionary vanguard. Spent much of his life in prison.

Léon Blum (French: 1872–1950). Disciple and heir of Jaurès. Rebuilt SFIO in 1920s. Headed a Popular Front government in 1936. Deported to Germany in 1943, returned, headed a socialist cabinet in 1946.

Willy Brandt (German: born 1913). SPD leader. Served in Bundestag and as mayor of West Berlin. Minister of Foreign Affairs in the 1966–1969 coalition cabinet, began the "opening to the east" that brought him the Nobel Peace Prize. Named Chancellor after the SPD's 1969 victory.

Paul Brousse (French: 1844–1913). Opponent of Second Empire. Participant in First International and Paris Commune. After 1882 headed a reformist (Possibilist) party. Active as Paris Municipal Councilman and as a deputy.

G. D. H. Cole (English: 1889–1959). Economist, socialist, and labor historian. Leading exponent of guild socialism. Chairman and then President of the Fabian Society.

Stafford Cripps (English: 1889–1952). Left-wing Labour Party leader. Expelled in 1939 for advocating a popular front with the Communists (readmitted in 1945). Member of Churchill's wartime cabinet and holder of ministerial posts in the postwar Labour government.

Marcel Déat (French: 1894–1955). Leading spokesman of "neo-socialism" within SFIO. Served as Minister of Labor in the Vichy regime.

Friedrich Ebert (German: 1871–1925). Trade union leader and SPD delegate to Reichstag. Supported German war effort. In 1919 became first President of the German republic.

Kurt Eisner (German: 1867–1919). Editor of *Vorwärts* and USPD leader. Best known for his abortive revolutionary Bavarian republic in winter of 1918–1919. Assassinated by an extreme rightist.

Friedrich Engels (German: 1820–1895). Together with Marx founded modern socialism and communism. The son of a textile manufacturer, he described working-class conditions in England. Met Marx in Paris in 1844 and collaborated with him on the *Communist Manifesto* of 1848. After failure of the German Revolution he spent the rest of his life in England. Aided Marx financially. Important in both First and Second Internationals and editor of the second and third volumes of *Capital*.

Paul Faure (French: 1878–1960). Associated with Jules Guesde. After the 1920 schism he served as Secretary-General of the SFIO. A deputy after 1924. His pacifism persuaded him to accept Munich and the defeat of 1940.

Hugh Gaitskell (English: 1906–1963). Labour MP in 1945 and Attlee's successor in 1955. Known for his efforts to revise the more socialist-sounding parts of his party's program.

Jules Guesde (French: 1845–1922). Born Mathieu Basile. Introduced and popularized Marxism in the French labor movement. Served as minister in a 1914 national coalition government.

Keir Hardie (Scot: 1856–1915). Miners' organizer and labor leader. First labor candidate for Parliament. Founder of ILP and its first chairman.

Arthur Henderson (English: 1863–1935). Three times Chairman of the Labour Party. Member of coalition cabinet 1915–1917 and two Labour governments between the wars. In 1931 refused to join MacDonald's National Union government.

Alexander Herzen (Russian: 1812–1870). Early populist socialist. Imprisoned 1834. Lived abroad since 1847. Propagandized by means of novels, tracts, and the newspaper *Kolikol* (The Bell).

Rudolf Hilferding (Austrian: 1877–1941). The economics expert of Austro-Marxism. Joined the USPD but opposed the KPD. Became German citizen and was Stresemann's finance minister in 1923.

Henry Hyndman (English: 1842–1921). Founded the Marxist Social Democratic Federation in 1881 and served as chairman of the British Socialist Party in 1911. Though more of a sect than a party, his Federation provided training for numerous working-class militants.

Jean Jaurès (French: 1859–1914). Former teacher of philosophy. Important socialist deputy and journalist in the 1890s and, after his defense of Dreyfus, party leader. Though a Marxist, he furthered French socialism's idealistic heritage and stress on individual rights. Antimilitarist; was assassinated by nationalist fanatic in 1914.

Karl Kautsky (German: 1854–1938). Longtime theoretician of SPD and drafter of its Erfurt Program. Important in Second International. Cofounder of USPD. A defender of Marxist "orthodoxy," he opposed both Bernstein's revisionism and Lenin's bolshevism.

George Lansbury (English: 1859–1940). Left-wing socialist and champion of London poor. Editor of the *Herald,* an important Labour party newspaper. Leader of party 1931–1935. Cited for his pacifism during the rise of fascism.

Ferdinand Lassalle (German: 1825–1864). Early German socialist theorist and organizer. In contrast to Marx, emphasized the role of the state and nationalism. Also favored state development of cooperatives. Helped establish first workers' political party in Germany (1863), an antecedent of the SPD.

Vladimir Ilyich Lenin (Russian: 1870–1924). Born Ulianov. Studied Marx and renounced law practice. Left Russia after second exile in Siberia. An advocate of a disciplined party of professional revolutionaries, he fought Plekhanov, Kautsky, and less radical Marxists. Successfully led the Bolshevik Revolution of November, 1917 and presided over the government until his death.

Karl Liebknecht (German: 1871–1919). Son of Wilhelm Liebknecht Prominent antimilitarist and revolutionary SPD member. Cofounder of Spartacists. Murdered with Rosa Luxemburg in January, 1919 when Berlin uprising was crushed.

Wilhelm Liebknecht (German: 1826–1900). Exiled for participation in 1848 Revolution. Associated with Marx. With Bebel founded first German Marxist party, which with addition of Lassalleans became the SPD. Long-time Reichstag member.

Rosa Luxemburg (Polish: 1870 or 1871–1919). Important advocate of revolution within SPD. Opposed formation of separate Polish socialist party. Relied on revolutionary spontaneity of masses and rejected Lenin's elitism. Killed in Spartacist uprising of January, 1919.

Ramsay MacDonald (Scot: 1866–1937). Fabian and one of founders of the Labour party. MP in 1906. Took pacifist stand in 1914. Prime Minister and Foreign Secretary in first Labour government in 1924. Came to lose what little socialist ardor he had. Again PM in 1929, but preferred a National Coalition (conservative-supported) cabinet to one that was socialist. Disavowed by his party.

Hendrik de Man (Belgian: 1885–1953). Both theorist and politician. Substituted a sociopsychological for a materialist explanation of working-class mentality. His *Labor Plan* sought to win middle-class support against finance capitalism. Minister in 1935. Increasingly authoritarian and neutralist, urged a collaborationist policy in 1940.

Tom Mann (English: 1856–1941). Socialist and labor leader. Leader of 1889 London dock strike. ILP Secretary, 1894–1897. Turned to syndicalism; in 1920 one of founders of British Communist party.

Benoît Malon (French: 1841–1893). Self-educated laborer. In First International. As deputy from Seine Department voted against peace with Germany in February, 1871. Communard. As editor of influential *Revue socialiste* helped implant a humanistic element in French socialism.

Karl Marx (German: 1818–1883). Chief theorist of modern socialism and communism. Turned from law to philosophy. Substituted materialism for the idealism in Hegel's thought. In Paris in the early 1840s attacked Proudhon's individualistic radicalism. Joined Communist League in 1847. With Engels wrote the *Communist Manifesto* stressing the class-struggle concept. After the aborted German revolution, lived a life of poverty in London. Besides writing extensively, helped to found the First International and advised numerous socialists on theoretical and organizational matters.

Alexandre Millerand (French: 1859–1943). Leader of parliamentary socialists in 1890s. Defended reformism in Saint-Mandé Speech, 1896. First socialist to enter regularly constituted bourgeois cabinet (1899–1902) and responsible for substantial labor reforms. Repudiated and expelled by party, he became an ardent nationalist.

Guy Mollet (French: born 1905). Teacher, war prisoner, resistance fighter. As Premier after Republican Front victory of 1956 also supported efforts to keep Algeria French. Secretary-General of SFIO since 1946 and member of various governments, he initially supported De Gaulle in 1958.

Pietro Nenni (Italian: born 1891). PSI leader. In government 1945–1946. Favored policy of collaborating with communists until 1957.

Fernand Pelloutier (French: 1867–1901). Revolutionary syndicalist. Secretary of Federation of Labor Exchanges.

Georgi V. Plekhanov (Russian: 1857–1918). Considered "Father of Russian Marxism." Broke with Populism and denounced individual acts of terror. Began to publish *Iskra* with Lenin in 1900. Became a Menshevik leader. Supported war effort in 1914. Opposed November revolution.

Pierre-Joseph Proudhon (French: 1809–1865). Socialist and anarchist theorist. Best known for publication, *What Is Property?* (in which he attacked its abuses and not the institution) and for his disputes with Marx. Advocated a libertarian and antistatist socialism won by peaceful and largely nonpolitical means.

Karl Renner (Austrian: 1870–1950). Wrote on nationalities question. First Chancellor of Austrian republic, 1918–1920. Imprisoned as socialist leader 1934. Chancellor and then President of the Second Republic after 1945.

Giuseppe Saragat (Italian: born 1898). As PSI member held various government posts after 1944. Broke with Nenni and formed separate Italian Democratic Socialist party (PSDI) cooperating with Christian Democrats. President of the Republic 1964–1971.

Philip Scheidemann (German: 1865–1939). SPD leader. Minister in the Provisional Government of 1918. First Chancellor of the Republic in 1919.

Kurt Schumacher (German: 1895–1952). Leader of SPD delegates to Reichstag, 1930–1933. Spent over ten years in concentration camps. Party chairman after 1946. Supported both class-struggle concept and a reunified Germany.

George Bernard Shaw (Irish: 1856–1940). Dramatist, essayist, and social critic. Member of executive committee of Fabian Society. Editor of *Fabian Essays* (1889).

Joseph Stalin (Russian: 1879–1953). Born Dzhugashvili. Russian revolutionary. Commissar for Nationalities after Bolsheviks took power. As Secretary General of the party's Central Committee, developed support and won control of the party after Lenin's death.

Leon Trotsky (Russian: 1879–1940). Born Lev Bronstein. Russian revolutionary and theoretician. With Lenin organized Bolshevik Revolution and implemented his doctrine of "permanent revolution." Commissar of War in civil wars. Ousted by Stalin. Assassinated in 1940.

Edouard Vaillant (French: 1840–1915). Member of First International and Paris Commune. Became Paris Municipal Councilman in 1884. Deputy from Paris from 1893 to death. Led Blanquist faction in French socialism.

Emile Vandervelde (Belgian: 1866–1938). Socialist leader and states-man. Member of several governments and important in Second Interna-tional.

Georg von Vollmar (German: 1850–1922). Chief of Bavarian delega-tion to Reichstag in 1890s. Wanted SPD to adopt reformist nationalist route to power.

Sydney Webb (English: 1858–1943). Economist, social reformer, and cofounder of Fabian Society. With his wife Beatrice Webb (1859–1947), published extensively on social and labor questions. MP in 1922 and Secre-tary of State in 1929.

Harold Wilson (English: born 1916). Succeeded Gaitskell as head of Labour Party in 1963. Prime Minister 1964–1970. Charged with attempting little significant social change.

Index